# To Live and Die a WASP

ALSO BY WILLIAM M. MILLER

*Eugene Ely, Daredevil Aviator*

*Silent City on the Hill*

# To Live and Die A WASP

*38 women pilots who died in WWII*

WILLIAM M. MILLER

Miller, William M., 1946-
To Live and Die a WASP: 38 women
pilots who died in WWII / William M. Miller.
Includes bibliographical references and index.

1. Women Airforce Service Pilots (U.S.). 2. Women's Air Force Service Pilots (U.S.). 3. WASP. 4. Women in aeronautics. 5. Women air pilots. 6. World War, (1939-1945—Aerial Operations). 7. World War, 1939-1945—Participation, Female. I. Title.
940.544973

Front cover: Wilda Winfield in a BT13, Air Force photo
020927-O-9999A-001. "Sad WASP," W. Miller.
Rear cover: WASP Wings, Air Force photo.
WASP Congressional Gold Medal, U.S. Mint photo.



ISBN-10:1523803819
ISBN-13:978-1523803811

# DEDICATION

To the brave women of the World
who seldom get the thanks they deserve.
and
To my wife Debbie who is always there and
always knows how to make our lives better.

# CONTENTS

"These women have given their lives in the performance of arduous and exacting duties without being able to see and feel the final results of their work. … We shall always keep and remember the brave heritage of the women who gave their lives. It is the heritage of faith in victory and in the ultimate freedom of humanity."

- *General Barton Yount, Commanding the Army Air Force Training Command, December 7, 1944.*

# [1]

## GRAND FIGHTERS

"I hope that poor woman fainted before she crashed," Paula Williams said.

Everyone else in the survey crew was scanning the ground, littered with the broken and melted remnants of the shattered airplane—all but Williams. She was looking up, unable to hold back her tears. Here, on this remote Oregon mountaintop, scene of a 57-year-old aviation tragedy, the tops of cedar trees still remained ripped away and those ancient moments of horror were being relived in Williams' imagination.

"All the cedars were sheared off at an angle," she said. "Even though the trees were growing new tops, you could still see where the airplane had smashed right through them. I'll never forget seeing that flight path. It was right there in the trees, forever marking her final, terrible descent."[1]

The doomed woman was Paula Loop, a pilot with the Women Airforce Service Pilots, the WASP. She was ferrying a military trainer aircraft from Enid, Oklahoma to Seattle, Washington. In July 1944, just a few weeks shy of her 28th birthday, and 330 miles away from her destination, she died alone in a fiery crash.[2]

Williams, a forester with the U. S. Forest Service, had only been working a few days at her new duty station in 2001, when she was assigned to a survey crew that would inspect the crash site and prepare a report that would allow removal of some of the plane's parts.[3]

Paula Loop's trainer airplane, a BT-13 *Valiant*, had begun slicing through those tall cedars in the middle of the afternoon. The left wing, nearly intact, sheared off from the fuselage and dropped about 150 feet from where the airplane ultimately struck the ground. The 60-gallon left wing fuel tank, still attached to the plane, erupted on impact, its contents exploding in a violent fire that quickly turned the remaining fuselage into a twisted skeleton framework of metal.

Why Paula's plane had suddenly crashed, just a few minutes after refueling and takeoff from the Medford, Oregon airport, was never determined. The weather was good; a sunny July day with light winds and temperature in the low 80s. The best guess was that Paula was unable to recover from a sudden down-slope wind as she was about to cross over the mountaintop. Officials were sure she died instantly on impact.[4]

In 2003, two years after that Forest Service survey, the Oregon Aviation Historical Society returned to the crash site and removed the remaining two major pieces of the plane; a tubular portion of the fuselage and the nine-cylinder, 450 horsepower Pratt & Whitney radial engine.

Paula Ruth Loop was born in 1916 about 15 miles from the family farm in Manchester, Oklahoma. She was the first child of Elton Loop and Nettie Bartlett. She grew up near the town of Wakita, on the 160 acres claimed by her grandfather, George Loop, in the Oklahoma land rush of 1893. As the oldest child, Paula soon learned how to milk cows, can fruits and vegetables, sew, clean house, cook and take on all the chores expected of a farm child. She was a hard worker and when her three brothers and sisters began to arrive in 1920, she easily moved into the role of babysitter and attentive teacher. Her younger sister, Genevieve, remembered Paula's exceptional talent for ironing. "How beautifully Paula ironed," she said, "and with those old, sad irons, yet!"[5]

Life was hard on the farm and rarely was there any extra money. Mrs. Loop sewed all the childrens' clothes and everyone had to pitch in whenever possible to keep the farm afloat. Even so, Paula's parents made sure that all their children went to school and worked hard for a better life. Paula did not disappoint. She not only graduated from Manchester High School, she began working her way through college. Almost immediately, she enrolled at the Northwestern State Teachers College, 50 miles west in Alva, Oklahoma. After two years of study, Paula transferred to the Oklahoma College for Women in Chickasha, just about 135 miles south of home. Two years later, she graduated with a Bachelor of Science degree in Commerce, what today we would call a business degree. However, Paula wasn't done with her education. She began taking graduate courses at Oklahoma Agricultural and Mechanical College in Stillwater, pursuing a Masters Degree, but apparently, the economic strain of the Great Depression was just too much. While trying to find a teaching position, she went to work as a secretary in Ponca City, Oklahoma. It was in Ponca City where her final fate was sealed.[6]

In early 1939, President Roosevelt asked Congress for $7.3 million to establish a Civilian Pilot Training program administered by the Civil Aeronautics Authority (CAA), forerunner of today's Federal Aviation Administration. Europe was already moving toward war and there was a sense that if war broke out, the United States might need more pilots for self defense and also combat pilots if the country was drawn into the conflict. Officials in the United States were aware that civilian pilot training was already well underway in several countries, particularly in German and Italy. By summer, Congress authorized nearly $5.7 million for the current fiscal year and a maximum $7 million annually for the following four years. Roosevelt signed the bill June 27, 1939.[7]

Initially, the Civilian Pilot Training Act authorized ground school and aerial training for students attending hundreds of colleges and universities across the country, but eventually it also provided ground school courses to a few people who lived near participating colleges. The 72 hours of ground school introduced students to the history of flight, the theory of flight, aerial navigation, meteorology, aircraft engines, instruments, radio, and civilian aviation rules. At the nearest airport with a flying school, students received 35 to 50 hours of flight training. Colleges could charge students up to $40 for the ground school course and the government added an additional $20 for each student. Flying school operators received government grants of $270 to $290 for flight training. The training program had two goals—to encourage development of civil aviation and to create a large pool of reserve pilots to call upon during a national emergency. None of that helped Paula who had already left school. Until the program accepted non-students, she was grounded.[8]

Finally, in December 1939, CAA announced that it would offer 700 flight scholarships to non-college students between the ages of 18 and 25 who didn't have access to the pilot training program. Local sponsors in 70 towns were allowed to select the students who would compete for a scholarship, and luckily for Paula, one of those towns was Ponca City. The city's school district and the local chamber of commerce sponsored the ground school and chose the students, including Paula, and the flight instructors. Students paid $30, which include a medical examination, ground school expenses, and insurance, with all other costs paid for by the CAA. At the end of the ground training, a competitive examination determined which 10 students received free flight training. There was one restriction. Of the final ten selected, only one could be a woman. Officials justified the requirement by saying it was the same class proportion allowed under the college program.[9]

Maintaining a grade point average of 94.9, Paula was the first Oklahoma woman to receive one of the flight scholarships, entitling her to 35 hours of flight training at the Ponca City Municipal Airport. After her solo flight on September 22, 1940, she received her private pilot's license.[10]

Soon, she took a job as an English teacher in Arnett, Oklahoma, where she worked for almost two years. There, she also taught music and was director of the high school plays. Following the bombing of Pearl Harbor in December 1941, Paula wanted to do something to help the war effort. Back in Ponca City, the Darr School of Aeronautics had begun training British aviation cadets. When the U.S. War Department took over the training in April 1942, Paula decided that that's where she really wanted to be. She decided to finish teaching her high school classes and then resign. By that fall, she was a Link Trainer instructor at the Ponca City aviation school. Link Trainers were grounded flight simulators in which pilots learned to fly, especially at night, without the danger of a crash.[11]

Her link training didn't last long. With the announcement in September of a training program that would allow women to fly military aircraft, Paula, and eventually over a thousand other women, were finally able to use their flying ability in support of the United States war effort. She applied and met all qualifications, the most stringent of which was proving that she had flown over 200 hours. On December 13, 1942, she reported for training at the Howard Hughes Airport, Ellington Field, Houston, Texas. She was a student pilot in the second class given by the Army Air Force Women's Flying Training Detachment. Six months later, her class graduated and Paula reported to the 3rd Ferrying Group at Romulus Army Air Field, near Detroit, Michigan. There, for nearly a year, she would ferry smaller bombers, fighters, and training aircraft to locations all over the country, and sometimes fly as copilot on larger craft. In June 1944, having flown for over 1,000 hours in the U.S. and Canada, she was transferred closer to home—the 33rd Ferrying Group, at Fairfax Army Field near Kansas City, Kansas.[12]

One of her first assignments, after arriving was to ferry a BT-13 *Valiant* two-seat trainer, from Enid, Oklahoma to Seattle, Washington. Flying solo, she crossed the southwest, stopping about every 425 miles for fuel. While flying between Albuquerque and Kingman, Arizona, she flew over a train wreck near Williams, Arizona that she described in a brief letter to her family as "Terrible." Three passengers and a railroad fireman had been killed just before midnight, July 3, when a Santa Fe Chief passenger train derailed. Twelve of its 14 cars had left the tracks, with four of them crushed together. Later reports said the train was traveling downhill, into a curve, at as much as 40 miles an hour faster than it should have been going.[13]

Orders said WASPs could not fly at night and so Paula would often spend a few minutes on the ground each evening writing a short letter home. At about 5:30 in the early evening of July 6, she reached the Victorville Army Air Field in California. She wrote that after having a meal of "Gooood" [sic] steak and peas, she got a ride into the nearby town of Adelanto for a few hours of relaxation. The next morning, it was a flight up the Central Valley of California, finally stopping in Sacramento for fuel. "Wonderfully cool here," she wrote. Apparently, someone told her that the temperatures were always so moderate in the area that officers could wear winter uniforms all year long. It was obviously a joke, as anyone who's been in Sacramento during the hot summer months would know. Paula had arrived in the morning when pleasant temperatures were likely still in the mid 60s. By afternoon, the thermometer was peaking at 100°. "Next stop Medford, Oregon and then Seattle," she wrote. The last words the Loop family ever heard from their daughter.[14]

At about 3:30 in the afternoon, July 7, 1944, Lowell Ash, a fire guard with the U.S. Forest Service, was the first to spot the fire. From his fire lookout, just north of the Rogue River in Trail, Oregon, he and a small crew rushed northwest over a narrow mountain highway to the scene. From there they hiked four miles into the forest. While quickly putting out the small forest fire, they discovered the wrecked airplane and Paula's body. By 7:30 that evening, Army personnel recovered Paula and took her to Camp White, an army training base about 5 miles north of Medford. Paula's friend and fellow WASP, Jerry Hardman, came to escort Paula's casket home to her parents in Oklahoma.

WASPs were civilian employees of the government, with no military benefits or courtesies. The Army did not pay to send her home—that was up to her family and friends. Eleven days after her death, the whole town turned out for her burial in Wakita Cemetery. Although the Army didn't consider her a veteran, Paula had served her country, and so, her parents draped her casket with an American flag. They embedded her WASP silver wings into her headstone.[15]

Paula Loop was the 26th woman to die while flying as a WASP.

Eleven more would join her before the end of the year. Each suffered horrific deaths, deaths seldom described to loved ones. Death certificates tell of fractured skulls, necks, arms, and legs, sometimes accompanied by lacerations of the skull and brain; even decapitation, and complete evisceration of the brain or other organs of the body. A coroner's notation of "multiple crushing of the body" could include chest, arms, legs, and skulls, with multiple internal injuries. Then, there were the 3rd degree burns and "charring of the entire body." Perhaps the kindest cause of death on a death certificate was a coroner's brief determination that death was the result of "multiple injuries incurred in an airplane crash."[16]

Most of these women had grown up idolizing and following the exploits of Ruth Nichols, Amelia Earhart, Jacqueline Cochran, and others; and yet, few of them ever thought they would get a chance to fly. However, flying clubs that allowed women and young girl members were popping up across the country, and in the spring of 1939, with the government planning for civilian pilot training, a new optimism was taking flight.

"In the wars to come," syndicated columnist, Bert Andrews, wrote that May, "be on your guard against Amazons with wings!" Andrews was predicting that women, at least women in other countries, might soon be flying combat missions during wartime. To those skeptics who laughed at the idea, he reminded his readers that those were the same cynics who ridiculed "the prophets who were rash enough to predict that someday women would be allowed to walk up to polling places in this America and cast their ballots just as men did." Andrews sought the opinion of some of the more notable women fliers of the day and found that most didn't think American women would soon be fighting in aerial combat, but rather, most agreed it was about time the government gave serious thought to training women pilots for wartime duties.[17]

"Of course women are capable of behind the lines work," Elizabeth "Betty" Gillies told Andrews. "I suppose that if the time should come when there was a shortage of men, and women had to take up bombers and pursuit planes, they could do that too. But right now it's hard for me to visualize them on the firing line." Gillies began flying in 1928 and was one of the first women to sign up for what would eventually be called the WASP.[18]

Jackie Cochran, already a well-known businesswoman, competitive flier, and soon to be one of the major forces behind creation of the WASP, was thinking ahead. "Women should have a chance to prove themselves in time of war," she told Andrews. "If they do not actually get training in the Army air schools, the government should establish a special school for their training. … In the next war, we shall probably see them flying the ambulance planes. I can't see them on the firing line, but they should receive every kind of training for defense, in case of attacks during peaceful pursuits."[19]

The last word went to Geraldine Masinter, a San Francisco woman who paid for her flight training out of her stenographer's salary and who would become a WASP, studying in the same class as Paula Loop. "It will take a long time for women to win a definite place in the Air Corps—maybe in twenty years," she said. "But if America ever needs them they'll make grand fighters—women always have."[20]

It would take much more than twenty years for American women to fly into aerial combat, but even so, much sooner than these ladies could have expected, their country was about to come calling.

# [2]

## JACKIE—"A PLUCKY FLIER"

Other than their love of flying, in many ways, the two women most responsible for formation of the WASP couldn't have been more different. Jacqueline Cochran was born into poverty, while Nancy Love was the daughter of a wealthy physician. Cochran never went to college, had barely two years in elementary school, and said she taught herself what she needed to know. Nancy attended private schools and was a Vassar coed. Both women were methodical and tenacious in their life decisions, but Jackie was more aggressive and vocal, loaded with uncontainable personality. Nancy was private, soft spoken, diplomatic, and gently efficient.

Long before she changed her name in the late 1920s, Jackie Cochran was born in Muskogee, Florida as Bessie Lee Pittman. Perhaps embarrassed by her poverty, bitter, and blaming her parents for her troubles, she creatively fashioned a personal biography. It emphasized her turbulent childhood and how her determined quest to escape poverty and achieve monetary success, took root at such an early age. Some, and perhaps much of what she said in a 1954 *Life* magazine article and her subsequent book, *The Stars at Noon*, about those hardscrabble years, may well have happened, but they also may have been distorted childhood memories. It's difficult to believe that a pre-teen girl would have all the abilities, physical and mental, that Jackie claims in surprising detail, and yet, she did manage to escape and succeed; and one wishes to believe every word. Her subsequent success as a businesswoman and aviator is a true Horatio Alger story; a story good enough to not need what often reads like a celebrity news release, rather than a truthful memory. Her account skips over a marriage and the death of a child, but it's the severe rejection of her parents, especially her mother, that is most disturbing.

"At the age of six I overheard my Mama telling a friend that I was not really her daughter at all," Jackie said. "My Mama was slovenly and lazy, and her meanness varied from a normal high pitch when things were going well to a feverish level when we were on half rations, which was most of the time. The knowledge that I did not belong to her gave me a sense of happiness and exhilaration." Jackie told of an independent little girl who refused to go to school and a girl no one was able to control. "Even then, no one could whip me and get away with it for long," she said. "Mama used to pick on me. I thought because I was the smallest." She tells of the time her mother was furious after sending Jackie to the store for ice and discovering it had all melted away before Jackie got home. "For this bad conduct, Mama decided to whip me. I picked up a big chunk of firewood and we talked things out, with my eyes flashing fire. She never touched me again."[1]

No matter what Jackie said or believed, family members insist that Jackie was never an adopted orphan. She was born May 11, 1906, to Ira and Mary Pittman. Ira was a skilled but illiterate millwright who seemed always on the move, taking his family with him throughout the panhandle of Florida, helping to set up and maintain small sawmills. Jackie was the youngest of their five children and she remembered hating the constant moving between mill towns; a life she called "living on Sawdust Road."[2]

"My life in the sawmill towns of northern Florida was bleak and bitter and harsh," she said, "but it taught me independence and the necessity of fending for myself." She said she tried to run away with a circus. When that failed, she walked into a gypsy camp. "I had been warned that gypsies would steal children if given a chance. I wandered into their camp several times, but they kept chasing me away. Coming on top of the circus debacle this was a big disappointment."[3]

When she was 8, the family moved to Columbus, Georgia. "We heard that in the cotton mills a boom was on and everyone could work," she wrote. "So we made the long, cold train ride to Columbus. I went to work immediately in a cotton mill nearby." She was paid 6¢ an hour, working the 12-hour night shift, pushing a cart up and down the aisles and delivering bobbins of thread to the weavers. At the end of her first week, she had made $4.50. "I was supremely happy," she said. "I had no shoes, but I had dreams." Her dreams darkened a bit when her mother took all of her money away. "The next week I took the initiative," Jackie said. "I gave Mama $3 and kept $1.50 for myself. With it, I made a down payment on my first pair of shoes."[4]

Two years later, the 10-year-old accepted an "executive position." She became supervisor of 15 other children, teaching them how to inspect cloth. It was a short-lived career move. The workers went on strike and, for three months, Jackie said she kept herself busy by reading several hours a day, always with a dictionary by her side. "I read *Dracula*—not a very good book for a 10-year-old child, but I did not think of myself as a child." Finally, bored and disgusted with her inactivity, she talked with a forewoman from the factory who told her to find something else to do. The woman believed Jackie had more energy and ambition than any other worker she had ever seen. She sent Jackie to a beauty shop owner who owned three shops in the area. Jackie became the woman's apprentice and went to live with her new boss and her seven sons. She cooked meals and cleaned house for the family, and went to work every day at one of the shops, cleaning the booths, and mixing shampoos and conditioners. The woman taught her how to make wigs, dye hair, and give permanent waves. A few years later, when she was 14, Jackie left for Montgomery, Alabama, where she talked her way into a higher paying job in another beauty shop. "I kept on saving my money," she said, "learned to dance, and bought a Model-T Ford. The Model-T not only got me invitations to college parties, but gave me my first experience with engines."[5]

What Jackie neglects to say in her story is that by the beginning of 1920, when she was still 13 years old, she had already moved back to live with her mother and father in Paxton, Florida. By the end of that year, when she was finally 14, she was pregnant and getting married. That's when she actually moved to Montgomery. In the next five paragraphs of her 1954 reminiscence, she covers nine years of her life, leaving out significant details as she quickly recounts her career moves, conveniently ignoring her personal life. She said one of her beauty shop customers in Montgomery was able to get her into a nurses training course at the Montgomery hospital, where she stayed for three years. With newfound confidence, Jackie accepted a job with a sawmill district doctor in Bonifay, Florida. "I was going back to Sawdust Road as a modern Florence Nightingale," she said, "to help the people I knew needed help so much." She doesn't say how long she nursed to mill families, but eventually, she decided she didn't have enough strength or enough money to help the people who had "needed help so much." She had to get away "and make money," she said. "I went back into beauty parlor work, first in Pensacola, then in Biloxi, and Philadelphia; and soon I thought I was ready for the biggest city of all. I sold my car and set off for New York City." That was in 1929. Jackie Cochran's 1954 story had erased and deliberately omitted nine years of perhaps some of her most painful memories.[6]

While living in Paxton, Florida, Jackie met Robert Harvey Cochran, a nearly 25-year-old man who had just completed a two-year enlistment in the U.S. Navy and was now working as a machinist at the Pensacola Naval Shipyard. For over 10 years, Robert and his parents had been living in the small town of Noma, a little over 50 miles east of Paxton. By the end of summer, 1920, 14-year-old Jackie realized that she was pregnant and Robert was the father. The couple rushed across the Florida-Georgia state line and married on November 13 in Blakeley, Georgia. Robert Cochran, Jr. was born three months later. Doris Rich, author of a Jackie Cochran biography, said Jackie left the baby boy with Jackie's parents in Florida and Jackie and Robert moved to Montgomery. Jackie worked there as a hairdresser and nurse. Whether her baby ever lived with Jackie and Robert is unclear, and just how long they stayed together in Montgomery isn't known. One suspects that it was a troubled marriage, especially with Jackie's memories of "learning to dance" in Montgomery, and those "invitations to college parties." When Jackie said that she returned as a nurse to Sawdust Road in Bonifay, Florida, it may have marked her separation from Robert. Her parents were now living in DeFuniak Springs, Florida, not far from Bonifay, and, in 1925, that's where four-year old Robert Cochran, Jr. died. The Pittman family said that young Cochran had taken matches into a backyard outhouse and tried to light them. A flame set his clothes on fire and the boy died a painful death. They placed a heart-shaped headstone on his grave, inscribed with his name, birth and death dates, and an inscription—"Gone so soon my loved one."[7]

Jackie and Robert were divorced in 1927 and for the next couple of years Jackie returned to work in beauty shops. In 1929, she left for New York City. There, from a small room near Broadway and 79th Street, 23-year-old Jackie went looking for a job. She found it at Antoine's Saks Fifth Avenue salon. "The salon was more than packed with customers who liked high prices," she said. "I began making good money." She soon began alternating between New York and Antoine's Miami salon. With her spare time in Miami, she could always find "fun," including winning dance contests and even a prize for her needlework at the county fair. She became a very popular guest at dinner parties and, in April 1932, the girl who had walked on the dirt of Sawdust Road took her first step toward another wedding and a millionaire. Standing in the lobby of a Miami nightclub, waiting for a table and cocktails, Jackie watched as an attractive man walked past and disappeared into the cloakroom. "A little while later," she said, "I found the man sitting next to me at cocktails." It was Floyd Odlum.[8]

Odlum had come to New York in 1917 as a struggling young lawyer from Utah, with a new wife and a 3-month-old son. He began buying up failing companies, reorganizing them until they turned a profit, keeping some and selling others; until gradually he became a self-made millionaire. After the stock market crash and the ensuing Great Depression, Odlum would be one of the few people in the country who would turn economic adversity into a fortune.[9]

In that Miami nightclub, Jackie told Odlum how confining her work was and that she had dreams and hopes of getting away, selling cosmetics on the road, and eventually starting her own cosmetic company. With the Depression on and the competition so keen, Odlum told her that she would almost need wings to cover all the territory she must have to succeed. "To do that job well, you should learn to fly," he said. Two days later, Odlum made Jackie the guest of honor at his own private party and the two had more time to talk. Jackie was convinced, and when she returned to New York, she asked for a brief vacation. "The next day I was taking a free demonstration flight," Jackie said. "After three hours of instruction I soloed." In 17 days, she had her private pilot's license and a new career. "It wasn't any stunt at all, this learning to fly in so short a time," she said. "It was just a question of making up one's mind to do something and doing it."[10]

When Odlum and Jackie met, he had already been married nearly 20 years, but something was happening in that marriage and perhaps it all began with Jackie Cochran. In October 1935, Odlum's wife, Hortense, left New York for Nevada and obtained a quick divorce on grounds of extreme cruelty. Nine months later, Odlum and Jackie were married in a secret ceremony, not revealed until July 5, 1936, when the couple sailed from New York on a honeymoon cruise to England.[11]

By late spring 1934, now with a commercial transport license in hand, Jackie was preparing for her first air race, the McRobertson, London to Melbourne International. She had paid for construction of the airplane, purchased its 900-hp, Pratt & Whitney Hornet engine, and entered the machine in the competition. She was also paying for most, if not all, of the expenses, including shipping the plane to Europe. Even with her well paying position in the cosmetics world, one has to suspect that Floyd Odlum was providing secret and significant financial support. She arrived in London in mid-October, dubbed by the press as "the mystery woman entrant." She and her copilot, Wesley Smith, planned to fly between 25,000 and 35,000 feet, breathing with the help of an oxygen tank. The flight lasted less than a day. A problem with the wing flaps reduced the aircraft's speed to a point where there was no possibility of victory. Far behind the other contestants, they gave up in Romania. Before returning home, the first thing Jackie did after landing in Bucharest was to buy a dress and other accessories to replace her flight suit. There were reports that the flight actually ended because Jackie was afraid to finish the race. Ed Granville, one of the owners of the company that had built the airplane for Jackie and had accompanied her to England, empathically denied those reports. He said she had "proven herself a thorough sportswoman … A plucky flier."[12]

Jackie had become a dedicated aviator whose accomplishments, in time, would even surpass her friend, Amelia Earhart. Prior to the 1934 running of the London-Melbourne race, Jackie had tried to enter the Bendix Trophy race, the country's premier cross-country air competition; however, women were banned from entering. Instead, Jackie's plane, a Granville, Miller & DeLackner Model R-6H, built in Springfield, Massachusetts, and named the *Q.E.D.*, was flown to a third place finish in the Bendix. Jackie would fly the same plane in the London-Melbourne race later that year. Newspapers took note that the *Q.E.D.* was painted in "Cochran Green," noting that the dark green color was named in Jackie's honor by the company, because it had manufactured that same color for the first plane Jackie had learned to fly. In 1935, after heavy lobbying by Earhart and Jackie, the Bendix race began allowing women fliers and Jackie flew in that race, but mechanical troubles over Arizona forced her to turn back and give up. In 1937, after skipping 1936 because of mechanical problems with her airplane, Jackie took third place and $5,500 in the Bendix, while flying a Beechcraft D-17W. That same year she set the women's international speed record at 293 mph. In 1938, she became the second woman to ever win the Bendix, flying a Seversky AP-7A from Los Angeles to Cleveland in 8 hours, 10 minutes and 26 seconds, at an average of nearly 250 mph. She had finished 23 minutes ahead of her nearest competitor. By the end of the 1930s, because she was setting records in altitude and speed, Jackie was known as the best woman pilot in the United States—perhaps the world. When she died in 1980, she had accumulated more speed, altitude, and distance records than any pilot, male or female, in aviation history.[13]

By the end of 1939, talk of a possible war in Europe and the Japanese campaigns underway in the Far East, had already stimulated talk of how women fliers could help the nation's national defense.

President Roosevelt had signed the Civilian Pilot Training Act in June, and while it appeared peaceful in nature, it was a quiet acknowledgment that the country might eventually face an emergency. A month later, Peggy Salaman, a record holding British aviator, while visiting in Boston, said British women were ready to begin ferrying military planes should war break out and were signing up with the country's civil air guard. There were also news reports of Soviet women who were already flying combat missions. In Germany, women trained male pilots to fly. That fall, members of the Ninety-Nines, the first organization of women pilots in the United States, voted to create a women's aviation scholarship in memory of Amelia Earhart, the clubs first president. It would allow members to learn aerial navigation and blind flying in a four-week course with a twofold purpose—to organize women pilots to take over commercial airlines in the event of a national emergency and to relieve male pilots who might be called into the Air Corps. "We want to have a group of women pilots who can be useful under war or any other emergency," said Mary Nicholson, head of the New York-New Jersey division of the Ninety-Nines.[14]

Earlier, in September, after the Nazi invasion of Poland, Jackie had written a letter pleading her case to Eleanor Roosevelt, the president's wife. "The real bottle neck in the long run is likely to be trained pilots," Jackie said, noting that women aviators could do many things that would release male pilots for combat duty. "This requires organization, and not at the time of emergency, but in advance. We have about 650 licensed women pilots in this country. Most of them would be of little use today, but most of them could be of great use a few months hence if properly trained and organized." Although her letter outlined what would finally begin to take shape in 1942, for the moment, the Washington bureaucracy was unmoved.[15]

For the next two years, Jackie pressed even harder for the training of a large number of women pilots, convinced that the winning of any future war would require women fliers contributing their skills to the effort. "I draw the line at combat," she said, "American women could fight if they had to, but I don't approve the idea." She said that there were already 1500 licensed women pilots in the country, but perhaps only 200 of those would be able to handle large airplanes without additional training. "A nucleus of 1,000 women," she said, "would be a good start toward a really effective corps. An Army operated women's auxiliary air corps would not," she said, "be a powder puff social vehicle, but a source of hardworking, patient, and effective ground and aerial instructors, couriers, and ferry pilots." She urged that any program be set up on a very large scale and under efficient and strict supervision. "That kind of job belongs to the government," Jackie said, "and I hope the government doesn't delay any longer in assuming it. Effective results next year demand preparations this year."[16]

Running out of patience, Jackie decided it was time to demonstrate what a woman could do. She would ferry a U.S. Army bomber from Canada to England and, once there, study the women pilots already flying in the British Air Transport Auxiliary. First, she had to pass a flight exam required of all pilots ferrying large aircraft across the Atlantic. "The exam had me plain scared and so I boned up for six weeks before taking it," she said. Husband, Floyd Odlum, arranged with Northeast Airlines for Jackie to train for the exam by flying one of their two-motored transport planes without passengers. Check pilots at her Canadian training base would ride along and repeatedly run her through the captain's checkout procedures and other scenarios. Some in Canada didn't want women flying bombers and were hoping Jackie wouldn't pass that final exam, but she did. Earlier, General Henry Arnold, head of the Army Air Corps, said he approved of Jackie piloting a bomber; however, just before takeoff, Canadian officials designated her copilot and told her she could fly, but not takeoff or land the Lockheed *Hudson* bomber.[17]

The British Ministry of Aircraft Production had tried to keep the flight secret; however, the story of a woman taking part in a war was a story no one could hide. When Jackie landed, the authorities couldn't do much when British and American reporters rushed to Jackie and began shouting their questions. It was good news for Jackie who knew how to get the publicity she needed and wanted. "I'm feminine," she told them, refusing photographs until she had changed out of her flight clothes. After a quick change into a light summer dress with floral print and a pair of high-heel sandals, the flashbulbs began to pop. Her hair and makeup were as good as could be found on any Hollywood starlet. "I am not allowed to describe what I saw or exactly what we did," she said, "but I can say this trip was uneventful and unexciting—merely a ferry trip." She showed them some oranges, cigarettes, and three dozen pairs of nylons that she had brought to friends living in a wartime country with few chances to obtain such simple luxuries. Although she had not taken off or landed the plane, she had flown the entire 2,000 miles herself, accompanied only by a Canadian radioman and an American pilot, Captain Grafe Carlisle. "He did the navigating and I was at the controls the whole way over," Jackie said. Carlisle was quick to compliment Jackie. "I've never flown with a more competent pilot," he said. "Cochran is as good a pilot as any man I've ever flown with."[18]

"I have a busy schedule mapped out," she said. "Inspection tours to see the part women are playing in this war. I am particularly anxious, of course, to meet the women pilots who are ferrying for the R.A.F. in the women's auxiliary air force. Whatever knowledge I pick up regarding this phase of the war may be useful someday to our country." For the next few days she visited a number of women's auxiliary units and also a British fighter station, where she talked with British, French, Polish, and Norwegian pilots as they prepared to sweep over the English Channel looking for German aircraft.[19]

On July 1, 1941, after first flying back from England to Montreal, Canada, Jackie arrived at New York City's LaGuardia Airport in the same clothes she had worn for 29 hours. "All I can think of at the moment," she told reporters at a small news conference, held in her large apartment overlooking the East River, "is about forty-eight hours sleep." She had changed into "a silk afternoon dress" and was serving tea, "her blond curls swept up into a crown." She said she would make a detailed report for whatever government official would listen, about her bomber flight and what she had seen the British women fliers doing. "If I should be asked to do the organizing of America's women flyers myself, I am prepared to give all my time to the task."[20]

The next day, she met with the highest government official in the country, President Franklin Roosevelt and his wife Eleanor. She was a luncheon guest in the couples Hyde Park dining room. The Roosevelts, Jackie, and her husband, Floyd Odlum, knew each other well. Odlum had made significant contributions to Roosevelt's campaigns and was about to be appointed by the president as a department head in the Office of Production Management in Washington, D.C. The president, Jackie, and Eleanor discussed what Jackie had found out in England and, if war came, the possibility of organizing a non-combatant group of American women fliers who could release men for combat duty. Roosevelt asked Jackie to look into how she would organize and train them. He gave her a handwritten note addressed to the Assistant Secretary of War for Air, Robert Lovett, asking him to help Jackie with her research. Lovett referred her to General Arnold who in turn sent her to Colonel Robert Olds, Commanding Officer of the Army's newly formed Ferry Command.[21]

Strictly as a volunteer and given no clerical help, Jackie went to work in Colonel Olds' Washington, D.C. office. She brought seven of her own employees from New York City to help her sift through 300,000 Civil Aeronautics Administration forms. They checked the medical and flying records of the country's nearly 3,000 licensed women pilots to see if they could meet current ferry pilot requirements. Jackie found that barely 260 had accumulated at least 200 hours flying time, the minimum required. At the end of July, a questionnaire mailed to these women asked for detailed information about their flying experience, including types of aircraft flown, how much solo flying had been done since their last license was issued, their flight instrument rating, and if they had a radio license. The key question was, "Would you be interested in joining an organization which is government sponsored at a salary not less than $150 to start?" When the surveys returned, Jackie realized her dream of 200 or more qualified women pilots flying for the Army wasn't possible without significant training. "Except for not more than 100 licensed women pilots," she said, "the women were not usable without advanced training in most cases."[22]

In the midst of Jackie's fact-finding, Eleanor Roosevelt gave her support to Jackie's efforts, closing her August 5 syndicated newspaper column, "My Day," by posing a question. "I have been hearing lately how much women pilots are doing in England," she wrote. "They ferry planes to places of safety when they are not in use, and fill in so that men can get some rest when duty is neither combat duty nor dangerous service. I wonder if, in this country, in the CAA courses or in the services, we have begun to train women so they may perform such duties. It would seem to be wise to give women pilots this opportunity, since we know they have been so useful in other countries."[23]

The answer was no. On August 25, General Arnold rejected Jackie's recommendations for training women. "The use of women pilots serves no military purpose in a country which has adequate manpower at this time," Arnold wrote. He said he was concerned about placing women on air bases predominantly populated by men. "In view of the small number of women pilots and the large number of male pilots available," he said, "the obvious military advantage of training … as many male pilots as possible, and the serious problems presented by the use of women pilots, the above recommendations cannot at this time be favorably considered."[24]

Two months later, Arnold suggested that Jackie, who was likely still quite frustrated and angry, recruit some women fliers to ferry military airplanes in England for the British Air Transport Auxiliary (ATA). As leader of such a group of women, Jackie could see firsthand how the British were able to integrate women into flight positions at normally all male duty stations. With those lessons learned, she would be better able to form a similar group in the United States, if needed. Jackie contacted officials with the ATA and with the blessing of Arnold began recruiting candidates. In January, when Jackie and British officials had reached agreement on procedures, Colonel Olds, now a Brigadier General, told Jackie that he was going to start hiring women pilots on an individual basis, the same as he did with civilian male pilots. Jackie immediately complained to General Arnold. Olds would pay the women more than they would receive in Great Britain, she said, and that would make it difficult for her to recruit the best pilots for the ATA. Worst of all, she believed women pilots should be organized into a unit separate from male branches of the Army Air Corps and that they be led by women. "His plan," Jackie said, "should be put on ice for at least six months, or my program for England should be stopped."[25]

With her and her husband's relationship with the president, Jackie had a lot of influence at Army Air Forces Headquarters, particularly when she was upset. On the same day that Arnold received Jackie's letter, he sent his own letter to Olds, ordering him to stop. "As per instructions from me this date, you will make no plans or open negotiations for hiring women pilots until Miss Jacqueline Cochran has completed her present agreement with the British authorities and has returned to the United States."[26]

In the spring of 1942, after a physical examination, two weeks of training, and successfully passing flight tests in Canada, the first of Jackie's personally chosen American women pilots arrived in England. They had signed 18-month contracts, agreeing to ferry British military planes throughout Great Britain for roughly $4,000 a year. Upon arrival, Jackie was with them as they received uniforms and complete sets of flying gear, including helmets, gloves, boots, and parachutes. Before they began to fly, there was more ground school and aerial instruction to acquaint the women with British flying procedures and the aircraft they would be flying.[27]

Of the 25 women Cochran recruited, four would eventually return to the U.S. to join the WASP and one returned to become a WASP flight instructor. Only one of the 25 women lost their life while serving—Mary Nicholson, the first licensed woman pilot in North Carolina, a charter member of the Ninety-Nines, and private secretary to Jackie Cochran. She died in May 1943 when the propeller flew off her plane. Mary attempted an emergency landing in a farmer's field, but the weather was poor and visibility limited. She crashed into a farm building and the aircraft erupted in flames. Aline Rhonie was the only American woman who would fly for the British after first serving as a WASP, one of the original five women pilots accepted in 1942 into the

Women's Auxiliary Ferrying Squadron, headed by Nancy Love. After just a few months, she left the WASP for England and privately joined the ATA.[28]

In the United States, pressure was mounting on the Army and the Congress to use women pilots in the war effort. Eleanor Roosevelt added her voice in her September 1, 1942, "My Day" column. She wondered why the CAA said women were not psychologically fit to be pilots, when she had seen pictures of women teaching men to fly and had admired the bravery of women flying for the ATA in Britain. "I believe if the war goes on long enough," she said, "and women are patient, opportunity will come knocking on their doors. However, there is just a chance that this is not a time when women should be patient. We are in a war and we need to fight it with all our ability and every weapon possible. Women pilots are a weapon waiting to be used."[29]

Jackie returned to the United States, arriving on September 10. The British had asked her to recruit more women pilots for the ATA. On the very day she landed, the formation of the Women's Auxiliary Ferrying Squadron (WAFS) was announced. It wasn't a complete surprise. She had heard from her husband before she left London that there was serious talk about forming a women's aviation unit. But Jackie was furious. After all, Arnold had ordered his subordinates to stop all planning until Jackie returned from England. The next day she was in General Arnold's office demanding an explanation. Arnold claimed he hadn't known in advance of the announcement, and said his subordinates had organized the squadron without his authorization. It's a claim difficult to believe. Military men, especially in wartime, weren't in the habit of establishing experimental programs without first checking with their commander for approval. Arnold was well aware of the plans, as subsequent reports show. Just a month earlier, Arnold had responded to Congressman William Poage, who had wanted to know if the Army planned to use women pilots. "It gives me great pleasure," Arnold said "to inform you that the Air Transport Command ... is giving consideration to the use of women fliers as ferrying pilots and is attempting to carry out a program of that nature."[30]

Arnold ordered his subordinates to come up with a plan that would be acceptable to Jackie. Over the next couple of days, a consensus was reached that more women pilots would be needed soon and, based on Jackie's previous research, most of those women would need more training. Rather than eliminate the ferrying squadron altogether, or burden it with a training mission, Jackie recommended "a training program be started separately and promptly." Announcement of the

Women's Flying Training Detachment with Jackie Cochran at its head came on September 14, 1942. "I am delighted," Jackie said, "that the more than 3,000 licensed women pilots in America are going to have an opportunity to prove their competence to serve in their chosen field in the war." In Jackie's mind, this was just a temporary compromise. She believed that all women's pilot programs within the Army Air Force were hers, and she was going to make sure that was the way it would be.[31]

**Great Britain was the first country to employ women to ferry military aircraft. In 1942, Jacqueline "Jackie" Cochran, seen here wearing her British Air Transport Auxiliary uniform, organized a group of American women to fly for the ATA and used that experience when forming the WASPs. –** ***Department of Defense photo.***

# [3]

## NANCY

While Jackie Cochran was advocating for an ever increasing force of women pilots who could be trained to aid the war effort, Nancy Love favored a small, extremely qualified corps of women who could quickly learn military customs and procedures, and would only need a few weeks' introduction to the airplanes they would fly. While Jackie Cochran was talking to newspapers and the president of the United States, Nancy was working with other women pilots, all hoping to organize an auxiliary air corps that would use their aviation skills, should the country be pulled into the European war.[1]

In May 1940, after completing her own survey of America's women pilots, using the same files Jackie Cochran would scan a year later, Nancy sent a letter to Colonel Robert Olds reporting what she had found. At the time, Olds was working in the War Plans Division of the Army Air Corps. Nancy said that she had found at least 49 women who she felt had excellent skills and were already more than qualified to fly larger and heavier military aircraft. "I really think this list is up to handling pretty complicated stuff," she wrote. "Most of them have in the neighborhood of a thousand hours or more—mostly more, and have flown a great many types of ships."[2]

Within days, the Plans Division was working out a strategy that would recruit 100 or more women pilots to begin ferrying single engine airplanes in the various Army transport squadrons. Refresher training was proposed and even commissioning the women as 2nd Lieutenants in the Army Air Corps. At the end of June, the plans were sent to General Arnold who quickly disapproved them, saying that women should only be used as commercial airline copilots to free some of those men for Army service. It seems war was still an ocean and over a year away, and for now, there was no need—especially no need for women fliers.[3]

Nancy Harkness Love was only 26 years old, but she had more hours flying an airplane than just about every licensed woman pilot in the country. She was born on Valentine's Day 1914, in Houghton, Michigan. Legally, Nancy was Hannah Lincoln Harkness, but because her father preferred to call her Nancy, the name stuck. Barely 13 years old in 1927, and while on a tour of Europe, Nancy saw Charles Lindbergh land in Paris after his historic transatlantic flight. One would think that she would have been impressed, but she wasn't. Aviation wouldn't captivate her imagination and become her passion until three years later, when she was 16. Back at home and on summer break from her studies at the Milton Academy, a girl's prep school in Milton, Massachusetts, Nancy saw a barnstorming pilot flying overhead. When he landed, she rushed to the nearby landing field. For a "Penny a Pound" she bought a ride with the barnstormer who flew her around the field. She rushed home for more money and "I bought another ride," she said. "Then I bought a stunt ride." The $5 stunt ride took her over the city and out over the water of Portage Lake. "I was hooked," she said. "I went home and told my father I wanted to learn how to fly." Her father, a successful physician, was more than willing to indulge his only daughter's dreams. He told her if she wanted to fly he would support her, even though her mother disapproved. But he made it clear that if she wanted to fly, she had better do it well or she shouldn't do it at all.[4]

Nancy's barnstorming pilot may have been one of the students trained by the Upper Peninsula Airways Company. The U.P.A. had built an airport on Michigan's Upper Peninsula near the town of Escanaba two years earlier. The company began to offer flying lessons, aerial tours, and commercial transportation services, and by May 1930, announced creation of the "Upper Peninsula Air College." The company expected nearly 25 or more aviation students to take flying lessons with them before the end of the year. That same month, they announced they had added the Fleet biplane that Nancy would learn to fly in, and not coincidentally, they also had hired Jimmy Hansen, the young man who would be Nancy's instructor. Jimmy owned that biplane.[5]

Throughout her life, Nancy would say that Jimmy Hansen was only two years older than she was, but in fact he was 4 ½ years older. He was born in Pennsylvania, June 1, 1909, to Klaus Hansen and his wife

Nannie. Klaus was a Norwegian immigrant who, after two years at the University of Illinois, became an independent consulting electrical engineer, offering his consulting and designing skills to firms such as Westinghouse Electric and the Louis Allis Company. Klaus was also an inventor, filing the first of his many electrical patents in 1921, shortly after the family had moved to Milwaukee. There, he was consulting engineer for the Harnischfeger Corporation, maker of mining and industrial equipment. Jimmy and his brother Ralph worked there as welders. Klaus' family life was more than comfortable and when his son, Jimmy, soloed and got his pilot's license, Klaus bought him the Fleet biplane as a reward.[6]

The story has always been that James Hansen was just a kid, barely older than Nancy and with little experience. "I don't think he knew what made the plane stay in the air," she said. "At least he never told me. My instructions were just to 'keep up the flying speed.'" Nancy recalled that Jimmy had a brand new license and that she was his first student, but that wasn't completely accurate. After his first solo flight in 1929, Jimmy flew as often as possible and had reached the 200 plus flight hours required for his transport and pilot instructor licenses. He may still have been a shaky pilot, but he certainly wasn't a novice. In May 1930, with both his licenses in hand, Jimmy flew his Fleet biplane to Michigan to become an instructor for the Upper Peninsula Airways Company. Perhaps Nancy probably remembered Jimmy as an inexperienced pilot because of the way he flew.[7]

When Jimmy agreed to teach Nancy to fly, surely he never told her about his accident. Three months earlier, and less than two weeks after he started as an instructor, he was flying with a ground instructor from the aviation school as his copilot. Perhaps it was a check flight to see if Jimmy was actually qualified to be an instructor. On the ground, the chief pilot for the school had noticed the airplane circling the city at an altitude lower than rules permitted. By the time the chief took off to intercept the plane, Jimmy had already lost control and crashed into the bay, a half mile east of Escanaba. Jimmy and the airplane survived, but the copilot drowned. Perhaps that's why some have said the Fleet biplane was in bad shape when Nancy first climbed into it; although, Nancy remembered Jimmy's biplane affectionately. "It was a darned nice plane," she later told a reporter.[8]

Nancy was a motivated student. "I wanted to fly right off," she said. "I'm no super genius, you understand, but I concentrated hard and I learned fast. I soloed after only five hours of training." That was August 31, 1930. In November, she passed her examination on the first try and became one of the youngest licensed women pilots in the country.[9]

When Jimmy returned home, and before Nancy returned to school, she followed him to Milwaukee and stayed with relatives so she could continue her flying lessons. A decade and a few years later, when Nancy took command of the Women's Auxiliary Ferrying Squadron, their paths briefly crossed again. By then, Jimmy Hansen was a ferry pilot himself who had started out as a civilian, but was now a lieutenant in the Army Air Corps, and married with a 6-year-old daughter. Early in January 1943, while Jimmy was flying solo near Columbus, Ohio in a Douglas A-20B light bomber, an onboard bomb exploded in flight and Jimmy crashed and died.[10]

It wasn't very long after earning her pilot's license that Nancy took a break from her studies and innocently headed off on her first cross-country flight—150 plus miles between Boston and Poughkeepsie, New York. Flying a closed cabin plane with two fellow students and their luggage on board, she was planning a visit with friends who were studying at Vassar College. "The ship was far too large and complicated for my fifteen solo hours," Nancy said. Heading generally west, she instantly recognized that she had no idea how to read a compass, and just as quickly realized she was in trouble. She couldn't see through the fast approaching clouds and so began a descent. Then the oil gage suddenly shattered, blowing black oil all over her windshield. She put her head out a side window and, while silently hoping the engine wouldn't stop, she made a safe and perhaps a miraculous landing in a coal yard. "When you have just made a forced landing in a coal yard," said a story about Nancy in the Vassar College newspaper, "so small that your plane has to be taken apart to extricate it, and your prep school has warned you that any more flying will result in immediate expulsion ...life is definitely complicated." Not long after her coal yard adventure, Nancy took a flight over a boy's prep school not far from the Milton Academy and, in her youthful enthusiasm, she decided to impress the boys with a buzzing of their campus. Unfortunately, she was late pulling up from her dive and her wheels grazed the chapel just enough to do some minor damage to its bell tower roof.[11]

Life didn't get any simpler when Nancy entered Vassar in the fall of 1931. In her spare time, she began taking ground school and aerial lessons at the Poughkeepsie airport. She quickly added enough additional flying hours to ultimately qualify for a commercial and then a transport license. When she had accumulated 100 hours and finally turned 18, the minimum age required, Vassar's only pilot qualified for a "hire license," allowing her to charge passengers for air excursions. Many of her passengers were Vassar students and the extra money she earned was poured back into her quest for that commercial license, a license held by fewer than 50 women in the entire country.[12]

Less than a month and a half after her 18th birthday, Nancy was in the final stages of her commercial training, flying in the front seat of a Great Lakes *Sport Trainer* biplane, and taking instruction from the pilot, John Miller. They had been in the air just over 20 minutes and Miller was bringing them down for a landing. Miller was in his final turn, a glide with little power. As he straightened out he tried to power up the motor, but it didn't respond. The biplane crashed into a tree and fell backward, while the motor was torn away and landed 25 feet further on. The plane settled bottom side up across a stone wall. Nancy released her safety belt and fell to the earth, striking her head, but otherwise unhurt. Miller followed a few seconds later, bleeding from his head and face after his goggles had shattered when his head slammed into the plane's control board. Rushed to the Vassar hospital, injuries seemed minor, but eventually he lost his left eye.

Nancy was back in the air 10 days later, just 11 days after that she received her commercial license. It was the first time she got extensive national coverage and a nickname. She was now, "Pretty Nancy Harkness of Houghton, Michigan, 'the flying freshman' 'the first and only aviatrix at Vassar.'" The photograph accompanying the news articles, showed Nancy in her flying clothes, including leather cap and goggles. It was one of a series that Nancy had taken earlier, in and about the Great Lakes biplane before it crashed, not after she got her commercial license, as the articles said. In August 1933, when she finally logged 200 hours, had passed all exams, and claimed her transport license, the identical picture again made newspapers across the country.[13]

Nancy dreamed of demonstrating and selling airplanes to prospective customers, but also thought she might try her hand at being a stunt pilot, or owning an airport of her own. "Aviation is a young field," said an article in her college newspaper, "and most of the people in it are young too, so Nancy can grow up with aviation." But growing up with aviation would take money and by the end of 1933, the depression had finally taken its toll on the Harkness family finances. Nancy's father couldn't afford Vassar anymore and Nancy had to drop out. She went to New York City to study at a secretarial school, looking to find some sort of job and hoping one day to fly again and take aviation classes. On one of those job hunting trips in the Boston area she met Robert Love. Love had learned to fly in 1929 and had attended Princeton and the Massachusetts Institute of Technology, but dropped out to pursue his love of aviation. In 1932, he had established his own company, Inter City Aviation, at the Boston Municipal Airport. He offered charter flights, pilot training, and conducted a fledgling airplane sales business. After seeing Nancy fly, Love hired the 20-year-old to not only demonstrate airplanes and fly charter flights for his company, but also to entice others to buy an airplane. "I sold only two planes," she would later say, "but you mustn't forget that one plane is equal to lots of automobiles and one sale means a lot more." Love was impressed with Nancy's flying abilities, but it wasn't love at first sight. "She's OK," Love told a reporter. "She's not just somebody who flies."[14]

"Miss Harkness is quite reserved," said a reporter, "but like all pilots, warms up to the topic of flying. ... It is anticipated that when this latest employee of the I.C.A. becomes a little better acquainted, she is going to be more than busy with her grey demonstrator, which by the way is the only ambulance plane in New England." The demonstrator airplane wouldn't be the only thing keeping Nancy "more than busy." A romance was blooming, and barely a year later, in August 1935, Nancy's parents announced the engagement of their daughter, Hannah Lincoln Harkness to Robert McLure Love. They married January 11, 1936, and taking turns at the controls, flew to California for their honeymoon. "Absolutely equal division of flying time," she said.[15]

Just after announcing her engagement, Nancy signed on with Phoebe Omelie who had been working on a plan with the Bureau of Air Commerce that would mark the roofs of buildings and towers, and place directional signs on the landscape, to designate airways that aviators could follow when navigating cross-country. Omelie was an aviation pioneer and, in 1927, the first woman in the country awarded a transport pilot's license. Nancy covered the east coast for Omelie and instead of flying from town to town trying to convince local governments and chambers of commerce to participate in the program, she rode trains. "Imagine," she said, "and me a pilot." Before she had to resign in November 1935 because her mother became sick, news reports said Nancy had already arranged placement of nearly 300 markers in Massachusetts alone.[16]

Returning from their honeymoon in late January 1936, the Loves went back to the hard work of keeping Inter City Airlines in business during the still difficult economic times. In September, Nancy decided to enter her first and last major air competition, the Amelia Earhart Trophy Race, held in Los Angeles. She won $75 while finishing fifth in a field of eight women, completing the 25-mile race around pylons in less than 17 minutes. She lost to the winner by only 45 seconds. A subsequent second place finish in a minor Detroit race ended Nancy's competitive streak. "I've led a humdrum aviation career," she would later say.[17]

Nancy was more interested in promoting women in aviation than competing in air races or making a name for herself. But even so, she was beginning to attract more attention from the press. When one reporter asked if flying took courage and might be too dangerous for women, Nancy, usually so calm and cool, came as close to frustrated anger as anyone was likely to see. "Courage?" she said. "Flying is simple. It's stupid to call it daredevilish. I've never wanted to fly to the South Pole or land a seaplane in a bathtub." She said she was tired of the "hero worshippers" of women pilots. She wanted "a campaign to teach women they are safer in a good airplane than they are in an automobile under bad traffic conditions." If a woman had time to learn French, "she has time to learn to fly."[18]

In the interest of easier and safer flying, Nancy agreed to test fly and demonstrate a new airplane of unusual design that was known as the Gwinn *Aircar.* Designed "for the man in the street" by aircraft engineer Joseph Marr Gwinn, Jr., the *Aircar* took its name from its many similarities to an automobile. It was about the same size as a large automobile and, allowing for its wingspan, could fit in a three-car garage. Inside a two-seat cabin, the pilot steered the stubby shaped craft with an inclined, automobile-like steering wheel. It not only controlled the plane's elevator control, but also its ailerons that were used for rudderless turns in the air and for steering on the ground. It featured a right foot accelerator on the floorboard, a foot pedal that controlled the landing gear's brakes, and a left foot pedal to control the wing flaps during takeoffs and landings. Rather than a two-wheel undercarriage, the *Aircar* landed on a more stable tricycle landing gear. Gwinn believed the machine incorporated unusual safety characteristics and he boasted that the "improper use of controls cannot produce loss of control, stall, or spin." He also promised that students would learn to fly in half the usual time.[19]

As special sales representative for the company, Nancy took the *Aircar* out on a few short exhibition tours. Initially only two *Aircar*s had been produced, and after the death of Nancy's fellow Aircar test pilot, Frank Hawks in 1938, the concept was all but dead. Yet, even as late as 1940, listings in aviation magazines still named Nancy "Director of the Gwinn Aircar Company."[20]

By 1939, Bob and Nancy Love had built up Inter City Aviation from a company with just two airplanes and eight employees to one that now had twelve planes and a staff of 50. The flying school was nearly always busy and there was hangar space for rent to accommodate up to 30 airplanes. The company signed contracts to make aerial surveys, take up newspaper reporters, and fly passengers anywhere they wanted to go. They not only sold planes, but also rented them. "Bob and Nancy get more fun out of flying than the Marx brothers would have in the White House in an election year," said Hamilton Thornquist, a reporter for *Popular Aviation* magazine. "They haven't found the pot of gold yet, but they've had a lot of fun flying around the rainbow."[21]

With the German invasion of Poland in September 1939, war began to engulf Europe. Nancy, a member of the Massachusetts Civil Air Patrol, began organizing a women's auxiliary air corps. Should the United States be pulled into war, these women pilots would be ready to replace men in flying jobs that would otherwise keep potential combat pilots out of the service. Nancy was also one of several women who ferried military planes destined for the Allies in Europe, and was the only woman to ferry a bomber. Because the United States was still officially neutral in the war, the bomber and the other planes only flew to the Canadian border, where they were hand-pulled or towed into Canada by truck, or with teams of horses. It was while flying these ferrying flights that Nancy began talking with members of the Army Air Corps Ferrying Command. Perhaps those talks prompted her to do some research and resulted in a May 1940 letter to Colonel Robert Olds, suggesting that women be used to ferry military aircraft. However, it was too soon. Military officials believed there were more than enough men to handle distribution of the few airplanes that were being manufactured. Until the Japanese attack on Pearl Harbor a year and a half later, there would be lots of talk about women pilots, but very little foresight and even less action.[22]

Nancy's husband, Robert, enlisted as an officer in the Army Air Corps in April 1941. Early in 1942, he was transferred to Army Ferrying Command Headquarters; prompting Nancy to resign from the Massachusetts National Guard and join him in Washington, D.C. In March, she found a civil service position in the Operations Office of the Ferrying Command's Northeast Sector. The job was in Baltimore, and rather than drive from Washington, Nancy flew her own airplane in a daily, 80-mile roundtrip commute. She kept tabs on how many planes were being produced in American factories and where in the U.S. or overseas they were being sent. With ever increasing wartime aircraft production levels in the country, it was obvious that soon the Ferrying Command wouldn't have enough male pilots to ferry them. Nancy was once again recommending the use of women pilots, but it would take a chance meeting at a Washington water cooler to turn talk into action.[23]

Colonel William Tunner, was commander of the Domestic Wing of the Ferrying Command, where Major Robert Love was working as an Administrative Executive. Although Tunner had never met Nancy and didn't even know who she was, he realized he had a major problem. "It was, of course," he said, "the delivery of all the planes which were now pouring off the assembly line." Compounding his troubles was the complexity of the war's battlefront locations. The same model of airplane might need many modifications to operate efficiently in varied climate and combat conditions. Modifications at the original factory would have slowed production, and so modification centers were set up across the country. Planes were being flown from the factory to a modification center, adding more trips to the Ferrying Command's schedule and putting a further drain on the limited number of male pilots available.[24]

"The greatest continuing hassle in the Ferrying Division [whether to use women pilots]—the one which caused ripples of anger, frustration, and indignation," Tunner said, "began in a moment's chitchat at the water cooler." Tunner was talking with Robert Love one day, and in their light conversation, Robert mentioned that he hoped his wife had gotten to work safely that morning, casually adding that Nancy commuted by airplane every day. "Good Lord," Tunner said. "I'm combing the woods for pilots and here's one right under my nose." He asked if there were many more women like Nancy. "Why don't you ask her yourself?" Robert said. Tunner met Nancy and the planning began.[25]

The Loves and their aviation skills were doing all they could in support of the war effort. Barely a year after his enlistment, Robert had risen from 2nd Lieutenant to Lieutenant Colonel, and in June 1942 was named the Ferrying Command's Deputy Chief of Staff. On September 10, 1942, Nancy Harkness Love was publicly named Director of Women Pilots for the Army's latest "experiment"—the Women's Auxiliary Ferrying Squadron (WAFS). Women pilots were finally going to war.[26]

When Nancy Harkness Love became director of the U.S. Women's Auxiliary Ferry Squadron in September 1942, she was only 28 years old. Beginning with her first squadron of women pilots at New Castle Army Airfield, near Wilmington, Delaware, her responsibilities quickly grew. Within nine months, she was commanding an additional three squadrons of WAFS—at Love Field, in Dallas, Texas, Romulus Airbase near Detroit, Michigan, and at Long Beach Army Airfield in California. - *National Archives photo 535775*

# [4]

## THE EXPERIMENT BEGINS

It began as a 90-day experiment that would last nearly 2 ½ years.

"Don't present us as a glamour outfit," Nancy Love told a reporter. "We're not. There's no room or time for glamour in the WAFS. We've got a serious job to do and we'll do it."

Sitting behind a simple wood desk that was barely large enough for a stenographer, let alone the Director of Women Pilots, Nancy had a few minutes to talk to a reporter in a barren room she called her office. The reporter was instantly fascinated and surprised when he met her. "She is amazingly young, still in her twenties," he said. "Here is a slim, tall, and gracious girl with ash blond hair."[1]

Nearly every reporter, man or woman, mentioned that Nancy was "extremely good looking—slender and girlish." Some noted her "large blue eyes" and a few were surprised with the touch of gray in her hair. Overall, they seemed to admire her directness and unassuming manner—"running the war without fuss and feathers," they called it. "Mrs. Love is no brusque and brittle big shot," said another, "nor is she the drilly type. She is gentle and understanding and dead in earnest." A fellow male pilot said that she was liked by both men and women. "She is something very special," he said. After her appointment, Nancy tolerated the inevitable flurry of interviews and photographs, but drew the line when photographers tried to make her into a glamour girl. In one photo session, a photographer kept shouting at her to, "Give us a smile! A big one! Show your teeth!" Finally, Nancy had had enough. She shook her head and said, "I look awful grinning, and besides, I don't think this is a grinning matter."[2]

With the war on, Nancy was only concerned with two things—the women pilots she was responsible for and flying. "She talks, thinks, and dreams flying every minute," said a friend. "She talks of her girls with pride and enthusiasm," said a reporter, "and yet, in everything she says there is a note of thoughtfulness, as if she never forgets, even for a second, the hard grueling, often dangerous war job her girls are being called on to do." Nancy said she believed that women pilots were more conservative than men and had fewer accidents; although, she admitted that they might be more careful because women pilots were more likely to be criticized by men. She was proud that her women could finally do something for their country. "They have been working so hard for so long to get any sort of recognition," she said. "They want to do something worthwhile and they've got something to offer."[3]

Early on, there was hope that they could recruit as many as 50 or even 100 women pilots for the ferrying squadron, but ultimately, because this was still only an experiment to see if women could do the job, only 25 were finally accepted. "Our rigid requirements limit the number available to us," Nancy said. The women had to hold a commercial pilot's license, must have flown at least 500 certified hours, and be rated to fly aircraft with a minimum 200-hp engine. In addition, they had to be an American citizen, 21-35 years old and a high school graduate. There were sincere efforts made to allow the women to become commissioned officers, but Congressional legislation that had created the Women's Army Corp (WACs) had no provisions allowing the commissioning of women flying officers or flight pay. Rather than delay the program while waiting for subsequent legislation, the recruited women pilots would be civilian employees, paid $250 a month, and given officer privileges without officer benefits. "We may join the officers club and eat in the officers mess," Nancy said, "but of course, we won't be here much. We'll be out on the road most of the time." She added that she personally expected to fly "as many of the ferrying trips as my duties will allow."[4]

Home base was just to the southeast of Wilmington, Delaware, along the Delaware River, at the New Castle Army Air Base. The Army Air Corps had taken over the former Wilmington Airport not long after the U.S. declared war. The conversion into a military base had been quick; although, the plan hadn't included women. In June, when Colonel Tunner visited New Castle, he found a barracks large enough for over 70 women. It was perfect because it was isolated from most of the other buildings on base, especially from all the men's barracks. However, beginning the experiment with only 25 WAFS would require extensive and costly modifications to such a large building. Tunner asked for something smaller. The solution was to have the men who were living in the Bachelor Officer Quarters moved out to the larger barracks, and then let the women take over the vacated BOQ. The result was 44 rooms that needed very little renovation.[5]

Although the drab green barracks seemed older than their years, Nancy was delighted. "These are our headquarters, not plain barracks," she said. "We've been assigned to bachelor officers quarters—real snooty. I've talked the colonel into giving us a full length mirror on each of the two floors." Each woman had her own small room that sometimes included a visit from a frantic little mouse or its family. The Army equipped the rooms with an army cot, a maple chest of drawers, a pine wardrobe, a chair, and a blue scatter rug. The women's responsibility was to "add a feminine frill or two;" easily accomplished by adding a few crocheted bedspreads and dressing table accessories. "There's only one bathroom on each floor," Nancy said, "so we will have to stand in line for the shower—it will be just like going back to college." It was as close as they could come to their rooms they left at home. The WAFS paid 75 cents a day for the room and 50 cents a meal at the Officers Mess. Nancy seemed most proud of the venetian blinds on all the windows. "I think we're the only outfit on an Army base that has venetian blinds," she said. "You see, we're surrounded by men and, before we got the blinds, we had to undress in the dark or in the hallways. Couldn't embarrass the men," she said with a smile.[6]

It took nearly two months of reviewing applications, subsequent interviews, and check flights confirming a woman's flying ability, before the first 20 WAFS were qualified. It took another month and a half before the full complement of 28 women were on base. Although the basic flying requirement was 500 hours, most of these women had actually flown more hours than the majority of male pilots in the command. Their average flight time was 1,162 hours. Nancy herself had logged over 1,200 hours.[7]

After the WAFS program was announced in September, the first regulation issued at New Castle Air Base declared that men and women pilots in training would be treated the same—"They will all be designated Civilian Pilots," it said. While in training, their day officially began at 7 a.m., when all pilots, men and women, had to be on the flight line for roll call. The women could sleep as late as they wanted as long as they made it to roll call on time. It all depended on how long it took them to get dressed. After their four weeks of training, roll call was moved to 8:00. When their day ended at 4:00 in the afternoon, the women were free and not subject to any curfew. Colonel Baker, commander of the 2nd Ferrying Group at New Castle, sensitive to any scandalous behavior that would damage the reputation of the experiment, ordered men and women to stay away from each other. But on a base where there were 400 men to every WAF, that was impractical. Although there never were any reports of bad behavior, there were always frequent groups of men and women gathering in the Officers Club for drinks and friendly conversation. "The girls never lack dates," Nancy said. "That is, when there is time for dates."[8]

It was an arduous program including calisthenics and close order drill. The study portion of the women's four-week training period would cover Army history, military theory, Army customs and courtesies, meteorology, and navigation. Along with an introduction to military aircraft, the women would also have at least 25 hours of practice flight time. "Of course, we are not part of the Army," Nancy said. "We're in Civil Service. But since we work with and for the Army, we have to learn to follow Army regulations and learn Army flying patterns." That meant the women would have to learn a new way to fly. "There are prescribed methods to be followed," Nancy said. "If you're flying with others, you learn to fly in specified formations. All of that takes time to learn and it's a hard grind."[9]

When the four weeks were up, the WAFS were ready to fly and weren't given any special ceremony. "There is only one ceremony," Nancy said. "The girl goes into Wilmington and orders her uniform. Up to that time, she's been kicking around in coveralls. The uniform is the symbol of her right to wear wings."[10]

Although they were civilians and not really part of the Army, Colonel Baker, recommended that all of the WAFS wear a uniform when on base or while flying. He couldn't order civilians to wear a uniform, but Nancy liked the idea and quickly endorsed it. Even though the WAFS would have to pay for their own uniform, the women bought them and wore them proudly. Ever since their arrival they had been wearing a rainbow hodgepodge of civilian and oversized military clothing, so, the new uniform not only gave them a quick morale boost, it also was a recognition of their service to their country. Nancy had contacted a Wilmington tailor who agreed to measure the women and create a greenish-gray uniform for them. It was a single breasted, four-button, belted jacket with matching skirt and trousers of wool serge. For formal occasions a white shirt was worn, and when a WAF was traveling or on duty, she wore a khaki shirt. Attached on the upper left shoulder of the jacket was the standard Army Air Forces Headquarters insignia, featuring a star with wings. Below it was placed a blue half circle patch with the letters "WAFS" written across it. Air Transport wings were pinned over the left breast pocket and smaller Air Corps wings graced both lapels. Regulation shoes were plain brown in an oxford style when wearing pants and a pump when wearing skirts. Topped with a garrison cap matching the material of the uniform, accompanied with a brown leather purse and gloves, the dress uniform was complete.[11]

When their four weeks of training were over and the WAFS finally put on their uniforms, their excited anticipation was temporarily and literally dampened. "Unfortunately it rained," Cornelia Fort said, "so we were like the original 'all dressed up & nowhere to go.'" The next day, Cornelia and five others received orders, put on their uniforms, and began delivering airplanes.[12]

Whether it was a short flight of perhaps a hundred miles, or a thousand miles across the country with many stops along the way, the WAFS were almost constantly on the move and always on their own. Anywhere along the route, if a plane wasn't ready for delivery when a WAF arrived, or if severe weather had set in, it was the woman's responsibility to find a place to stay until she could fly again. Perhaps worst of all, the problem of returning to New Castle was often monumental. Eventually, a transportation system was established; however, in 1942 and the early part of 1943, a WAF had to find her own way back to base. That meant either commercial airlines that gave her priority seating, or railroads and busses that didn't. Male ferrying pilots could hitch a free ride, known as a "hop," on a military airplane headed in the right direction, but the Transportation Command, afraid of mixing the sexes in isolated locations, closed that option to the women. Once back at New Castle, the WAF reported to Air Corps Supply to return her parachute and other equipment, and then visited the Finance Office for expense reimbursement. After some much needed sleep, she would return to the ready room, where she could study and wait for her next assignment. She never had long to wait.[13]

Although there had been a lot of publicity about the WAFS, the women frequently met people who were mystified when they saw them and just had to ask who they were and what they did. According to a government report, a typical conversation pestering the WAFS in their early days went something like this. "Someone would ask a WAF what her uniform was for. She would reply that she ferried planes for the government. The interested person would then ask incredulously, 'All by yourself?' The WAF would reply in the affirmative. The final question would then be, 'Who pilots the plane?'"[14]

Even newspaper writers were sometimes at a loss. In 1943, Oscar Schisgall, a prolific freelance writer, was ready to board a plane for Washington, D.C. when he learned his reservation had been cancelled. A priority passenger was taking his place. "I knew this was a war necessity and I was willing to take it with good grace," Schisgall said. "Yet, I couldn't help asking, 'Who's getting my seat?'" The man at the gate nodded toward "a girl in a trim gray uniform, wearing trousers, instead of a skirt." "The lady, sir" the man said. Schisgall saw the Air Transport Command wings on the woman's coat hanging over her arm—"a bulky, fur-lined coat—the kind you'd expect to be used in an open cockpit during a blizzard." She was looking intently at an airline time schedule. "When she lifted her face," Schisgall said, "I saw that she was tired—desperately tired. She looked as if she hadn't slept in days."

Schisgall asked what outfit she belonged to. "WAFS," said the gatekeeper. "Women's Auxiliary Ferrying Squadron. The sooner we can get her back to her base at New Castle, Delaware, the sooner she'll be able to deliver another one." Schisgall watched her go through the gate and climb aboard the plane. "I wondered at her weariness," he said. "Wondered how many flights she'd made in the past few days." He was sure she couldn't be more than 23 or 24 years old. "She was quite small," he said. "It was astonishing—humbling, too—to think of a girl like that flying Army planes to points all over the country—alone in the skies, hour after hour, flying through rain and sleet and snow and clouds. … For weeks the memory of her tired face kept recurring."[15]

In late 1942, Nancy began setting up three additional women's ferrying groups in Dallas, Detroit, and Long Beach, California, each situated near factories producing military airplanes WAFS were qualified to fly. Once more women could be trained, the Air Corps planned to have 30 WAFS stationed at Wilmington, and 15 WAFS at each of the other locations. All of them would be highly skilled women fliers who would only need a few weeks of training at New Castle before joining the ferrying force.[16]

There was some concern about the pilots Jackie Cochran was already training in Texas, especially when eventually new trainees were only required to have 35 hours of flying time instead of the original 200. Transport Command officers were comfortably confident that they had the authority to hire their own pilots and the right to reject any of Jackie's pilots if the women couldn't meet command requirements. Then, on January 25, 1943, word came down to the Air Transportation Command from the Ferry Division Headquarters—"no women pilots would be hired other than graduates of the training school." A month and a half later, Army Air Forces Headquarters directed ATC to hire any graduate of Jackie's flight training school and consider them qualified to ferry trainer aircraft anywhere within the United States.[17]

Perhaps one unidentified and worried ATC officer had been right all along when he said, "Miss Cochran will take it inch by inch and try to move in on us."[18]

# [5]

## HOUSTON—"THE GUINEA PIGS"

In the winter of 1942, the Rice Hotel lobby was nothing less than a tangled swarm of humanity, dozens of civilians, military men, and civil service workers trapped in a smoky haze. "Houston's busiest hotel is the Rice," said Marjorie Kumler. "It has more men in uniform per square inch in the lobby than any other hotel in the city. The majority are cadets—there are about 5,000 at Ellington Field, eighteen miles away—and there are Naval officers, Army men, Marines, and Coast Guard!"[1]

Marjorie and 28 other women had received telegrams telling them they'd been selected for Army Air Corps training. They had until November 16 to report to their new commanding officer at the Rice Hotel. Marjorie lived in California and paid her own way to Houston, as had the other women selected. Because they would be civil service employees, the government wasn't going to pay their expenses. "Bring such street clothing as you deem desirable," the telegram read, "with funds for living expenses for thirty days." Pay would be $150 while in training, and after successfully completing the Army's instructional course, they would receive $250 a month, and be certified Army utility pilots, ready to ferry planes anywhere in the country.[2]

Within days of the September 14, 1942 announcement that Jackie Cochran was developing a training program for women pilots, applications began flooding Army Air Corps Headquarters. Because the plan was considered an experiment and was still in the planning stage, to ensure success, Jackie wanted the best women pilots available. Rather than having the program fail at the outset, applicants were required to have at least 200 hours flying time. As their applications came in, qualified applicants received an assessment interview by a recruiting officer. In many cases, that interviewer was Jackie. "The selection," Jackie said, "was entirely a matter of choosing clean-cut, stable appearing young girls, of the proper age, educational background, and height, who could show the required number of flying hours, properly noted, and certified in a log book." If the field interview looked promising, the next step was a physical examination. The women received more forms to fill out and from all information gathered, Jackie made the final decision.[3]

Marjorie's orders told her to report to her commanding officer at the Rice Hotel; however, the C.O. hadn't arrived yet and the desk clerk directed Marjorie to a room where a civil service clerk was handing out yet another form. "By the time I got there," Marjorie said, "two or three dozen other selectees had arrived." Marjorie took the form, squeezed into a seat around a small coffee table, and began to fill it out—in quadruplicate.[4]

Suddenly there was a flurry at the door, announcing the arrival of the commanding officer, accompanied by Jackie Cochran and her entourage. "She was neat and tailored, even to her lapel ornament," Marjorie said, "which was a small silver propeller, [with] a large rosette diamond in the center." Leaning on a chair, Jackie welcomed her women. "You girls are the first women to be selected for training by the Army Air Forces," she said. "You are all experienced pilots. There isn't a girl in this room who has less than 250 hours, and most of you have much more. If things don't run smoothly at first, just remember that you will have the honor and distinction of being the first." She assured them that the government needed them badly and she hoped they would finish Army training in two and a half to three months. She introduced a man who took their fingerprints and then she said goodbye. Late in the afternoon when processing finally ended, the women were issued a summer style man's flight suit, a regulation wool sweater, and a standard issue A-2 leather flight jacket. They then raised their right hands and took the oath of office. Now they were Civilian Student Pilots in class 43-W-1, 319th Army Air Forces Flight Training Detachment, Houston—more commonly known as the Women's Flying Training Detachment. The 43-W-1 designated them as the first class who would graduate in 1943.[5]

In mid 1942, the country's flight training programs were rapidly taking over available air bases and Jackie had to scramble to find a location for her school. Aviation Enterprises, Ltd. had been running a Civilian Pilot Training program at the Houston Municipal Airport, but with their contract running out they gladly agreed to train Jackie's women to fly.[6]

It was a decidedly diverse collection of women who boarded the bright blue bus that took them to the Houston Airport. They were dressed in tailored suits, wildly printed dresses, slacks, sweaters, and coats; some wearing sandals, or colorful high-heel pumps, and even a few pairs of cowgirl boots. The old bus rocked as they climbed aboard and filled every seat. "Only a week before," Marjorie said, "we had been nurses, flight instructors, radio announcers, reporters, secretaries, designers, photographers, debutants, wives, and mothers. Overnight we had become flying guinea pigs in an experiment to see whether women could take it."[7]

Houston Municipal Airport sat just to the west of Ellington Field, where the Army was training bomber pilots. It was a 14-mile trip from the hotel to the airport and the bus seemed content to savor each mile as if it were its last. "It ran off slower than the last horse in a maiden race at Pimlico," Marjorie said. Many of the locals still called Municipal Field Howard Hughes Airport, even though the name had changed nearly four years earlier. The City of Houston had acquired the private airfield and renamed it Houston Municipal Airport in June 1937. A year later, when Hughes returned to Houston after setting a new round the world speed record, city officials announced they were renaming Houston Municipal as Howard Hughes Airport, to honor the millionaire who had been a resident of Houston for years. However, four months later, while trying to get Federal money to improve the airport, the city council discovered that naming a federally funded project after a living person was prohibited. They needed the money, so they dropped the Hughes name and Houston Municipal Airport was back again.[8]

The center of training was the Aviation Enterprises' hangar and the offices that were located immediately south of the two-year-old passenger Air Terminal. Three frame buildings, arranged in a U-shape and enclosing a grassy area, would be the women's daytime home for the next four months. The center building served as headquarters for Aviation Enterprises and was off limits to trainees. The two buildings opposite each other and forming the legs of the U were the classrooms.[9]

Off the bus and assembled into one of the classrooms, Captain Paul Garrett, commanding officer of the flying detachment, greeted the women. "If he was glad to see us," Marjorie said, "he concealed it as though it were a military secret."[10]

"A lot of you girls," he said, "have come down here with a lot of time, and you may think that you are pretty hot pilots. But let me tell you that just because you may have 300 or 500 hours—you may even have 1,000 hours—it doesn't mean that you can fly. Maybe you haven't got anything but a collection of bad habits. If you think you're hot pilots, I'd advise you to forget it. You're here to learn the way the Army flies."

The lecture continued with the captain warning the women to be where they were supposed to be, do what they were supposed to do, and do it at the time they were supposed to do it. He closed by telling them the only three things that would guarantee they would "wash out" from training and be sent home. "The first is that you can't fly," he said. "The second is that you can't do ground school work. The third is that your attitude isn't good." For whatever reason, six of these 29 women wouldn't make it to graduation.[11]

There was nothing glorious about this start at Houston. First, there were no barracks. The job of finding housing for the women fell to Mrs. Leni Deaton, hired by Jackie as an administrative assistant. Officially, she was the Chief Establishment Officer, but really was more of housemother for the trainees. The quickest solution was to find rooms in private homes, but that presented a transportation problem. With the women scattered miles off base and roll call set at 7 a.m., how would they get to the base on time each morning? Aviation Enterprises decided to invest in a very used, yellow school bus—another transportation veteran, once owned by a Tyrolean band that had staggered its way from one beer blast to another in South Texas. The trainees would reunite each morning at a prearranged street corner and wait for the sputtering engine of the bus to make its earsplitting appearance. Frequent blown tires and mechanical breakdowns meant a rush to a phone booth for a call to Mrs. Deaton who, in turn, would rouse someone from Aviation Enterprises out of their still warm and comfortable beds, and send them off to the rescue. If no one came in time, the women improvised. "Hitchhiking to the airport, when our transportation broke down," Margaret said, "was as routine as our seven day week."[12]

Mandatory gas rationing began December 1, 1942, and it didn't take long to realize that rounding up the women each morning and taking them home when their day ended at 9 p.m. was costing too much for fuel. Mrs. Deaton solved the problem. She found an auto tourist camp closer to the base that was willing to rent a section of its cabins for the trainees. When new classes of women began to arrive, she rented two more auto camps. Each camp had a student in charge and the rooms were subject to inspection at any time.[13]

With no mess hall, the airport cafe served up breakfast. The food wasn't very good, and because the women not only paid for their own lodging, they also paid for their meals, some of the trainees decided to take their early morning hunger to a pleasant little restaurant that they had discovered out on the highway. Eventually, a former non-commissioned officer's club at the airport became the trainee mess hall. Unfortunately, getting to the chow line was a one-mile hike to and from the classrooms.[14]

Trainees concerned with their appearance quickly discovered that preserving a semblance of beauty in an open cockpit while flying though Houston weather was impossible. Hairnets, the favorite "helmet" of the Guinea Pigs, couldn't come close to blocking the ravages of Texas dust on one's carefully coiffed hair. Fingernails would crack and polish would chip. Skin dried out in the gasoline fumes and took away any chance of having that "skin you love to touch." Even a chance morning look in the mirror could have a devastating effect. As one trainee said, one look and "morale gets lower than a Houston fog."[15]

While the upper echelons may have wished for dress uniformity, it would be many months before they would get it. Until then, the spirit of the trainees' individuality was irrepressible. Uniforms "consisted of whatever lay nearest to you on arising," said one trainee. The closest things to an official trainee uniform were the flight suits they wore while flying and the leftover mechanic's coveralls they were issued—all arriving in a not so figure flattering, men's 44 long. The women creatively tied ropes or wore belts around their waist to give the coveralls some sort of form and rolled up sleeves and cuffs. They called them Zoot Suits because the coveralls reminded them of the suits worn by young, primarily minority men, in the 1930s and '40s that had high-waisted, very baggy pants billowing out like parachutes below the waist, and were tight at the cuff. Zoot Suit jackets were also wide at the shoulders and very loose, with sleeves that completely covered the hands and reached the wearer's fingertips. It didn't take too much imagination to see the similarity.

The women finally did settle on a uniform look that was used until adoption of their official Santiago Blue uniforms in late 1943; however, there are two different stories about how that original look was chosen. One story says that just before the first class graduated, the women realized they would be marching at the ceremony with men in uniform

Until new uniforms finally arrive, Leonora "Noni" Horton Anderson (43-W-7) takes a moment to "cinch up" classmate Mildred "Mickey" Axton's "Zoot Suit." The baggy men's coveralls were available in a non-figure flattering "one size fits all"— a man's 44 Long. - *National Archive photo.*

who were Air Corps graduates. So as not to be embarrassed by their own lack of a uniform, the graduating women, along with their sisters from three other classes, decided to make their own. From the Ellington Post Exchange they each purchased a white, open collared, long sleeve shirt, a khaki overseas cap, and a pair of high-waisted khaki trousers. They called the trousers "General's Pants," either because of their "baggy seat," as one author says, or because they were worn on parade, while passing in review.[16]

The other and more believable story came from the women's training detachment newspaper. "The girl's 'General's Pants'—the khaki dress uniform," it said, "first made their appearance when it was reported that the field was about to be visited by top ranking officials from Washington." A frantic order for sufficient uniforms to dress the entire detachment arrived just four days before the rumored visit. Some 300 slacks needed quick alterations. It was a monumental task, but volunteers, working in shifts, got the job done—all 300 altered in just four days. Of course, in the spirit of the military's unofficial "hurry up and wait" ethic, the Washington officials never arrived.[17]

In a 1972 interview, Mrs. Deaton confirmed that the trainees were expecting a visit from Army Chief of Staff George C. Marshall who was bringing with him Lord Beaverbrook—Sir John Maxwell Aitken. Lord Beaverbrook, the British Lend-Lease Coordinator, had come to America to consult with the U.S. War Production Board. "Mrs. Cochran wanted the girls to look sharp in their new cotton gabardine slacks," Mrs. Deaton said, "some of which were rather ill-fitting. But the visiting dignitaries never showed up."[18]

There were at least a dozen styles of shoes worn throughout the day; including moccasins of many colors. The base newspaper said the moccasins felt best "after much marching up and down the shell roads, or when being trampled by the girl behind." There were slippers and ordinary oxfords, toeless and heelless sandals, sneakers, and yes, those cowgirl boots. What with flying, physical training, close order drill, and just walking around the flight line, a nightly application of shoe polish was the only way to camouflage worn out heels, scuffed leather, and fraying stitches. There were so many complaints about their shoes in letters home that when Christmas packages arrived, instead of the hoped for food and other treats, many of the ladies were unwrapping a new pair of shoes. Aching feet led many a trainee to slip out of her shoes for a few moments of barefoot bliss, but that "footloose and fancy free fad" finally inspired a notice that was posted on the bulletin board. "Shoes will be worn on the flight line at all times."[19]

Newspapers had told America that Jackie Cochran was going to train women pilots, but that's about all Americans knew. "There's a great deal of mystery surrounding Jacqueline Cochran's army training school for women pilots," said one newspaper story. "No publicity of any kind," Margret Kumler said. The women could not talk to the press or anyone else about their training. Margaret said the women wrote the word "confidential" on every letter home, "even if it said only that we had liver and onions for lunch." Even the residents of Houston didn't have an idea what the women were doing. "Some deduced from the way we looked that we were girl welders," Margaret said. Although still separate from Nancy Love's WAFS, the Houston Detachment was following the Ferrying Command's orders. In October 1942, the command had ordered all widespread publicity stopped until "substantial results of the experiment may be observed." The command was concerned that publicity had been interfering with operations and was inconsistent with the goals of the women's pilot program.[20]

Just because they were going to learn the Army way to fly didn't mean trainees were going to fly the latest pursuit aircraft or even the newest trainers. The planes were all obsolete or surplus civilian craft obtained from various airfields and rarely could one find two planes of the same model. Painted over in olive drab, with U.S. emblems attached, the aircraft needed constant maintenance, and just trying to keep them in the air was difficult.[21]

A few days after she arrived, Marjorie Kumler took her first flight. She remembered her instructor, Sydney, pulling her out of the assembly room and telling her it was her time to fly. They stopped off at the supply depot in the hanger, where Marjorie signed out a 26-pound bundle of "straps, buckles, and bunting with a cushion to match"—her parachute—and walked to the line. She climbed into a two-seat trainer and after a preliminary check, Sydney shouted, "Let's go!" She opened the throttle and began to roll. "As I look back on it," she said, "that was my last carefree moment." The wheels left the ground and Sydney began to instruct. "Hold your airspeed. … Make a 90-degree turn right. … Now left. .. Now right again." Marjorie had never been so busy in an airplane. Sydney took the controls and showed her a clearing turn—a maneuver that allows a pilot to be sure there is no other air traffic or obstructions in the area. He suddenly banked steeply to the right; rolled around 90 degrees, leveled out, and then banked steeply left, rolled around another 90 degrees, and leveled out again. "The blood drained from my head," Marjorie said. "All the muscles in my face pulled long. I was pressed down in the seat and the earth was swirling underneath me. … Naturally he got a great kick out of my reaction, so he did it a couple of more times."[22]

Halfway through her first try at a clearing turn, Marjorie suddenly found herself headed straight at another plane. Sydney yelled, "Watch out for that A6!" Marjorie snapped the plane into a sharp turn and gave it full throttle. She missed the A6 by a few hundred feet. The sky was swarming with planes at all altitudes in the practice area, an area the women shared with the cadets in training at Ellington Field. "When you emerged from some violent maneuver and saw a lot of dark specks," she said, "those weren't spots before your eyes. Those were airplanes."

They flew a bunch of demonstration stalls and spins that showed Marjorie how a pilot could recover control. On that final "neck twisting dive, my heart wasn't in it," she said. "I had gone from excitement to fatigue to indifference." They repeated the same routine, over and over, day after day, in good weather and bad, until it all became routine. Marjorie and the other women were finally flying the Army way.

Flying cross-country was when the trainees had the most fun; often surprising male pilots with their flying skill. Just before graduation, Marjorie landed an AT-6, *Texan*, advanced trainer at Yoakum Field, an isolated dirt runway on the Texas prairie, about 120 miles southwest of Houston. As she sat in the shade under her wing, waiting for her control officer and the rest of the women to arrive, a young Army captain landed his AT-6. He walked over to Marjorie, introduced himself and asked if she were guarding the plane. She said yes, she was. "Where's the pilot," he asked. "I'm the pilot," she said. Judging by the captain's laugh it was obvious that he didn't believe her. "I realized," Marjorie said, "I didn't cut a very military figure in my cowboy boots, frontier pants, and green shirt." Just then, Miller, her male control officer, landed his plane. She told Miller that she couldn't convince the captain that she was actually flying the AT. Miller looked surprised. He strolled over toward the captain and they exchanged cigarettes. The captain was waiting for the rest of his boys who were flying in from Randolph Field, and when Miller told him the rest of his women fliers would also be arriving soon, the two men agreed on a bet. "I'll match my boys against your girls," the captain said. "If it's a girl, I'll bet she bounces the landing." Miller was sure she wouldn't and was confident enough to put up a dollar bet on every landing. "That was a bad day for the captain, and Miller was all smiles," Marjorie said. "The girls couldn't miss." Luckily for the captain, even though the boys kept bouncing in, it was easy enough to collect a dollar from each of his boys to pay off his ill advised bet.[23]

For 23 weeks, the Guinea Pigs worked through some long and busy days. There was plenty of flying, but most of the day was filled up with ground school, Link training, drill, and calisthenics. Early on, everything was still an experiment, and the women found the schedule changing almost daily. Finally, it settled down. They completed at least 115 hours of flying and 180 hours of ground school. For Marjorie and most of the other trainees, ground school was the absolute worst. With three hours a day of mathematics and physics, Marjorie was lost. The instructors set up a special class for her and the others who were falling behind. "After a few weeks," she said, "I found myself doing the same homework as the fourth grader in the house where I boarded." For three additional hours a day they studied engine mechanics, the theory of flight, meteorology, and navigation, while also receiving an introduction to Army organization, its courtesies and customs, military ceremonies, and how to safeguard military information. Each day ended at 9 p.m. when the mandatory study hall closed.[24]

Whenever there were a few minutes in between activities, the women would head for some relaxation in a small room they called "the collapse room." Inside was an Army double bunk bed where the trainees would squeeze together to spread the latest rumor or air their latest complaint. The women had given themselves a nickname that would only last until the flying program moved to Avenger Field in Sweetwater, Texas. They pronounced the Women's Flying Training Detachment initials, W.F.T.D., as "Woofted," and happily declared themselves as "Woofteddys."[25]

The Guinea Pigs decided they wanted a mascot, preferably a female, and she suddenly appeared in 1942 Christmastime newspapers. Columnist Walter Winchell was out of the country and had asked Walt Disney to write something for Winchell's newspaper column. Disney wrote about Gremlins and the animated film he planned to make, based on a story written by British children's author Roald Dahl. He even included a few drawings. The Gremlins were mischievous mythical creatures, all male, that British R.A.F. fliers had been blaming for aircraft sabotage for two years. In early 1942, the story had reached America. Apparently, as the story went, the Brits had made the Gremlins mad by chopping down the little creatures' forest home to build an aircraft factory. In retaliation, the Gremlins ran amuck on British airplanes. With suction cups on Gremlin feet, pilots said Gremlins could walk up walls, hang from the ceiling, and stroll outside the plane from wing to wing—all while the plane was still flying. The little devils jammed triggers on machine guns, tore parachutes, and ate through critical control cables. They could foul a spark plug, or block radio communications, and even keep a landing gear from coming down. Bullet holes in a fuselage or gas tank were obviously the work of an industrious Gremlin with a boring bit. Everyone agreed. These were nasty little devils—but the Guinea Pigs weren't interested in a male mascot.

As the Gremlin legend grew and observation of the life and habits of the Gremlins became more "scientific," a female version of the species was discovered—Fifinellas. "From all reports," Disney said, "the Fifinella is a honey—really an eye full. She has wizard curves, all in the right places." Much like a queen bee's entourage of worker bees, the Gremlins adored Fifinellas, but they weren't interested in the boys at all and only needed to be well taken care of. "The boys tell us," Disney said, "that you'll never catch a Fifinella drilling holes in your wing, cutting your parachute straps, or draining the alcohol from your compass." If you treated a Fifinella right, she would keep the Gremlins so awestruck they'd be too spellbound to do any damage. "All a Fifinella has to do," Disney said, "is hop aboard a plane for a joyride and the Gremlins will follow her in droves."[26]

There she was, a Fifinella drawing right on the newspaper page. Would Disney give the Houston women permission to use her as their mascot? Well, of course, but Disney did better than that. In answer to their telegrammed request he not only gave them permission at no cost, but had his artists create a new drawing of a blond Fifinella with wings. She soared through the sky wearing red boots, a red blouse, yellow pants, and oversized goggles. The flying women cheered their new mascot and used her everywhere. Houston Airport was now Fifinella Field. Their unit newspaper would be The *Fifinella Gazette*, and they wore a Fifinella patch on their flight jackets. "Watch out fellas!" they said. "Them Fifinellas, like the gals of 319$^{th}$, are taking to the air."[27]

The weather and two accidents delayed the March 15 graduation of Jackie Cochran's very first class of women fliers. The wet winter had been so bad in Houston that whenever there was a clearing the Guinea Pigs climbed back into their planes, flying six to eight hours a day, just trying to catch up and finish their required hours of flight time. Marjorie Kumler began to reflect on how the Guinea Pigs had changed. "Any resemblance we bore to our former selves was purely coincidental," she said. They were "wearing G.I. flying suits instead of dresses and carrying a parachute instead of a purse." Conversations were about "crosswind landings or instrument letdowns." They were "flying the Army's advanced trainers instead of driving a car" and "turning down a fashion magazine to study manuals explaining engine maintenance and aerodynamics." It all "seemed as bland and ordinary," she said, "as taking off in the morning to have lunch at an airport 300 miles away or getting up at noon to fly all night." The Guinea Pigs of 43-W-1 had paved the way, and with lessons well learned, their class never lost a pilot during the war.[28]

Class 43-W-2 arrived in Houston and began training, December 13, 1942. Each of the 51 women was in awe of their older sisters. Forty-three of them graduated and three, including Paula Loop, would die. On January 16, 1943, the third class to learn the Army way to fly began their studies. Only 43 would make it through training and two of them would die.[29]

When class 43-W-4 began training February 16, 1943, about half of the 156 women went to the newest flight training facility for women, Avenger Field in Sweetwater, Texas. The other half went to Houston, the last class of women pilots to train there. They were welcomed in the Houston detachment's newspaper with warnings of what was to come—the thousand and one things they never experienced before. "Old timers who have been on Fifinella Field for thirty days or more are glad to see each new class role in," they said. "You'll be deglamorized speedily. You'll acquire sore muscles you never knew you had. It won't be long before you lose that city slicker pallor and acquire a farmer's leathery neck." They would "sleep like a horse, eat like a dog, and fly until it pops out of your ears." Nevertheless, they told them to take heart; they too would soon be old timers. "By the time 43-W-5 arrives, kids, you'll know a lot of swell people who right now are saying welcome to you."[30]

Of the 112 graduates from 43-W-4, six would die, including the first of 38 women who would perish while flying for their country. She—was 33-year-old Margaret Oldenburg.

WASP trainees from Class 43-W-4 listen as their instructor prepares them for flight.
- Air Force photo 050407 F 1234P 009

# [6]

## SISTERS BEGIN TO FALL

It had been a relatively quiet Sunday afternoon. A few of the women had taken advantage of the improved weather to fly some training flights. Margy Oldenburg had talked to her husband in California by phone at noon and then checked out a parachute and met Norris Morgan, her civilian instructor, on the flight line. They would fly a Fairchild PT-19, a basic trainer airplane used to introduce pilots to military aircraft before moving them up to more demanding planes.

Margy Oldenburg began her training in Houston, February 16, 1943, just 19 days earlier. At 33 she was one of the older student pilots, and at first, a bit shy. But soon she was entertaining small groups of trainees by singing the Hawaiian songs she had learned while visiting friends on the islands. "She had a smile for everyone," one student said. Born Margaret Burrows Sanford near Cleveland, Ohio in 1909, the youngest daughter of Percy and Mary Sanford, her family had moved to New York by 1915. Her father was an accountant on Wall Street for the National City Bank of New York. In 1919, he filed a patent on an improved ink-feeding device for fountain pens. Sometime, after 1925 the family moved to the San Francisco Bay area where Margy attended the University of California and graduated in 1931.[1]

Margy married Jacob Oldenburg in late 1940. Jack, as he preferred to be called, was a salesman for a metal works company and had left his home in Ohio just a few years before. He was a member of the United States Naval Reserve and once he was commissioned an officer in October 1942, he asked for a leave of absence from his civilian job. At the time, he was a member of the Structural Engineers Association of Northern California. In early 1943, just weeks before Margy's fatal training flight, he received his commission as an Ensign in the regular Navy with a duty station at Port Chicago, just northeast and across the bay from San Francisco.[2]

Norris Morgan, Margy's instructor, had been flying since 1933. Born and raised in Galva, Illinois, Morgan was a graduate of the University of Illinois, Urbana-Champaign, with a degree in agricultural engineering. After graduation, he worked with his uncles in Illinois' first hybrid seed company, known simply as Morgan Brothers. Norris made the area's first airmail flight in May 1938 by flying 31 miles with 16 pounds of mail from the Morgan family pastures, north of Galva, to Moline. He made two stops along the way to pick up another eight pounds of mail. By 1942 he had nearly 700 hours in the air, most of it on business and inspection trips for the company, or aerial seeding of the Morgan family's many commercial production fields that were scattered throughout the area.[3]

In late 1942, 41-year-old Norris Morgan volunteered for wartime duty as a civilian flight instructor, and while he attended the Instructors School at Randolph Field, near San Antonio, Texas, his wife, Margaret, and three children stayed in Galva. Once Norris completed his training and arrived at the WASP detachment, Margaret advertised in the local Galva newspaper for a passenger who would help drive her and the children to Houston. On Monday, February 14, they left Galva for what would be her final two weeks together with Norris.[4]

Just about 6 in the evening, March 7, 1942, the base siren in Houston began to wail an emergency call. Because it was a Sunday, many of the women trainees had already left the Houston base for home. Those who remained had never heard the siren sound that way before, because now it was announcing an accident, and there hadn't been an accident at Houston since classes began the previous November. An unexplained spin had suddenly sent Margy's PT-19 hurling straight down into a pasture seven miles southeast of the Houston Airport. She and Norris smashed into the ground at such speed that both of them died instantly.[5]

Mrs. Deaton made the rounds of the auto courts where the trainees were living and explained what had happened to those who didn't already know. She stressed that no one was to write home about the accident or tell anyone else what had happened. The military didn't want any publicity, but initially lost control of the story. In reporting the crash and the deaths, the Associated Press was able to identify Norris Morgan as an instructor at the 319th Detachment who was flying with "a woman student pilot," still unidentified until next of kin were notified. The United Press apparently had better sources. They identified Margaret Oldenburg as wife of a Navy ensign, "a young Navy wife who was studying to become a Ferry Command pilot," and that she had only been in training for a short time. They also wrote extensively about Norris. Both versions of the story flashed across the country's newspapers.[6]

Margy's fellow trainees took up a collection for wreathes and flowers; while Jackie Cochran arranged to have Margy Oldenburg's remains shipped home for burial in Oakland, California. The Morgan family brought Norris Morgan home to the family plot in the Galva town cemetery.[7]

The women of the 319th were still in shock. Margy Oldenburg was the first of their sisters to die. They had known the dangers before they signed up, and yet, they never really believed there would ever be any trouble. Now they would try to remember to fly carefully. They would exude confidence in their flying abilities to family and to everyone on the outside. They were sure that this need not happen again, but inside, in their deepest thoughts, they hoped that they'd never make a mistake.

The Guinea Pigs were scheduled to graduate on March 15, eight days after Margy's accident; however, the ceremony was delayed for over a month. Some said the delay was because Jackie Cochran had wanted to make sure the ceremony would be more impressive, so that it would ensure better publicity for the training program. More likely was the fact that the Army had already decided the women would have to fly more hours before graduation, and in the unsettled Texas weather, the Guinea Pigs were still struggling to fly those hours. In addition, it seems likely that the deaths of Margy Oldenburg and Norris Morgan also had a huge impact on the delay decision; and the death of Cornelia Fort, two weeks after Margy, had even more.[8]

One of the most experienced women pilots in America, Cornelia was the second woman to join Nancy Love's WAFS. Two days after training at New Castle Air Base was over, October 22, 1942, Cornelia and five other WAFS arrived at Piper Aircraft Headquarters in Lock Haven, Pennsylvania. From there they began their very first official ferrying flight, flying six Piper L4B Grasshopper light reconnaissance planes, 115 miles east and over the Allegheny Mountains to Allentown. Early the next morning, after resting overnight, they were in the air again, completing their delivery mission in the afternoon at Mitchell Field on the Hempstead Plains of New York's Long Island.[9]

Cornelia was born into Nashville aristocracy—one of the wealthiest and most influential families in the state. Her father, Dr. Rufus Fort, was a well-known surgeon with memberships in most of the important medical associations of the country. He was also a businessman and investor, but probably best known as an award winning breeder of Jersey cattle, a passion he pursued on 365 acres of Fortland Farms, the acres that surrounded Fortland, his Colonial mansion. Sitting high on the bluffs at the edge of Nashville, Fortland's 24 rooms and its white-columned veranda overlooked the Cumberland River. Mr. Fort had modeled the home after Arlington House, General Robert E. Lee's former home, in today's Arlington National Cemetery. Rufus married Louise Clark in 1909, a marriage that was probably a little surprising to his relatives, as Miss Clark was a Northern lady from Boston. Born February 5, 1919, Cornelia was the couple's fourth child and first girl.10

Hers was a privileged life that didn't always sit well with Cornelia, especially as she grew older and the social expectations of her parents grew even more restrictive. She had started her education in the public schools of Nashville, but in the seventh grade her father enrolled her at Ward-Belmont, an exclusive Nashville women's finishing school. Then it was on to Ogontz School for Young Ladies, a private and exclusive institution located a few miles north of Philadelphia. Amelia Earhart had been a student there and perhaps was the inspiration for Cornelia's later desire to fly. She spent her final two years of school at Sarah Lawrence College near New York City. Her father was opposed to the northern school; however, Cornelia and her mother finally convinced him to give in. During Christmas break in 1939, her senior year at Lawrence, Cornelia underwent what was for her a very unpleasant rite of passage—introduction to an audience of hundreds of Nashville society members as a new debutante. In Cornelia's mind, debutante wasn't exactly a promising career move that would lead to much of anything.11

When she was five years old, Cornelia heard her father take her older brothers aside and make them all swear that they would never fly an airplane. Apparently, it didn't cross his mind to give Cornelia that same oath. Who would have ever thought a five-year-old girl would want to grow up and be a pilot—but she did. After an exciting airplane ride at an airfield near Nashville, Cornelia began taking flying lessons. In early 1940, while she was flying, Cornelia's father became seriously ill and after 10 weeks of suffering, he died. Cornelia had never told him about her flying. On April 27, just a month after her father's death, she had made her first solo flight and now, all she wanted to do was fly. On June 10, she earned her pilot's license and in celebration flew off on a 2,000 mile, one-day, round robin flight that took her as far west as St.

Louis and as far south as the Mississippi Delta. She quickly qualified for her commercial license and a few months later, March 10, 1941; she received her instructor's rating.[12]

Not satisfied just to teach flying, Cornelia wanted to improve her skills. She wrote to flying schools across the country asking for a teaching job and quickly received a telegram from Massey & Ransom Flying Service out of Fort Collins, Colorado. They told her she was hired sight unseen and told her to report at once. She should have been happy, but Massey & Ransom had sent the telegram to "MR. Cornelia Fort," and that pushed Cornelia to tears. Maybe they wouldn't hire a woman. Her mother convinced her to respond to the telegram and confess that she was a woman. Cornelia's answer came the next day. "Mr. or Miss or Mrs., we do not care what you are. If interested please report at once."[13]

Flying at the higher altitudes near the Rocky Mountains would give her a chance to try the thinner air almost never reached by light craft flying from sea level. "I'm flying off the side of the Rocky Mountains," she wrote in an article for her college magazine, "where the air is tricky and vicious. One learns plenty and fast." Her Civilian Pilot Training students kept her busy, but Cornelia was tireless. For the next six months she worked six days a week, and sometimes seven, her days filled with long hours; waking up at 4:30 and going nearly nonstop until 8:00 that evening. She didn't care. It didn't matter. It was all worth it as long as she had just one student who really was burning to learn, or "one little girl who claps her hands and shouts 'roller-coaster!'" She was simply in love with flying. "One sun-drenched flight at sunrise, one trip chasing a rainbow, or one cool, deeply quiet flight up the canyon at dusk," she said, "are perhaps reasons enough."[14]

In August 1941, a letter arrived from the Andrew Flying Service, based in Honolulu at the John Rodgers Airport. They offered her a job. War was building in the Western Pacific and with fears that Hawaii might eventually be invaded by the Japanese, Andrews was seeing a surge in students from the Army, Navy, and also from civilian workers, all wanting to become a part of the Civilian Pilot Training program. Cornelia quit Massey & Ransom and returned briefly to Nashville to pack. From there she drove west to San Diego and bought passage aboard the S.S. Mariposa, one of four luxury ocean liners owned by the Matson Lines, known as the "White Fleet." She arrived in Honolulu on October 1, 1941, after an uneventful eight-day voyage.[15]

"I'm of two minds about Honolulu," she said in a letter home just a month before the bombing of Pearl Harbor. "It is truly beautiful and such weather as could never be found anywhere." Yet now, Honolulu was becoming a boomtown that Cornelia hated "Hectic and full of petty and not so petty irritations," she said. She was proud of what she had learned, and happy and content that she had found a way to earn a living for herself, "with my hands and the skill that they can produce." Nevertheless, whatever she felt was wrong with Hawaii, she knew if she left and returned to the mainland, she would be leaving the best job she could ever have. "A very pleasant atmosphere," she said, "a good salary, but by far, best of all, are the planes I fly. Big and fast." Yes, the best job in the world, "unless the national emergency creates a still better one."[16]

At dawn on Sunday, December 7, 1941, Cornelia left her apartment across from the Royal Hawaiian Hotel and drove to John Rodgers Field for another day of takeoff and landing practice with one of her students. Just after 6:30, up in the air in one of the company's yellow Interstate Cadets, with her student at the controls and flying in for another touch and go landing, Cornelia looked casually around. "I saw a plane coming closer," she said. "It was in violation of the air traffic rules." She waited for the plane to give ground as it was required to do, but when it didn't, "I jerked the controls away from my student and jammed the throttle wide open to pull above the oncoming plane," she said. "He passed so close under us that our celluloid windows rattled violently and I looked down to see what kind of plane it was." With a large red sun along its fuselage and on its wings there was no doubt—Japanese! She could see smoke rising from the harbor and Cornelia tried to convince herself it was only an exercise—a simple drill. "Then I looked way up and saw the formations of silver bombers riding in," she said. "Something detached itself from an airplane and came glistening down. My eyes followed it down, down, and even with knowledge pounding in my mind, my heart turned convulsively when the bomb exploded in the middle of the harbor."[17]

Now it was a dash for the relative safety of the ground. A shadow passed over and a burst of bullets spattered around and into her plane's body. "Suddenly," she said, "that little wedge of sky above Hickam Field and Pearl Harbor was the busiest, fullest piece of sky I ever saw." Her student was mystified, and when Cornelia landed, still running across the field toward the hangar with machine gun fire strafing the ground in front of her, the oblivious student asked her when he would ever be able to solo. Her response was curt and to the point. "Not today, brother. NOT TODAY!" No one on the ground believed her frantic story until a mechanic came up to say Robert Tyce, manager of the K-T Flying Service at the airport, had been shot in the head and was dead. "My student let out one gasp and disappeared," Cornelia said. "He never did pay me for that half hour instruction."[18]

In less than two years, Cornelia had amassed over 900 hours of certified flying time, but now the military banned all civilian flying in Hawaii. Cornelia was grounded. Worse, with war declared, returning to the United States mainland wasn't going to be easy. In January 1942, weary of the delay and worried about the war, she wrote a letter to her mother, never intending to mail it. "In writing this letter, which if delivered will be my last; I'm filled neither with a feeling of morbidity nor a prescience of disaster. But the ocean voyage I will be making shortly has elements of danger, and if I lose my life before seeing you again, dearest, I wanted to say aloha and send you my love forever and forever." She included a long list of the things she loved in life and closed with a solemn goodbye. "If I die violently, who can say it was before my time? I should have dearly loved to have had a husband and children. My talents in that line would have been pretty good, but if that was not to be, I want no one to grieve for me."

"I was happiest in the sky—at dawn when the quietness of the air was like a caress, when the noon sun beat down, and at dusk when the sky was drenched with the fading light. Think of me there, and remember me, I hope, as I shall you."[19]

When she finally returned safely in late February 1942, reporters rushed for an interview. They were fascinated with her story of that devastating morning and how she had coped while trapped on the island. "I've been trying to come home ever since [the attack]," she said. "It's not that I didn't like Honolulu or was afraid, but I felt I could be doing something more constructive for my country than knitting socks." She had little to say about her plans, but according to one reporter, "it is whispered she wants to ferry planes for the Army." She also considered joining Cochran's women in England, but instead decided to see if talks about forming a women's ferrying group would actually lead somewhere. Early in September, she received a telegram from Nancy Love asking her to come to Delaware and join a group of women. It was Cornelia's dream come true.[20]

Although Cornelia's mother tried to support her daughter's need to fly, she never really liked it. When she asked Cornelia if she really felt she had to do this kind of flying, this ferrying work, Cornelia said yes. "It's something so deep inside of me," she said. "A need so vital to my happiness as sunshine and sleep. I want more than I ever wanted anything in my life to be really good, to be a scientific pilot and command respect from all comers in aviation—but even more important—for my own satisfaction."[21]

During the first week of February 1943, Cornelia received orders to report to the 6th Ferrying Group in Long Beach, California. Within days, she checked out in the 450 horsepower BT-13, the biggest and fastest plane she had ever flown. Before the end of the month, she had flown the 1,304 miles between Long Beach and Dallas in a day and a half, and delivered her first BT-13. She was thrilled at the machine's speed when compared with the slow trainers she had been flying out of New Castle. "I was making a good speed of 180 instead of 60," she said. In less than two weeks, she was already flying her third trip over the southern deserts on her way to Texas. She was eager to finish this mission and complete two more BT-13 delivery flights; required if she wanted to train on "the newest and fastest pursuit plane," the P-51 Mustang. After landing in Dallas the weather changed for the worse and the usual seven-hour commercial airline flight back home to Long Beach took a grueling 26 hours. "We were all too exhausted to move," she said.[22]

A few weeks later, barely a month after Cornelia's 24th birthday, she and six male Army Air Corps pilots took off on another BT-13 flight to Dallas. On March 21, 1943, at their final refueling stop in Midland, Texas, Cornelia agreed to try practice flying in close formation, a maneuver forbidden to ferry pilots, and a maneuver Cornelia had never tried. The flight group had just passed by the Sweetwater airfield, where Jackie Cochran's women were learning to fly. They were a few miles south of Merkel, Texas, less than 140 miles from Dallas. The BT-13 didn't have a retractable landing gear and, according to the Army Air Force accident report, Cornelia and flight leader, Frank Stamme, were flying close together at about 140 miles an hour. Stamme's landing gear suddenly struck Cornelia's left wing. The tip of her wing broke off and six feet of its front edge was ripped away. Stamme was able to continue on, but Cornelia immediately veered right into a series of spinning rolls that ended in a high-speed, inverted vertical dive, straight into the ground. Apparently, Cornelia never tried, or was unable to regain control. The emergency hatch release on the plane's canopy had never opened and even after the crash, it remained locked. The Air Force report found that "marks outlining the wings were very distinct on the ground, and the engine was buried approximately two feet into the ground, and showed no movement after impact." Cornelia was horribly mutilated.[23]

Some people blamed Cornelia for the accident and others blamed

Stamme; however, the Army couldn't find anyone at fault. Although Stamme had less than 300 hours flying time, most of that had been in heavier aircraft, heavier than most of the airplanes Cornelia had ever flown in her 1,100 plus hours. It was obvious they had flown too close, but why? Stamme denied that he had been showing off, or had been flirting with Cornelia, but accusations against him continued for years. Stamme had joined the Army just before the outbreak of the war, on November 5, 1941. He married a year after Cornelia's accident and lived until 1987, dying at age 67.[24]

Cornelia's remains came home to Nashville by train. She lies near her father in the Mt. Olivet Cemetery. Tennessee Governor Prentice Cooper sent yellow roses to the funeral that was held in the Christ Church Cathedral. Cornelia was the second woman pilot to die, the first member of the WAFS to fall, and the first woman pilot to die while on active duty while flying for her country.

A month later and two months after their originally scheduled graduation, the 23 Guinea Pigs of Class 43-W-1 who had survived training, returned to the supply room to check in their parachutes for the last time. "It is the graduation of the famed Guinea Pigs," said the detachment's newspaper. "The long awaited, once mourned day, the day we knew would never come. It is not so long since we heard a certain Senior Woofted mutter something about 72 more times to go, while she grunted and groaned at calisthenics. Pretty soon there won't be any more 43-W-1's clambering into ATs, or yelling because they can't find their mail, or walking around in a daze wondering WHEN somebody was going to TELL them SOMETHING about WHERE they'd BE and WHAT, after graduation."[25]

After assembling on the flight line, the women boarded Army busses that took them to Ellington Field for graduation rehearsal. "As we drove through the base, all the bombardiers and navigators were swarming over their barracks, washing windows," Marjorie Kumler said. "Cadets whistled and yoo-hooed. There were hundreds of cadets, maybe thousands. Everyone was giggling and smiling and, even cruising by at twenty miles an hour, the girls could pick out the best-looking cadets and cry, 'Mamma, I want that one!'"[26]

Once they reached the Ellington parade ground, their physical trainer, Lt. Alfred Fleishman, shouted them through their marching paces. It was one of the hottest days of spring with the temperature reaching 79 degrees by mid afternoon, but the grueling succession of marching commands, "by the squad," "by the column," "file from the left," and "file from the right," continued for hours. "When we finally dragged ourselves into the busses and started back to our own—our native airport," Marjorie said, "we were weary and subdued." Even the sight of a good-looking soldier couldn't stir the exhausted women's passions. "A stop sign held us motionless for a minute," Marjorie remembered, "and everyone's eyes fell naturally on a perfect Adonis of a cadet, standing in a barracks doorway. But the bus was leaden quiet."[27]

"The next afternoon the microphones budded and the bunting billowed in the breeze," Marjorie said. At 2:30 in the afternoon, April 23, 1943, the ceremony began. All 23 members of the Guinea Pig class sat in 12 airplanes on the flight line at Ellington Field, behind the crowd, and facing the speaker's platform. With the Universal Newsreel cameras rolling and a martial introduction from the Ellington Field Marching Band, Lt. Joseph Lumpkin, Public Relations Officer at Ellington Field, opened the program. "This occasion sets forth a new milestone in the wartime aviation program of America," he said. "Since that fateful day at Pearl Harbor, the women of our land have been training themselves in every conceivable line of war work in order to put an additional shoulder to the wheels of war." Lumpkin reminded the audience that the average age of this first graduating class was 26, and that each woman had well over 400 hours in the air. "These 23 women who will leave this platform today with their new and specially designed silver wings, make up a unique group," he said. "There will never be another group just like them."[28]

As graduation day had approached, Mrs. Deaton realized that the graduates should receive wings at the ceremony, just as graduating men fliers did. But they were civil service employees, not eligible for Army Air Corps wings, so what to do? Mrs. Deaton went to the base commander, Major Farmer, who ordered her to find some way to get some sort of wings made in time. But how were they to pay for them? Mrs. Deaton couldn't locate Jackie Cochran and, with time running out, she called Floyd Odlum, Jackie's husband. Odlum gave his enthusiastic approval and told Mrs. Deaton to send him the bill. Mrs. Deaton and Lt. Fleishman rushed to the Post Exchange to buy Army Air Corps wings. They had a local jeweler buff out the central shield on the wings until each had a smooth finish, and then they had them engraved to commemorate the class—"319th" above and "W-1" below.[29]

"Among those attending this ceremony today," Lt. Lumpkin said, "are some of the undergraduates of the women's Flying Training Program. They're here to wish their flying sisters Godspeed in their new adventure, following work well done." The band began playing a march, as women of Houston's second, third, and fourth classes marched in toward the speaker's platform. The music stopped and the trainees performed a brief demonstration drill before sitting down.[30]

The Guinea Pigs dismounted from the 12 airplanes, quickly assembling into military formation. Led by Dorothy Young, at 5 feet, the shortest woman in the class, they marched to the front of the speaker's platform. "We were neat and tidy in white shirts and khaki slacks," Marjorie Kumler said, "and there was a fanfare and flourish as we marched on the field." They saluted and then stood at attention as Colonel Walter Reid, Ellington Field's commander, wished them success. "It is their distinct privilege," he said, "to create the precedents by which their fellow fliers to come will conduct themselves."[31]

Major General Gerald Brant, Commanding the Army Air Force Gulf Coast Training Center and principal speaker of the day, said he would not make a formal speech. "I prepared one, but instead of reading it to you I'm just going to say a few of the things I've been thinking as I've been watching you. I guess you've done it again. You've shown us that one of the things we thought was a male prerogative can be done just as well by women. You girls who have just completed training have shown that you can take the training that men take, and can achieve the same degree of flying efficiency." Brandt closed with brief humor. "If Hitler could see what he is up against now, the war might be shortened considerably. We are proud of you."[32]

"Jacqueline Cochran added God's blessing to that," Marjorie Kumler remembered. "She said that we, as the experimental class, had proved ourselves in training. We now had to prove ourselves in the job." Jackie closed her remarks by saying that for her the graduation exercises were "the proudest moment of my life."[33]

As Major Farmer called each graduate's name, the Guinea Pigs climbed the stairs to the platform. General Brandt gave each their diploma, congratulated them, and shook their hand. Jackie Cochran pinned most of the wings onto the left side of the women's white shirts; although, for Marjorie Kumler and a few of the other women, Colonel Reid did the honors. As he pinned Marjorie, Reid was nervous. "I've done this for hundreds of cadets," he told her, "but I've never pinned wings on a woman before. If I stick you, for heaven's sake, don't jump. My wife is in the front row and I'd never live it down." Fellow graduate, Mary Lou Colbert, was the exception. She received her wings and a kiss from her father, Rear Admiral Leo Colbert, who was Director of the United States Coast and Geodetic Survey.[34]

The band played "Off We Go …," the Song of the Army Air Corps, and then, in honor of the graduates, the Navigator and Bombardier Wings of the Air Force Preflight School at Ellington Field marched in review. The ceremonies ended with the playing and singing of the Star Spangled Banner. After all these weeks of nearly non-stop training, the women finally had a ten-day leave before reporting to their duty stations.

Although three more classes remained in Houston, the Guinea Pigs were the only women who would ever graduate there. The Guinea Pigs left for their Ferrying Command assignments. They were among the best pilots, man or woman, in the country, and they were lucky. All 23 would survive the war, one of the few classes that didn't lose a single pilot.

Two women had already lost their lives and 36 more would follow in quick succession. For now, training was moving 350 miles northwest to Sweetwater, Texas, and from across the country, letters were pouring in. Thousands of American women wanted their chance at the stick.[35]

# [7]

## HOME SWEETWATER, HOME

Early in the year, the winds can get wild on the West Texas prairies—and the weather? It's even more unpredictable. Texans call it the "changeable season." It begins around the first part of February and doesn't stop until summer, if at all. Just about anything can happen at any time. Start with nose-numbing sleet at breakfast, wait for a boiling sandstorm by noon, and end with dry, hot sweats at suppertime. Then there's that uniquely Texas experience—the "Blue Norther," when the northern sky suddenly turns dark blue, almost black, and a hot, summery day drowns away in wind whipped rain. Then temperatures dive 30 degrees in less than an hour. Dust storms rapidly rip up ready-for-planting topsoil. Their red and brown clouds loom into the sky as they gobble across the prairie, scraping against paint and skin, smothering the air, and pushing cloth protected noses indoors for a fruitless escape.

It was here, 200 miles west of Fort Worth, at Avenger Field, near Sweetwater, Texas, where Jackie Cochran was moving her school for women pilots. "It's hard to imagine another spot in the universe where there is so much of so many different kinds of weather in so short a time," said one trainee. "Arriving at 7:45 in the morning we find the sky covered with thick, black clouds. Anywhere else we would say—'No flying today. Might as well go home'—and we'd be right." But that isn't West Texas. "By 8 o'clock the sun is breaking through the clouds and by 8:30 there's not a cloud in the sky." Just when they begin to fly, the wind suddenly shifts, the clouds rush back, and by 9:00 o'clock the rain pours down. It's a quick landing and a taxi to the hangar, where they set the brake and dismount. By then the sky is clear again and they climb back into their plane and take off. After only a couple of well formed and quick patterns in the air, they must come down again. But now the sky is suddenly clear and blue. They say to themselves that maybe the weather will now stay good for an entire week. "We hang up the mike, pick up our chute, and climb out of the cockpit into a pea soup fog. Only fools and newcomers predict the weather in Texas."[1]

Avenger Field began in 1929 as the Sweetwater Municipal Airport, a $50,000 project approved by local voters. A year later, floodlights added along its two dirt runways brought in two passenger airlines to serve the city with daily flights. Nevertheless, the country's sudden economic depression almost immediately reduced flight activity so dramatically that revenue was barely enough for maintenance. Until the city hired Ray Baumgardner as airport manager in 1937, occasional discussions of how to revive the airfield went nowhere. Baumgardner was a private pilot and had managed at least three other airports. He knew how to generate activity—75-cent airplane rides for birds-eye views of the city and flight training for $3 an hour. He bragged that he could train most students to fly solo for just $60. He also provided an air ambulance service for 30 cents a mile and carried hunters high over the prairie, in search of coyotes and eagles to shoot.[2]

By the summer of 1939, city officials had converted the airport's dirt runways to all weather asphalt. A year later, a Sweetwater delegation went to an airport development conference in Dallas, hoping to secure some of the federal money Congress was expected to approve for municipal airport improvements. The city had already developed an airport improvement plan estimated to cost about $125,000. At the conference, they learned that funding was available, but only if the Works Progress Administration approved the project.[3]

By the spring of 1941, the estimated cost of their airport project had climbed to $190,000, and yet Sweetwater had WPA approval to solicit construction bids. That fall, to meet Civil Aeronautics Authority standards, they began grading the entire airport grounds and strengthening both runways with a new base and adding two 4-inch layers of asphalt. Because the weather suddenly turned too cold to allow mixing of the asphalt, final touches on the project waited until March 1942, just in time to announce that the government had finally promised the city a flying school. Not the basic training school for Air Corps pilots that city officials had hoped for, but a school for training British pilots.[4]

On April 1, Sweetwater officials signed a contract to build the aviation training facility, just northwest of the municipal airport hangar.

The projected cost was $300,000, the money coming from funds allocated by the Lend-Lease Act of September 1941 that covered the cost of any training of British pilots in the United States. When finally completed in 1943, construction of the airfield had gone $153,000 over budget.

Three weeks into June, Victor Nelson, engineer for the contractors, Joe Plosser and Charles Prince, put a couple hundred men to work on the project. Eighty-five days after Plosser and Prince agreed to a contract, the field was officially activated. Workers had completed three barracks, a mess hall, several administration buildings, a tower, an emergency hospital, and two hangars.[5]

While dirt was still flying, Plosser and Prince decided to involve Sweetwater residents in the construction project. They announced a contest to name the new airfield and offered a $50 prize to the winner. "The name submitted," they said, "should be symbolic of a fighting air force. As a suggestion, some airfields now have such names as Thunderbird, War Eagle, Falcon, etc." Residents could enter as many names as they could think of and the contest was open to everyone, "Every woman, man, or child of Sweetwater."[6]

Residents had one week in early May to submit their entries for judging by a select panel of Sweetwater residents. At the noon meeting of the Sweetwater Rotary Club, on May 13, Plosser and Prince were on hand to hear the winning entry announced by newly elected Sweetwater mayor, Jonah Lawrence. Grace Faver, a schoolteacher and 50-year-old widow, received the $50 Savings Bond prize for her suggested name, "The Avenger."[7]

The first British pilot trainees arrived at Avenger Field June 20, 1942. To dedicate the field and welcome the men of the R.A.F., the City of Sweetwater sponsored a 4$^{th}$ of July event at the town's football stadium. To open the ceremonies, over 8,000 people looked up in awe as bombers from the Midland, Texas Army flying school flew over in close formation. Next in the air came flight instructors from Avenger and other training schools who began demonstrating several aerobatic routines. Riders on horseback rode into the stadium carrying a colorful parade of flags that represented all 26 of the Allied nations at war. After riding around the field, they handed the flags to a troop of Boy Scouts who marched them into a giant "V" for victory at the center of the field. After a brief speech by British Wing Commander Frederick Moxham and others, a USO group presented a stage show and British cadets sang some of their favorite English songs.[8]

Less than a week later, Sweetwater was in a panic. No sooner had the British settled in than they received orders to leave within a month, and no one would say why they had to leave so suddenly or what would happen to Avenger Field. Finally, on July 10, the British command in Washington, D.C. announced they were consolidating their American training schools and returning two bases back to the Air Force, one in California and Sweetwater's Avenger Field. Although not initially confirmed, rumor said American pilot trainees would replace the British. Early in August, the official announcement revealed that the current class of British trainees would finish their training at Avenger and American cadets would join them. On August 14, Sweetwater said their final goodbyes to the Brits with a farewell party at the local USO club. Now, Avenger was all American and all men, but that wouldn't last much longer. Jackie's women were on their way.[9]

On February 21, 1943, half of class 43-W-4 were already training in Houston and wouldn't reunite with the rest of their class at Avenger until April. The women trainees at Avenger Field were designated the 318th Women's Pilot Training Detachment. For the next six weeks, until the male pilots finished their training, the women represented the female portion of the nation's only coeducational military flying school. While men and women trainees shared the air while flying over Sweetwater, their barracks were widely separated. They ate at opposite ends of the same mess hall, yet shared mealtime dates with each other on Saturdays and Sundays. Until flying hours were over, they were forbidden to walk around the Avenger Field aviation campus. Even then, they could only have a brief stay in the base canteen and only drink Coca Cola. Jackie Cochran wanted no impropriety that could tarnish the reputation of the women's flying program. Of course, that didn't stop a few curious glances and a word or two exchanged between men and women as they passed by each other. But alas for the ladies, by April 6, the last of the men were gone.[10]

While the Guinea Pigs were preparing to graduate in Houston, a financial scandal involving the building of Avenger Field was on trial in an Abilene, Texas federal courtroom. The Justice Department accused the Plosser-Prince Company of fraud and of conspiring with others, including Victor Nelson, the engineer on the project, to receive secret rebates and kickbacks. They were also accused of preparing and collecting from the government on fake invoices. When the Federal Grand Jury handed down its indictment in January 1943, attorneys in the Coast Training Command Headquarters recommended cancellation of the Plosser-Prince contract. "Although these individuals have not been proven guilty," they said in their letter, "with the adverse publicity, it is not considered in the interests of the training program to continue this school with the present operators." On April 3, just a couple of weeks before the trial began, the Plosser-Prince contract ended and the very next day, Aviation Enterprises signed on to manage Avenger Field and run the women's flight program. Three weeks later, Plosser and Prince were acquitted. They wanted their contract back, but the Training Command refused. Jackie Cochran was happy with Aviation Enterprises and she apparently had the final say.[11]

It was already apparent to military officials that Houston with its inadequate facilities would soon become too crowded and, without a significant building program, would be unable to train the number of women pilots previously planned. Rather than open an additional school at another airport, Avenger Field became the place where all women pilots would now train. It required $765,000 for additional improvements, including constructing a new runway, and widening and lengthening the two existing runways.[12]

On April 5, after completing primary training and almost a month before the Guinea Pigs graduated at Ellington Field in Houston, the half class of 43-W-4 that had studied there, made their way by air to Sweetwater to complete their training. It was "a hair-raising but astonishingly uneventful PT-19 hop." This was the youngest class at Houston and they had fewer hours in the air than their predecessors. Their formation was loose and scattered, at one point it stretched across at least eight Texas counties. Trainees at Avenger Field sat on a fence near the flight line, waiting for the women to land. Some of the women took bets on how hard and how high each incoming trainee would bounce once she struck the runway, but it was a disappointing day for Sweetwater's lady gamblers. The trainees landed in sequence without a bounce among them. "I don't think any of us who were on the flight line that day," said trainee Mary Bowles, "will ever forget the wonder and pride we felt at seeing those ships come out of the southwest, their sun-splendid wings bearing true to Avenger Field."[13]

Nearly two months later, May 26, 1943, women from class 43-W-2, Paula Loop's class, climbed into the cockpits of the AT-6 *Texans* and AT-17 *Bobcats* that had finally arrived at Houston. They took off and flew them to Sweetwater for their graduation. Two days later, they were the first graduating class to march the flight line at Avenger Field. It was also the first time the public came to an open house. Not only did hundreds of civilians from Sweetwater and the surrounding area see the graduation ceremonies, they also got to inspect the hangars, barracks, mess hall, and the women's recreation areas.[14]

Reporting for duty at the Avenger Field entrance gate, on the prairie near Sweetwater, Texas. – *Air Force photo B-36520-AC.*

In mid-June, Nancy Love made her first and only trip to Sweetwater, along with her boss, Colonel Tunner, commander of the Domestic Ferrying Command. They wanted to meet with the trainees and let them know what to expect when they graduated and got their assignment to one of the four women's ferrying groups. "I wish to say how much I am impressed at seeing this group of girls," Nancy told them. She said it would be a military style of life, full of discipline, and although they held no commission, they received officer courtesy and could use the officers club. Their uniform had also changed. "We no longer have the drab gray uniform," she said. "We now have uniforms the same color and material as officers, to which will be added—after the War Department approves—an officer's blouse, skirt, as well as slacks and overseas cap." The winter uniform would be basically the same, but cut from wool. "You will wear slacks 90 per cent of the time and skirts only for formal occasions." During that first week after assignment, she told them they would learn how to fill out the paper work required when delivering an airplane. "The trips are long," Nancy said, "averaging about 1,000 miles. On the trip you are completely responsible for the ship assigned to you, including finding a guard each evening." So a plane could always be located, the women had to send a report to their home base every time they stopped. "You are on duty seven days a week," Nancy said. "When you return from a trip you are given a reasonable length of time off to take care of your personal affairs and do your laundry, which has proved to be quite a problem." After answering a few questions, Nancy and Col. Tunner left, continuing on their tour of all eight ferry divisions.[15]

The 44 remaining members of class 43-W-3, "The Lost Platoon," the only class left at Houston, flew their formation of BT-13 trainers into Avenger Field on May 18. All that remained for them was a little less than two months of advanced training. They had never had the chance to be the senior class at Houston. In April, they had even seen their junior class (43-W-4) fly away before them to Avenger Field. Because of the military airplane shortage in Houston, the Lost Platoon was stuck flying Piper *Cubs*, waiting impatiently for weeks on end until they could inherit the Guinea Pigs' BT-13s. When their class finally flew into Sweetwater that May, no one seemed to want them around, and in the flurry of activity in their last training days, they were just isolated strangers to the other trainees—indeed—a Lost Platoon. Like any other class of trainees, they wondered if they would really graduate on time, especially when their base assignments didn't come through until the day before their graduation ceremony. Yet, right on schedule, on July 3, they pulled on their General's Pants and marched proudly in front of a few hundred parents, relatives, and friends who were invited to the ceremony.

Brigadier General Thomas Blackburn, commander of the 31st Flying Training Wing, warned them that things were not going to be easy. "All your life," he said, "you've been told nice things. I want to tell you some things that may disillusion you a bit." He told them how difficult and exhausting ferrying planes would be. How strict the military discipline would be and how they would find "uncompromising competition" from the men who were also ferrying planes. "You'll be in competition with men in a field they have always considered to be their own," he said. "But we know your training here is hard, and when you get through it, you are qualified as a competent ferry pilot."

**Jacqueline Cochran pins wings on new WASP graduate Isabel Fenton (43-W-3) on July 3, 1943, at Avenger Field, Sweetwater, Texas. - National Archives photo 080305-F-0000B-004.**

Jackie addressed the audience, saying, "These girls are not going to replace men in the Army Air Force. The pilots trained at Avenger Field will, I know, leave the heroics to the heroes. Carrying out the job of delivering planes wherever they're told will be their reward." Then, Jackie pinned silver wings on their white shirts.[16]

The festive atmosphere came to an abrupt end on June 7, 1943, when Avenger Field trainees faced their first fatality. Just before midnight, Jane Champlin was on a nighttime, cross-country training flight near Westbrook, Texas, almost 40 miles west of Sweetwater. With her in a BT-13 was her instructor, Henry Awbrey. Her roommate, Jennie Hrestu, was flying nearby. Early the next morning, after flying for over two hours, an exhausted Jennie returned to Avenger Field. Although Jane still hadn't returned, Jennie wasn't concerned. Awbrey had a reputation among the women of getting lost, and rumor said that once on a training flight he had even fallen asleep. Besides, Jennie was just too tired to care. The next morning, at the flight line assembly, everyone heard that Jane was dead. Although there were no witnesses, investigators believed that Jane was making a turn when she lost control, perhaps the engine catching fire, and neither she nor Awbrey reacted quickly enough to avert disaster. They smashed into the earth and the plane burst into flames.[17]

Jane Dolores Champlin was born May 14, 1917, in Chicago to David and Katherine Champlin. When her father died a month before Jane's 14th birthday, her mother took Jane and her brother to live with their aunt in St. Louis. Jane graduated from Saint Louis University in 1937 with a degree in Sociology. While working as a secretary for the Railway Express Agency in St. Louis she took flying lessons and when she heard of Jackie Cochran's aviation school for women, she signed up.[18]

The evening after the crash, Jane received a rosary service at the Sweetwater funeral home. At sunrise the next morning, 250 trainees attended a requiem high mass pronounced by Father Joseph Ballarin of Sweetwater's Holy Family Catholic Church. That evening her body left for burial next to her father in St. Louis. "We'll miss you Jane," said the editor of the detachment newspaper, "but we won't forget you—the way you made us laugh, the many friends you found among all our classes, or the cause for which you made your sacrifice."[19]

In 1949, Saint Louis University renamed the Lucerne Hotel, just across the street from the school, Champlin Hall, in Jane's honor. Built for the 1904 World's Fair and later acquired by the university, the hotel had been converted into a women's residence building. Sadly, Jane's honor only lasted seven years. In 1956, the university converted

Champlin Hall into offices and a bookstore.[20]

Henry Awbrey had been a flight instructor at Houston and arrived in Sweetwater with class 43-W-2. He was 43 when he died. Josephine, his wife, came from Dallas to accompany his body to Clovis, New Mexico for burial. The detachment newspaper offered a simple pilot's goodbye wish, "happy landings."[21]

For the women who had begun their training at Houston, life was quite different at Sweetwater. Now there were plenty of military airplanes to fly and overall, Avenger Field was more comfortable. There were no long bus rides from auto courts each morning and at Sweetwater, trainees lived in long barracks divided into bays, six trainees to a bay. Each bay included six standard metal Army cots, complete with a 5 to 6-inch thick cotton filled mattress, olive drab, wool Army blanket, a lightly feather-stuffed pillow, and linens that were changed once a week. Beside each bed was a tall, two-door, double section locker with drawers, where trainees stored clothing and personal items. In the center of the bay sat a long, double sided table with a short privacy partition down its center, used for community studying and personal projects. Straw seats on the six wooden chairs offered a semblance of comfort. A simple bathroom between adjoining bays was equipped with two toilets, two sinks, and two showers. "The chance of being lonely is quite remote," said one trainee. "One even has a companion in the shower." Deanie Parrish (44-W-4) was shocked at the lack of privacy. "I had grown up in a house with six kids," she said, "but that had not prepared me for constantly being around all those people."[22]

Even with the differences, much like Houston, there wasn't much free time in the women's day. Reveille cracked through an exhausted sleep at 6:15 in the morning, followed by breakfast in the mess hall at 6:45, and assembly on the flight line at 7:30. While one half of the trainees flew in the morning, the other half were studying math, navigation, physics, meteorology, and aircraft maintenance in ground school. After lunch, the trainees swapped places on the ground and in the sky. Drill practice or calisthenics, depending on the day, began at 5:00 o'clock and then at 6:30 the trainees rushed to the chow hall for supper. Following the evening meal, the post canteen was a favorite gathering spot for an hour of free time. There the women could find snacks, orange juice, milk shakes, soft drinks, and a jukebox, where they could swoon over the latest romantic tune and remember the fun of those pre-war dances. Mandatory study hall lasted from 8 until 10, when *Taps* sounded, and it all started over again.[23]

Reporting directly to Sweetwater for training wasn't much different from the women who had reported to Houston. While some drove a car from home or spent days on a bus, many of the women arrived on a Texas & Pacific train. From the depot at Oak and First streets they walked two blocks to the Blue Bonnet Hotel where they filled out their paperwork and were assigned a room. They spent the night at the hotel and early the next morning prepared for their 5-mile trip to Avenger Field. "Eager to impress," said Deanie Parrish, "we all appeared in dresses, with our hats, heels, and gloves." When their transportation arrived, it didn't match their more formal attire. "We looked out the window and saw old converted cattle trucks," Deanie said, "with wooden benches in the trailers for seats." A later class was lucky enough to get a real bus ride to Avenger Field, but apparently, they weren't as eager to impress with their appearance. "As the latest contingent of recruits swarmed into the finishing school of the lady war birds this morning," said the camp newspaper, "high heels and oxfords, silks and slacks, perky Lilly Dache fashions, gay print head-kerchiefs—all were in evidence at Avenger Field." Soon, it wouldn't matter what they were wearing. Be it fashionable clothing, snuggling in fur coats, or just casual sportswear, waiting in base supply there was an oversized Zoot Suit for each and every one.[24]

When they arrived at Avenger Field, Deanie's trainees were lucky enough to meet Jackie Cochran. "I always want you to remember that you are a lady," Jackie told them. "I want you to look and act like a lady." She told them to look left and then right and then offered a warning. "Two out of the three of you will wash out," she said. Jackie wasn't far off. Exactly half of Deanie's class never made it to graduation.[25]

Immediately after their arrival, the trainees marched to a flight program orientation and then to Avenger Field headquarters. After they took the oath of office and completed their official paperwork, they received their barracks assignment and were issued bedding. Once they settled into their new home, they marched to supply, where they received flight jackets, winter flying equipment, and yes, Zoot Suits. After lunch, there were more meetings and then measurements for the current dress uniform, General's Pants and white blouses.[26]

Within a day or two, not long after sunrise, they marched to the infirmary, where they lined up and one by one were shot—the dreaded immunizations against typhoid and tetanus, along with a few pricks on the shoulder against smallpox. "There is only one thing worse than shots," said a trainee, "and that is people not affected by them—

grinning, robust characters constantly flexing their left forearm muscles and chortling that they've never been sick a day in their life." Once the whole class had their shots, they assembled again to hear lectures from medical officers on hygiene and health. They learned that doctors and nurses will always be available at the infirmary and, over the coming months, dentists from the Army Air Base Hospital at Big Spring, Texas will make regular visits every four to six months.[27]

Although the basic structure of the original pilot training program remained, elements within were always changing to match the Army's needs. In April 1943, the flying time required to qualify for training at Sweetwater was now only 35 hours. Originally, when training began in Houston, applicants had to have at least 200 hours in the air. "The desire was to have the more experienced licensed women pilots in the earlier classes to help get the program off to a smooth start," Jackie Cochran said. "It was known from the beginning that the requirement of 200 hours would not permit the then objective of 500 trained women pilots to be obtained." With that objective in mind, required flying time "was quickly and successively reduced to 100 hours," she said, "then to 75 hours, and finally to 35 hours, where it remained until the end of the program." To one reporter the reason for the reduction was much simpler. "There will be one inescapable conclusion if the new requirements are relaxed to any great extent. It will be that the WAFS have found favor with the Army, and the Army wants more of the same."[28]

The 98 members of Class 43-W-8 began training at Avenger on July 5. They would not only be the last class to graduate in 1943, but would also be the first class to have an indoor graduation and the first to graduate at night. There would be no shivering in General's Pants on the flight line in December. The lucky 48, who actually made it all the way through training to graduation, also received the first official pair of WASP silver wings. However, as joyful as that graduation would be, training began with heartbreak. Less than a month after their arrival at Avenger Field the class lost another sister, 22-year-old Kathryn Lawrence.

Energetic Kathryn was Kay to her friends and family. Born in December 1920 to Frank and Chrissie Lawrence, Kay grew up in Grand Forks, North Dakota, not far from the Great Northern Railroad Depot. Her father was an engineer on the railroad and shortly after Kay's older brother, Frank Jr. was born in 1917, the family had moved to North Dakota from Washington state. After graduating from high school, Kay began working toward her Bachelor Degree in education at the University of North Dakota. At 5 feet 4 inches tall, 125 pound Kay didn't stand out in a crowd, but she still made the most of her college years, especially in athletics. She was a champion swimmer, and as an ice skater for the university, won the trophy for best woman speed skater on campus. As a cheerleader with the all-girl, Nodak Pep Squad, she was at every football and basketball game, making sure there was plenty of noise from the cheering fans.[29]

As a sophomore, in 1939, she signed up for the Civilian Pilot Training program, the only girl who wanted to fly out of the 100 collegians who had applied at five North Dakota Colleges. It brought her news coverage and her photograph in newspapers. "Cranking an airplane propeller is a woman's job for Kay Lawrence," said one headline. The university yearbook called her "Skybird Kay Lawrence," the girl who "flits through the air; not on a flying trapeze, not on wings of a song, but in a *Cub* two-seater, with a ponderously jovial Mert Howe perched on the tail." Mert was a star on the North Dakota Fighting Sioux football team, but his relationship with Kay will probably always remain a mystery. Kay passed all her ground and air tests for her pilot's license in April 1940, but with two more years of school remaining before graduation, there was little time to fly. After graduation in June 1942, Kay headed west for a job with Boeing Aircraft in Seattle.[30]

After learning that flight time requirements to join the flying detachment in Sweetwater were lower now, Kay met with a recruiter and headed for Avenger Field. It was just before 5:00 in the evening on August 4, 1943, when Kay's PT-19 trainer lifted off from the runway at Avenger Field. Hers was the eighth flight made that day in the very same airplane. In the month since she arrived, she had flown nearly 20 hours in this type of plane, but now she was soloing. Fifteen miles and a few minutes northwest of Avenger, something happened, and no one knows exactly what. Whether pilot error or mechanical failure, the plane spun out and crashed into the ground. Kay managed to jump, but her parachute never opened. Investigators believed that she had been too close to the ground when she jumped and didn't have time to pull her ripcord. The next day, a memorial service held at Sweetwater's Methodist Church, brought over 100 of her fellow trainees to remember her. She returned to Grand Forks for burial; her grave marked simply as "Kay."[31]

Two months later, her older brother, Frank, joined the Army, while her younger brother, William, lied about his age and joined the Marines. Frank survived the war, but not William. On September 15, 1944,

William, a private in the 1st Marine Division, hit the beach on Peleliu Island in the South Pacific. On the first day of battle, the withering fire coming from the Japanese who were entrenched in caves above the beach, took William's life. When he returned to North Dakota, they buried him next to Kay.

# [8]

## "WE REGRET TO INFORM YOU"

The people of Sweetwater weren't quite sure what to think of these women who were beginning to walk the streets of town in ever growing numbers. Residents had quickly taken to the R.A.F. trainees and the Army Air Corps cadets when they came to town on weekends, especially the town's young women who had sadly seen most of their eligible young men go off to war. But what were they to make of these women who had replaced the men? The local USO dances had once been lively affairs, but, except for a few men working at Avenger Field, the rest of the soldiers were all gone now. Sweetwater was a conservative town, not used to seeing women taking on men's jobs, and the new trainees themselves were uncomfortable with the reception they were receiving. Jackie Cochran's insistence on secrecy until the women trainees proved their value to the military had only added to the mystery.

At Jackie Cochran's request, community leaders began trying to find a way to integrate the women trainees with the residents. To encourage the local effort, Jackie agreed to an interview with the *Sweetwater Reporter*, the first newspaper interview she had ever given to discuss the training program. "I want our trainees to take an active part in the life of this community," she said, "to lead, as nearly possible, normal lives in keeping with their essential work at the field. I know I can count on the women and the other people of Sweetwater and the surrounding area to help me in what we consider one of the most important things that American women, or any other women, ever have tried to do." She asked that families invite the women to their churches and private homes, as they had done for the male cadets. "The girls have an exacting schedule," she reminded them, "and have only one night off a week, and then, only when they are not to fly the next day. Saturday nights are the only nights on which they can visit private homes."[1]

Residents responded. A War Bond drive began with seven men vying for the title "Victory Commander," the man who would be the official USO host for the women of Avenger Field. Residents earned votes to cast for their favorite "Commander" by buying bonds, the number of votes they earned based on how many bonds they bought. Trainees from Avenger Field volunteered to be campaign managers for each man and urged their fellow trainees to buy bonds and vote for that manager's candidate. During the campaign, a visit to the Double Heart Ranch, south of Sweetwater, gave the women a chance to ride horses, have their photographs taken wearing cowboy chaps, and feast on barbeque beef and beans, cooked over an outdoor fire. After a few bond campaign speeches, some of the boys demonstrated bull riding. That encouraged some of the women to stage an impromptu rodeo, roping calves and tying the young animals' legs together. When the campaign ended, the community pledged over $900,000 in War Bonds. At the coronation ceremony, Mary Wiggins, Avenger Field Group Commander of Women Pilot Trainees, a former Hollywood stuntwoman, and a trainee herself (43-W-4), crowned the "Victory Commander." In the coming months, trainees had a home away from home, as the people of Sweetwater finally began to embrace them.[2]

In late June 1943, Jackie became Director of Women Pilots and special assistant to Major General Barney Giles, chief of the air staff who answered directly to General Hap Arnold. It was a position Jackie had wanted for nearly a year and she believed it gave her control over all women pilots in the Air Force, including Nancy Love's original WAFS. "The school and trainees were justifiably drawing the conclusion," said a reporter, "that the Avenger project has progressed so well that army officials have chosen to trust Miss Cochran with increased responsibilities." At the same time, Colonel Tunner, wary of Jackie's influence, appointed Nancy Love executive of WAFS in the Ferrying Command. Even so, Jackie continued on, undeterred. She considered Nancy's appointment to be nothing more than that of "an advisor relating to the Ferrying Division." It seems likely that Jackie's political influence and Army connections had finally borne her some fruit. On August 20, 1943, General Arnold ordered all women pilots flying for the Army be designated Women Airforce Service Pilots and be known by the acronym WASP; including—all of the original WAFS recruited by Nancy Love.[3]

From her Pentagon office in Washington, D.C., Jackie was already eagerly expanding the role of her graduates. Among her duties, Jackie had authority to determine where women pilots should be used and the right to assign them to appropriate agencies and commands within the Air Force. No longer would WASPs be restricted to just ferrying airplanes. Soon, Sweetwater graduates began flight-testing new and repaired aircraft, flying cargo, training male cadets to fly, and completing other experimental assignments. They were scattered to various air bases and various commands throughout the country, releasing even more men to combat duty.

After appointment to her new position, Jackie wrote a letter to Major Robert Urban, Sweetwater commander, saying she was looking for the names of the best student pilots; the women with the best flying ability. "I have requested Mrs. Deaton to send me information concerning height, weight, and general deportment of twenty-five of the best girls," she said. "I am anxious that I get as many of the qualities desired as possible, as they will be setting the pace for many hundreds more to be used in this capacity if it works out." She told Urban the women would tow aerial targets at Camp Davis, but asked him to keep that subject confidential. She wanted to make sure that the trainees wouldn't know they might be assigned to duties other than ferrying aircraft.[4]

A July order from Air Force Headquarters told the Ferrying Command to transfer 25 of their women pilots to Jackie Cochran, Director of Women Pilots, for two weeks of unspecified temporary duty. The Ferrying Command asked what the women would be doing, but learned it was a military secret. Jackie supplied names of 23 women she wanted and left it to the Command to choose an additional two women, as long as they were at least 5 feet 4 inches tall. When the Command received a bill for the women's airfare to Camp Davis, North Carolina, it refused to pay, prompting a new order from Army Air Force headquarters amending the original order. The Ferrying Command would pay the bill and change the women's temporary duty status to detached service for 90 days. No matter how much the Ferrying Command complained, Jackie had the backing of headquarters, and with it, she could get just about anything she wanted.[5]

By September, there were just over 50 WASPs at Camp Davis, on an Army post populated by nearly 50,000 men. Camp Davis was about 30 miles northeast of Wilmington, North Carolina on the Atlantic coast and was an anti-aircraft artillery training school. The women flew planes as targets for the men. On any given day or night, the women would fly a number of different planes on target towing or tracking missions, including the Douglas A-24 *Banshee* and the Curtiss A-25 *Shrike* dive bombers. "WASPs are the prettiest clay pigeons an ack-ack gunner ever sighted," said a reporter. Four 90mm ground-based anti-aircraft batteries and machine guns, manned by trainees firing live shells, shot at a simulated cloth airplane. The airplane, a red, 6x35 foot, flag-like target was towed 3,000 feet behind the women's airplanes. Stiffening the flag was a loosely woven wire mesh. If the gunners were lucky, they hit the target enough times and with enough power, to see it burst into flame and fall into the ocean.[6]

"We would fly up and down the beach, and they would either track us or shoot at us, whatever the mission called for," said Dora Dougherty of class 43-W-3. "The gunfire never hit the fuselage, to my knowledge." Of course, those explosive black puffs that appeared around the target and sometimes came a bit too close to their airplane, reminded Dora and the other WASPs that this was live ammunition and the trainees on the ground "were playing for keeps."[7]

While visiting Camp Davis, a veteran pilot who had flown in the South Pacific against the Japanese, had a chance to see the WASPs in action. "I had about the same opinion of women pilots that some taxi drivers have of women motorists," he said. "Then, one day I was standing on the sands north of Camp Davis watching anti-aircraft drill." A plane flew by and the batteries opened up. "A pattern of ack-ack 100 yards square was being poured into the target," the veteran pilot said. "That pilot had a dirty assignment. A conk-out, a loss of flying speed, a sudden down or up draft, and that little plane would have been in the soup." He said he couldn't breathe easier until it was all over. "Nice flying," he told the officer who was standing next to him. "Yeah," the officer said, "pretty good for a 22-year-old girl who left flying school in June." The veteran pilot was "dumbfounded."[8]

Much less dangerous, but more monotonous for the WASPs, were the tracking missions—particularly at night. The women would fly set patterns, back and forth, hour after hour, at various altitudes, as targets for the coastal defense trainees. The trainees attempted first to discover the plane and then follow its course with aimed guns that they would never actually fire. "This work involves both visual and sound tracking," said a military spokesman, "and tracking through other devices that far transcend visual or aural means."[9]

When they first arrived at Camp Davis, the women faced six more weeks of training to acquaint themselves with the new airplanes and everything they needed to know about their new and unexpected assignment. Of course, there was still the never-ending study—more hours of navigation, meteorology, first aid, airplane maintenance, and Morse code. There also was more time in the Link trainers and what seemed like endless hours of everyone's perpetual "favorite," early morning exercise. The women had to get up early, early enough for their daily 6:45 morning. calisthenics. Between 7:15 and 7:30, they changed into their work clothes, tidied up the room for potential inspection, made their bed with tight hospital corners, ate breakfast, and then rushed to the flight line to check on the day's mission. There was no time, said a reporter, for "toying with curls or eye shadow."[10]

Rooms in the barracks were larger than at Sweetwater; quite similar to bachelor officer quarters. They tried to make their rooms feel as much like home as possible, sometimes adding a feminine touch to the standard Army furnishings with an occasional shopping trip to Wilmington. Lace hung off clothing cabinets, over windows as curtains, and served as doilies on dressing tables. It wasn't unusual to see a photograph of a husband, a loved one, or family member, keeping silent company nearby. GI cots were covered in colorful spreads and frilly pillows. There were throw rugs on the floors and mirrors on the walls, and yet, as one reporter noted, there was almost always a serious side to the room. "There are maps and charts—but no pinup boys—on the walls," he said. "There are a few modern novels on bed-head tables, but there are even more text books on weather, flying, and artillery."[11]

When the women weren't flying a mission, they sat in their private alert room, specially created as a somewhat comfortable lounge. A sign on the door warned off the curious. "WASP Nest!" it said. "Drones Keep Out or Suffer the Wrath of the Queen." Here they were "sweating a ship out," what they called waiting for a mission. Eyes glanced at the operation board and those with assignments moved out to their plane. Those WASP without a coveted mission would still hang out, hoping that something might pop up later. There was plenty of time for kidding around and occasional horseplay, a perennial part of almost every military experience.[12]

Depending on whether they were flying or not, the women had lunch at noon. The WASPs paid 75 cents a day for their meals, 25 cents each meal. On the bright side, there was always a good selection of food, "plenty of butter, and meat, and cream." Three hours of ground school followed their lunch, and an hour of calisthenics preceded the evening meal. Evenings offered peace and quiet in the barracks, a movie at the base theater, or a brief evening of music and perhaps

**"Sweating a ship out," these WASPs check to see if they are flying today. Target towing was probably the most dangerous assignment a woman could fly—live ammunition exploding just a few feet away from their aircraft. – *Air Force photo.***

dancing with some real men in the officers club, but it never lasted long. "We generally have to go to bed early," said June Ellington, of class 43-W-4. "Flying comes first, and you simply can't do it without proper rest."[13]

Because new airplanes went to the battlefront, the WASPs flew worn out machines, unfit for combat, retired from overseas action, and returned to the States for use as trainers. Spare parts were almost impossible to come by and mechanics could barely keep the aircraft flying, let alone safe enough to fly. When a WASP found something wrong with an airplane she reported it to maintenance. Regulations said the plane should be taken out of service until the repair was made, but instead "they'd just write what the problem was and off it would go again," said Ann Baumgartner (43-W-8). "And if you didn't read it beforehand, you didn't realize that something was about to fall off, or quit, or something." For 26-year-old Mabel Rawlinson the problem was a stubborn latch that wouldn't open on her A-24's canopy. A latch that should have saved her life in an emergency, but couldn't, and didn't.

Born March 19, 1917, to William and Nora Rawlinson, in a remote section of Delaware, Mabel was 8 years old when the family moved to Virginia. It was a simple, country life during the Great Depression and

Mabel, the fourth child and third daughter in a family of seven, helped with all the chores. Her mother taught school to help keep the family going. After graduating from high school, Mabel left for Michigan, living with an aunt and attending Western Michigan College in Kalamazoo. She graduated in 1939 with a Bachelor of Arts degree. After graduation, she worked as personal secretary to Kalamazoo's esteemed Chief Librarian Flora Roberts.[14]

In 1940, she began flying lessons at Western Michigan College as part of the Civilian Pilot Training program. She soloed on October 31 and as soon as she obtained her pilot's license joined the local Civil Air Patrol. She rose to the rank of sergeant with the patrol, accumulating well over 200 hours in the air before volunteering for Jackie Cochran's training detachment in Houston. Mabel was a member of The Lost Platoon, class 43-W-3. After graduation in July, she was one of the elite women that Jackie personally chose to send to Camp Davis.[15]

While still in her six-weeks of training, and just 18 days after she arrived in North Carolina, Mabel was flying her first night mission with flight instructor, Lieutenant Harvey Robillard, Jr. The 24-year old lieutenant studied ceramic engineering at LaSalle Institute and Alfred University in New York, but interrupted his studies in March 1942 to enlist in the Army Air Corps. The Air Force sent him to Randolph Field and then Brooks Field, both near San Antonio, for Flight Training and Combat Observer Training. There he also qualified as a flight instructor. When the first class of women pilots arrived at Avenger Field in 1943, Lt. Robillard was one of their flight instructors. That summer, when Jackie decided some of her students would tow targets in North Carolina, Robillard received his transfer to Camp Davis.[16]

It was a moonless night, just past 9 o'clock, and Mabel Rawlinson was in the front cockpit of an A-24 dive bomber. It was her first night flight in that type of plane, although she had been flying the A-24 in daylight. At the end of a normal flight, they were circling at about 2,000 feet, waiting for permission to land. "The tower called and told us to shoot a landing on Runway 4," Robillard told government investigators. Mabel entered the normal landing pattern and at 1,100 feet, reduced power, and let the airplane's wheels down. Within seconds, Robillard noticed that Mabel was moving the throttle back and forth and he realized that the engine was dead. "By that time we were at 700 feet and were across the runway, and there, turning to the left," he said. "I took over and told the student to jump." Halfway through a slow turn at low altitude, the A-24 began to stall, its wheels crashing through pine trees at the edge of the runway. The airplane shuddered for a moment and then struck the ground, about 300 feet from the end of the runway. Between the front and rear cockpits it separated into two segments and burst into flame. Thrown free of the blaze, Robillard lost consciousness. Mabel hadn't jumped. She was still alive—the malfunctioning emergency release latch trapping her in the blazing cockpit.[17]

Marion Hanrahan, (43-W-3) should have been flying that ill-fated A-24, but when her time came, she hadn't eaten supper and Mable offered to switch places with her. "We were in the dining room when we heard the siren that indicated a crash," Marion said. "When we ran out on the field we saw the front of her plane engulfed in fire and could hear Mabel screaming. It was a nightmare."[18]

Over the years, there have been many theories about the cause of the crash. Much later, Jackie Cochran even said that investigators found sugar in the gas tank and that she suspected sabotage. She said she didn't tell anyone at the time for fear the information might jeopardize the women's flight training program. Some say it was simple engine failure of a dilapidated machine, and others note that the fuel used in the plane was of a lower octane than required. There are even a few who say artillery fire might have hit Mabel's plane. Although these theories persist, especially Jackie's long-delayed sugar in the gas tank confession, no credible evidence has ever confirmed any of the stories.[19]

"I don't know exactly what it could be attributed to," said Dora Dougherty (43-W-3). "It was a very traumatic time for all of us there. I remember there was an old nurse who came over to our barracks. She had a couple bottles of beer and she sat on the end of the barracks watching the fire, drinking her beer, and singing old hymns … and just thinking the thoughts that we all thought." Dora said she had always known this sort of thing could happen, but she never expected its reality. "This was the first time that I had seen a friend die," she said. "So it was a trauma for me and I think for all of us."[20]

In the middle of the night, the telephone rang in the Rawlinson Michigan home. A loud voice read Mabel's mother and sister a telegram. "We regret to inform you that your daughter has been killed." The women at Camp Davis took up a collection to send Mabel's body home, accompanied by classmate Bertha Link. Five days after the accident, Mabel Virginia Rawlinson was home and at rest. Members of the Kalamazoo Civil Air Patrol were pallbearers for her flag draped casket. Following military tradition, members of the local National

Guard unit played *Taps* on a bugle and formed a six-man honor guard that fired three rifle volleys in salute to the fallen WASP. Air Patrol members offered their own salute with a flyover in their airplanes. General Arnold wrote a letter of condolence to Mabel's parents. "There is little I can say to console you in the loss of your daughter," he said, "but I trust that the memory of her devotion to her country will bring some measure of solace."[21]

Two days after Mabel's funeral, the confidence of the Sweetwater trainees was tested yet again, with another training catastrophe. It was August 30, 1943, and class 43-W-5 was in the homestretch, just 12 days before graduation. As the big day approached, they were tense and ecstatic all at the same time. Well into their advanced training, the women were flying cross-country in the Cessna UC-78B *Bobcat*, learning the power of multi-engine aircraft. Pilots called the *Bobcat* the "Bamboo Bomber" because of its wood wings and tail section, and its extensive wood and tubular metal framework that was covered in fabric. With dual steering wheels and room for three, it was the primary two-engine trainer for student pilots transitioning from single engine aircraft.[22]

Temperatures had reached 100° just north of Big Spring, Texas, and visibility was good, under partly cloudy skies. Helen Severson was at 2,000 feet, "flying under the hood," a training device that made sure she couldn't see anything but the flight instruments directly in front of her. The technique prepared a pilot to fly in the clouds or in conditions where it wasn't possible to see the surrounding countryside. To Helen's right was Peggy Seip who, with their instructor, Calvin Atwood, kept watch to be sure no other aircraft were in the area. They had left Sweetwater in the afternoon on a cross-country training flight around Big Spring with a planned return by 2 o'clock. It was the last anyone on the ground saw of them.[23]

When they hadn't returned by 5 o'clock, Avenger Field officials knew something must be wrong. They called to all of the nearby airfields to say they had a missing plane. A call came back from Big Spring Air Base that said a farmer had reported what looked like a crash in one of his fields.

When the Army crew finally arrived at dusk, they joined with sheriff's deputies in a search party led by the farmer. The man knew that the plane had fallen somewhere on the vast ranch owned by Repps Guitar, but he wasn't exactly sure where. When they arrived on the crash scene at 2:00 the next morning, they were stunned. There had been no fire. The plane had nosed in vertically with the left aileron laying a couple of hundred feet away from the main wreck and the right engine another couple of hundred feet away in the opposite direction. In between there were no marks on the ground. The plane had apparently just fallen apart in the sky. The bodies were horribly mangled, the coroner's gruesome description of their cause of death exactly the same for all three individuals. Identification of the victims would have been impossible without papers found in their clothing.[24]

Helen Josephine Severson died just three days before the first anniversary of her marriage to Robert Severson. Robert and Helen likely met while both were studying at South Dakota State College in Brookings, but the couple married at Ft. Benning, Georgia, where Robert was finishing his Air Corps training.[25]

Helen was the eldest child of Edwin and Amy Anderson, born November 16, 1918, in Marvin, South Dakota. Her father was in road construction and so the family moved quite frequently while Helen was young. A bright student, she was class valedictorian at her 1936 high school graduation from Summit, South Dakota's high school. When the family moved to Brookings later that year, Helen took a job with the local state planning office until she began her studies at South Dakota State College. During those college years, she worked in the registrar's office and as stenographer for the college library staff. It was during the summer, between her junior and senior year, that Helen began taking flying lessons with Cecil Schupe, department head for aviation mechanics at the college. Shupe told reporters that Helen was one of his best students. After Helen graduated with honors and a Bachelor Degree in Political Science, she attended the University of Illinois in Urbana, again graduating with honors in August 1942 with a Masters Degree in Library Science.[26]

Not long after her marriage to Robert, the Army sent him off to war in Europe. There he trained as an artillery spotter, flying in a light plane, observing enemy fortification, and directing mortar and artillery fire on the frontlines. Helen returned to Urbana and, with her previous aviation training, went to work as the assistant manager for the Urbana Airport. There she also trained with the local Civil Air Patrol. Her application for training with the WASPs was accepted and 24-year-old Helen reported to Avenger Field, to begin her training with class 44-W-5, March 26, 1943.[27]

Margaret June Seip was the second child and only daughter of Harry and Elizabeth Seip. She was born June 24, 1916, in Milwaukee, Wisconsin. While most of her friends knew her as Peggy, her younger brother called her Maggie. Hers was a comfortable life. By the time she graduated from college, her father had already risen from insurance salesman to become a vice president and Assistant Treasurer of the Northwestern National Life Insurance Company. After Maggie graduated from Wauwatosa High School, outside of Milwaukee, she earned a Bachelor Degree in English at Lawrence College, in Appleton, Wisconsin. Within days of her graduation in June 1938, she accompanied three other women on a voyage to Great Britain for a summer tour of Scotland and England. When she returned, she worked as the personnel director at Chapman's Department Store in Milwaukee. In her spare time, she took flying lessons at the Milwaukee Seadrome, located along the shores of Lake Michigan at Maitland Field. She qualified for her pilot's license in the fall of 1940. An active member of the 99s club of women aviators, she was also one of the first Wisconsin women to join the Civil Air Patrol, where she quickly rose to the rank of technical sergeant.[28]

In 1942, Maggie enrolled in the Link Trainer Instructors' School in Binghamton, New York, the same school Cornelia Fort had attended following her return from Hawaii after the attack on Pearl Harbor. She returned to Milwaukee in the summer of 1942 to work for Tony Lange, president of the Lange Aviation School and creator of the Milwaukee Seadrome. There she taught Army and Navy pilots to fly in Link Trainers at Milwaukee's Billy Mitchell and Curtiss-Wright fields.[29]

Twenty-two-year old Calvin Atwood, their instructor, died 190 miles southwest of his home. Born in Temple Hall, Texas, the family had moved north a few miles to Bryson before he was a teenager. His father, Luther, worked in the oil fields west of Fort Worth. Calvin graduated from Bryson High School and in 1939 entered North Texas Teacher's College in Denton, where he was one of the founding members of the Intercollegiate Flying Club. In July 1941, he enlisted in the Army Air Corps. After training, he came first to Houston and then Avenger Field as a flight instructor. Not long before he died, he married WASP Anna Frankman, a member of The Lost Platoon, 43-W-3, who was flying out of Love Field in Dallas.[30]

On the evening of the tragedy, even before discovery of the bodies, Avenger Field classmates gathered outside the barracks, offering prayers in the flower garden that Maggie and Helen had planted. The zinnias, petunias, and nasturtiums were in bloom, and the morning glories that Maggie had first planted when she arrived in Sweetwater, were beginning to climb the trellis on the barracks wall. "Peggy Seip may have had a smattering of agriculture at college," said a reporter.

Just a few weeks before her accident, Maggie also combined her expertise in Link Trainers with the English skills she had learned at

Lawrence College, to write an in-depth story for the camp newspaper about the Link simulators and Avenger Field's newly air-conditioned Link training room.[31]

Two days after the accident, in the dark, moonless hours before sunrise, trainees at Avenger Field left their beds, dressed, and without breakfast, arrived at Sweetwater's First Baptist Church. The 5:45 a.m. funeral service was to honor and remember Helen, Maggie, and Calvin. Already the trainees had heard the shocking story of chance that took Maggie Seip's life. Maggie had been on the operations board, scheduled to fly at about 3:00 in the afternoon. That would have been after Helen Severson and classmate, Marjorie Sanford, returned from their flight with Calvin Atkinson. But, just before takeoff, Sanford received a telephone call from her mother. Calvin Attwood told Sanford to take the call and asked Maggie to take Sanford's place. Minutes later, Maggie Seip was dead. After the memorial service, classmates returned to training, while the victim's bodies left for home and burial.[32]

Robert, Helen Severson's husband, was still in Europe. The Allies finally had control of Sicily and Robert had received the Air Medal after safely completing 25 observer flights against the enemy. By October 1944, he was with the advancing Allies inside Germany. A year and two months after Helen's death, it's unclear whether he was on another spotting mission or on a bombing run, but he died when ground fire shot down his plane. He now rests beside Helen in Greenwood Cemetery in Brookings, South Dakota.[33]

Back at Camp Davis, the trouble with A-24 flights continued. Just two days after Mabel Rawlinson died, Joyce Sherwood's engine stopped, forcing her and her instructor into a belly landing. With the propeller, engine, and nose of the aircraft ripping away, rescue crews rushed to the scene. "The ship skidded on the runway and the engine started sputtering," Sherwood said. "I was anxious when I saw the plane catching on fire, but I'd always had faith in planes and the guys who were taking care of them." Sherwood (43-W-3) and her instructor escaped from the crash and fire with minor injuries, but Betty Wood wouldn't be so lucky.[34]

On the day she graduated at Avenger Field with class 43-W-4, August 7, 1943, Betty Louise Taylor married one of her civilian flight instructors, Harry "Shorty" Wood. Harry got his nickname for the not so obvious reason—he was tall. Regulations forbid trainees from dating flight instructors, but Betty and Harry's wedding proved that love would top any military regulation every time. After her morning march on the flight line and receiving her wings from Jackie Cochran, Betty had most of the afternoon to get ready for the evening wedding service. Her mother and father, Thomas and Effa, had come from Auburn, California for both ceremonies. Her father would give his youngest daughter away and waited patiently while Betty, her mother, and classmate Violet Thurn prepared themselves. Violet was maid of honor and had chosen a white silk suit with a gardenia corsage. Effa Taylor wore a navy dress with white accessories and a yellow rose corsage, while Betty dressed in a white linen suit, white shoes, and wearing a white gardenia. Harry Wood waited nervously at the front of Sweetwater's First Presbyterian Church, his best man and school friend, Fred Nesber, at his side. Reverend Clifford Williams looked up the aisle as the organist began to play the *Wedding March*. Behind him, the church was decorated with ferns, various cut flowers, and dozens of white gladioli. Fellow trainees filled the pews and even Jackie Cochran was a witness to the double-ring ceremony. The evening ended with dinner at The Club Cafe's banquet hall for family and a few close friends, and then, Betty and Harry began their 10-day honeymoon in Sweetwater.[35]

Twenty-one-year-old Harry was born in Colorado and he attended Fort Collins High School. After graduation, he enrolled in Colorado State College, learning to fly in the college's extensive Civilian Pilots Training program that included advanced training and cross-country flights. After training in Texas, he qualified as a civilian flight instructor.[36]

Betty was born in Illinois and she grew up near Athens, a small community in the central part of the state. In 1940, while still a high school student in the nearby community of New Berlin, Betty's parents moved the family west and settled in Auburn, California. Betty finished her senior year at Placer Union High School and then began studies at Placer Junior College, now known as Sierra College. It wasn't a long commute between classes, the college and high school shared some of their facilities and a few of their instructors. While Betty studied, she worked as a store clerk and as an assistant in a doctor's office. She enrolled in the Civilian Pilot Training program at the college and learned to fly. A fellow student later remembered her as the most natural pilot enrolled in the class. Her application to the WASP program was accepted and Betty reported to Houston to begin her training with the 43-W-4 class.[37]

After their honeymoon, Harry returned to his training assignment at Sweetwater, while 22-year-old Betty headed for her duty station with the 5$^{th}$ Ferrying Group in Dallas. Initially scheduled for transition training to heavier aircraft, by September, new orders had assigned her to Camp Davis.[38]

On August 23, 1943, while making a landing following two hours of flying, one of Betty's wings touched the ground, forcing her to abort. Observers on the ground thought they heard her engine surge and cut out. They believed Betty was giving her A-24 full throttle, trying to climb and make a go-around attempt, but the throttle must have been sticking. The plane struck an embankment, the engine stalled, and the plane rolled over onto its top, crushing Betty. Almost every current report of the accident says that an Army chaplain was riding with her and that he too died; however, none of the newspaper stories reporting the accident at the time mentions anyone else dying or even flying with Betty that day. Another story says that the person flying with her escaped. It's likely that someone was with Betty, but if he was, why doesn't someone know his name? It's also puzzling that a chaplain would be in the cockpit behind her and not an instructor or a fellow WASP. Could the man's last name have been Chaplain? Apparently these are questions never asked before, and if asked, never answered. After nearly 75 years, there's little hope that we'll ever know for sure.[39]

When word of Betty's death reached Sweetwater, Harry Wood was on leave and in the air, on his way home to Fort Collins. Sweetwater forwarded the message to Fort Collins to await Harry's arrival. Until he landed, Harry didn't know that his wife of less than two months was dead.[40]

There was a delay in returning Betty's remains to California and she didn't arrive until after the memorial funeral service held in Auburn. Her parents chose to have her cremated and then interred in the mausoleum at East Lawn Memorial Park, in Sacramento.[41]

So far, eight WASPs had died, four in a single month. But the war was still going on and the worst had just begun.

# [9]

## GOLDEN EAGLES

Avenger Field, "out where the rattlesnake rattles and the buzzard builds its nest." It was a foreign land; a dusty, and sometimes muddy rancho on the West Texas plains. The native customs were definitely strange and the vast, flat surroundings severe. Trainees were dedicated to flying and to their country, but without a strong sense of humor, few of these women could have survived their months of training.[1]

A reporter for the detachment's newspaper, Dorothy Bancroft (44-W-6), tongue firmly in cheek, tried to ease the transition, welcoming a new class of trainees with a whimsical introduction to life at Avenger Field. Barracks, she said, "are spacious buildings on the hacienda order, divided into cozy apartments known as bays." With a few steps over "the concrete terrace," actually a narrow sidewalk outside the barracks, the trainee entered "a studio type living room with gothic arched ceiling, half timbered." Yes, they were here to fly Uncle Sam's wondrous airplanes, she said, but most of all "the big job here is the matter of living." She warned the newcomers that they could hardly believe how much of their "living" would now be devoted to housekeeping. In fact, the true secret was "Uncle Sam's chief wish for his little Fifinellas," simply "to teach them the art and science of becoming good housewives." That, she said, would ensure a cleaner and much more orderly world after the war was over.[2]

For Dorothy, each bay came furnished in the "Roman manner." Army cots were luxurious divans, "scattered about comfortably." The plain chests of drawers and pine wardrobes represented "beautiful woodwork of matching design." The desks, she said, would host "leisure hours of correspondence" and, of course, there was "central heating"—a fireplace, offering the perfect opportunity for a "midnight weenie roast."

Dorothy was sure the trainees were familiar with the servant problem facing the country at the time. "Unfortunately, we have had to dismiss a large portion of the household staff," she said. "This burden, my dears, you must share bravely, just as our mothers are doing at home." In the bathroom, the "no man's land" that the military called a latrine, she said the women would find many "devices of straw attached to a stick" that were known as brooms. "You career girls, I know, are unfamiliar with its uses, but Uncle Sam will see to it that you learn shortly."

"Friday night we regularly have an orgy," Dorothy said, "which sometimes lasts over until Saturday morning." It was an orgy of sweeping and mopping floors, while every shelf, nook, and cranny was dusted. Toilets were scrubbed, showers wiped down, personal items and clothing perfectly arranged, beds tightly made; never finishing until everything was spotless and ready for "the holy rite of Army Inspection."

"The Army Inspector is a three-toed, double-eyed, demon whose distinguishing mark is a white glove," Dorothy said. He comes out of his hibernation at 10 o'clock each Saturday morning, "thirsty for a chance to rub that white glove on all available table tops, locker tops, and venetian blind slats." If the glove remains white after each swipe, "he leaves in bitter defeat." However, should the glove come back gray or black, "he has found his heart's delight and gleefully chalks up demerits." Demerits, she said, was a game devised by Uncle Sam to make life "fuller, richer, and more exciting." Scored like golf, "the girl with the lowest score is the winner." WASP Betty Jane Williams (44-W-6) remembered those Saturday inspections. "If you had an apple in your locker," she said, "everyone got demerits."[3]

Anytime a superior officer found a violation of any of a long list of rules, a trainee could expect demerits. If a woman accumulated 75 demerits or more, she automatically "washed out." She was eliminated from the training program, requiring her to clear out her locker, return all government supplies, and leave Avenger Field within 24 hours. From there she had to find her own way home. Seven or more demerits in a week meant no weekend pass into town. Violations could be as simple as hair not properly combed (one demerit), or more serious infractions that included throwing food or utensils in the mess hall (five demerits), and trainees changing rooms or barracks without permission (seven demerits). The most serious offenses, such as absence from quarters without permission, talking back to a superior, neglect of duty, spreading gossip, not complying with orders, and harsh or abusive language, meant a trainee faced a board of officers. They questioned her about her violation, and if the offense was serious enough, or the trainee already had exhibited a bad record or attitude, the board could immediately wash her out and send her home.[4]

Dorothy Bancroft joked about a scenario where a woman returning late to Avenger Field tried to beat the curfew and avoid demerits. "Racing the deadline," she said, the trainee managed to slide "breathlessly" though the camp gate at the very last minute. "How much more exciting," Dorothy said, "than merely coming home from a date!"

Just a few months after Dorothy's story appeared in print, she needed to hold onto every bit of her wit and whimsy, as she endured an emergency operation for appendicitis; or, as she called it, "intestinal confusion." The operation and subsequent recovery forced her removal from class 44-W-2 and, in January 1944, she returned back to the beginning of training with class 44-W-6.[5]

By the end of summer 1943, Avenger Field was taking on the look of a boomtown and the extracurricular lives of the WASP trainees were improving. The Civil Aeronautics Administration's $765 million expansion at Avenger was already underway. The gymnasium was nearly finished, its maple floor soon to squeak under women's shoes as the trainees battled against each other in basketball, volleyball, and shuffleboard. "We are going to hope," said a trainee, "that in the near future, sports will become an integral part of our life at Avenger Field." The new gym was also going to be the camp theater, equipped with a motion picture projection room and a stage for traveling USO shows and other performances, including graduation ceremonies. On the flight line, thousands of square yards of additional runways, taxiways, aprons, and service roads were under construction. Contractors were refurbishing old buildings and building half-a-dozen new buildings that were almost ready. An extension to the Link Training room, insulated and air conditioned against the Texas heat was almost ready. With seven more flight simulators available, the growing number of trainees would easily be able to finish their required number of simulated flight hours.[6]

The Link Trainer was a wooden box about the size and shape of an airplane cockpit, painted in Army colors, yellow and blue, to match the real airplanes the women flew. Beneath the Link were four large bellows that allowed the simulator to bank in all directions. A vacuum

**Hazel Lee (43-W-4) practicing her flying in the Link trainer, a WWII flight simulator. – *Air Force photo.***

created by a three-quarter horsepower motor powered the bellows and, at the same time, operated the cockpit instruments. The Link turned left or right with the help of a front-mounted motor.[7]

Many of the WASP trainees had attended the Link Trainer Instructors School in New York before coming to Avenger Field. They had learned to setup and monitor ground based instrument flying missions for their students. Now, the women themselves were the students and they flew the missions. Although each had completed at least 30 hours of instructor training and flown an additional 30 hours inside the trainer at Instructors School, here in Sweetwater they were learning exactly how the Army wanted them to fly. The 30-hour course began with five hours of primary training, introducing the Link trainer and explaining how to "fly" it. Without visual clues, they coordinated their flying with instruments. One of the most important basic maneuvers they practiced was the standard rate turn, where the Link simulated a 360° turn in two minutes. During the turn, the trainee had to hold a steady altitude and bank angle, while controlling air speed. The turn remains the basis of all controlled turns a pilot makes.

Basic Link training takes up the next 15 hours. Students continue their flying with the addition of simulated rough air and changing weather conditions. They learn to use more instruments and begin practicing radio communications and radio navigation, their instructor playing the roles of control tower operator, weatherman, and radio range operator. The final 10 hours of training concentrates on advanced navigation by instruments, where trainees fly simulated cross-country flights from takeoff to landing. In an article Maggie Seip wrote before she died, she said almost all the women began their training with crashes. "After most of the instrument landings," she said, "the instructors usually call for the crash truck, as the student levels off fifty feet underground." A detailed record of each trainee's Link experience, including time spent flying, name of the instructor, the training exercises performed, and the grade for each exercise, becomes part of the woman's permanent record.[8]

In Sweetwater, the community had opened its arms to the "Avenger girls." One Sunday in June, any "girl aviation trainee" who wasn't flying and could get away from camp, received an invitation to morning church services and a home cooked Sunday afternoon dinner in a private home. It was Hospitality Day, Sweetwater's official welcome to the fliers. Some of the 400 trainees who came to town got a trip to Lake Sweetwater, others a dip in the municipal swimming pool, while still others had their pick of a movie—*Crash Dive* with Tyrone Power at the Texas Theater or Marlene Dietrich in *Pittsburgh* at the Ritz. It seems residents were now anxious to include the girls in everything.[9]

Rather than have the women wait in line for an available tennis court in the city park, school board officials invited the trainees to use the town's high school courts, as long as they brought their own rackets and balls. Within weeks, a tournament pitted some of the town's former high school tennis champions against the best of the Avenger trainees. The tussle ended in a "hard fought" victory for the "Avenger girls"—three matches to two over the "Sweetwater Swatters." Frances Grimes, winner of many collegiate tournaments in the East and Mid-Atlantic states, didn't play. Instead she coached the Avenger team to victory.[10]

The success of Hospitality Day convinced city officials to open the municipal swimming pool to Avenger cadets for swim classes. The Army thought all trainees should be able to swim, believing it would increase their confidence and safety when they eventually began ferrying planes over large bodies of water. At no charge, three days a week, for two hours in the afternoon, trainees got exclusive use of the pool. Officials also voted to give the women a one-third discount on pool admissions for the days when the women had free time and wanted to swim on their own.[11]

Helen Drake, a teenager during the war years, was fascinated with the WASPs she saw swimming at the pool. "These women were different," she said. "They were special. They were my idea of 'high class' women." In awe, Helen noted every detail. They were tan, self sufficient, and their makeup "had an elegance—a just rightness, which no local beauty salon could produce." Their speech was firm and bold, most of the time in a northern accent. They used words that no one ever used in Sweetwater, and most shocking of all— "They even cussed openly, something which no 'proper lady' in Sweetwater would ever do." The impressionable teenager would never forget them. "To me they will always be special," she said. "They will always be golden eagles who soar through my memories of other times and other places."[12]

As long as they were up-to-date with their flying and classes, and their demerits allowed, there was always a way for trainees to find a few special moments away from the pressures of training. There was the Fourth of July Watermelon Feast sponsored by the local USO. Because most of the women were from northern states, "where watermelons are pretty much a rarity," local residents thought the melons would be the perfect treat for the hard flying ladies. They were right. Four hundred fifty "girl fliers" managed to swallow 1,154 pounds of fresh Texas melon in a single evening. "They took them apart just like they'd been a cheap dish of caviar," said a reporter.[13]

Soon, nearby communities were inviting the women to other unique events. In mid-July, another 400 trainees boarded military busses on a Saturday night and headed to nearby Scurry County for the annual rodeo. There weren't enough horses to go around, but a few of the trainees were able to climb up behind a cowboy and ride with them into the arena. The man at the loudspeaker kept yelling challenges to the more bashful cowboys to ride their horse up to the pretty ladies in the Avenger fliers' section and "Git 'em." Even Mrs. Deaton, the Chief Establishment Officer at Avenger, rode her own horse into the arena, prompting the trainees not so quietly to urge Major Urban, Avenger's commander, to saddle up too, but he declined.[14]

Restrictions on publicity were easing. *Life* magazine had published a nine–page photo essay about the trainees, and newspaper interviews and stories were becoming more common. When the women heard that bandleader Fred Waring was going to salute the "Avenger Girls" on his coast-to-coast, national radio program, "Victory Tunes," they were thrilled. Word was that Waring's featured vocalist, Donna Dae, would sing one of the trainees' favorite songs. Immediately, Mrs.

Deaton started a survey to determine which song would be most popular with the women. The four most requested were: "All or Nothing at All," "Dark Eyes," "Coming in on a Wing and a Prayer," and the winner by a wide margin, for obvious reasons—"Don't Get Around Much Anymore." On Monday night, July 19, 1943, almost every ear in Sweetwater and at Avenger Field was leaning toward a radio. The WASPs got their salute from Waring, but they never heard their chosen song. "The air trainees and townspeople listened in; however," a local reporter said, "and accepted the on air tribute for the field and the personnel."[15]

Fall was just a few days away and it was football season in Texas. Daytime temperatures were still in the low 90s and weren't likely to cool off for quite a few more weeks. Texas is a football loving state and Sweetwater called itself "a football community," where "good patronage is expected." Hoping for good attendance from the surrounding military installations, especially by the women from Avenger Field, the Sweetwater school board cut the cost of admission for enlisted personnel in uniform and "the girls at the field" from 55¢ to 30¢. On Friday night, October 4, two busloads of trainees headed for Mustang Stadium, in downtown Sweetwater, to see their first game. It had rained all afternoon, there was mud everywhere, the bleachers were wet, and the women shivered through all four quarters. It was tough going, but the local boys pulled off a 33-0 victory. The drizzly rain and the cold north wind didn't help the situation for players, WASPs, or the other spectators. A few weeks later it was still cold, but it hadn't rained, and so "a load of enthusiastic and noisy Avenger Field girls," were on hand to watch the Mustangs trounce another opponent, 53-0. The women were an energetic pep squad for the local boys, constantly cheering the team, the officials, the water boy, and drooling over "an unidentified football hero on the Sweetwater team known only as Scotty." It would be a good season for the Sweetwater Mustangs, but their one loss that year would also lose them the championship.[16]

While trainees were suffering through that bone chilling Texas night in early October, Virginia "Ginny" Moffatt (43-W-2) was in Long Beach, California, getting ready for the next days' mission. Ginny's assignment after graduation in May was the 6$^{th}$ Ferrying Group, just 25 miles south of her Los Angeles home. Born May 31, 1912, in Wheatland, Wyoming, Ginny was one of the oldest WASPs selected for service. She was the fourth of five daughters born to Louis and Nettie Moffatt. Louis came to America from England at age 20 in 1891, settling near Cheyenne. He and Nettie married in 1901 and soon moved to Wheatland, a small community on the prairie, 70 miles north of Cheyenne. Louis was the town clerk and marshal. In 1909, he was one of the local organizers of Company I of the Wyoming National Guard. In January 1911 he received his commission as captain of the company, a rank he held until his death in 1917. A year earlier, Pancho Villa had invaded a small town in New Mexico, killing 17 Americans and torching the town. Wyoming volunteers, including Captain Moffatt, headed for the Mexican border to join a U.S. force that hoped to capture Villa. While there, stomach pains that had plagued Louis for months became unbearable and he returned to Wyoming for an operation. Four days later, Ginny's 46-year-old father was dead. A military escort of 100 men accompanied Nettie Moffatt back to Wheatland, where the entire town shutdown for the funeral.[17]

Left with five daughters, ranging in age from 2 to 15, Nettie leased the Wheatland fairgrounds and stables, where she opened a dairy farm. Early each morning, before school, the girls helped milk 12 cows, and then, while riding in Nettie's beat up Chevrolet, delivered the milk to their customers. With proceeds from the dairy, Louis' government pension, and the salaries she and eldest daughter, Hilda, earned as schoolteachers at the local rural schoolhouse, Nettie was able to support the family in comfort. By 1929, she and her three youngest girls moved out to Los Angeles, where Ginny graduated from John C. Fremont High School. Before joining the WASPs in Houston, she worked as a typist for Los Angeles County.[18]

Ginny graduated from Sweetwater in the same class as Paula Loop and, after her ten-day leave, she reported for duty in Long Beach on June 14, 1943. For months, she had flown ferrying flights all over the country, but on October 5$^{th}$ her mission was much simpler, delivering BT-15s to the Cal-Aero Airfield between Chino and Ontario, just over 30 miles away. Before the war, Cal-Aero had been a civilian flight school, but now the Army Air Force was training cadets there. It was late in the afternoon when 31-year-old Ginny began her landing approach to the runway. Perhaps tired from previous deliveries she had made that day, she came in too hard and overshot her landing. She began her climb into a go-around for another try at a landing. About a mile out from the airfield she started a turn, but at too steep of an angle. The plane stalled and spiraled into a dive, crashed in a walnut orchard, and burst into flame. Neither the Sweetwater nor the Avenger Field newspapers mentioned her death.[19]

That same week, class 43-W-6 was graduating from Sweetwater under a warning: "Camera Bugs Note. No pictures may be taken at the

W-6 graduation ceremonies, except those by authorized Army personnel." Tagged with the owner's name, all cameras were supposed to remain at the front gate until the ceremony ended, but authorities relented. Trainees were to advise their relatives that forbidden pictures included more than two airplanes grouped together, cockpit interior shots, and panoramic views of buildings or the airfield. Also off limits were pictures of damaged equipment or of the ongoing construction. Publicity rules had eased for the WASPs, but wartime security and secrecy were still strongly in effect.[20]

Every class would always have the same questions before they graduated. Where will we live? What will we do? What kind of planes will we fly? Perhaps the most exciting news came from Ohio, where 16 women from class 43-W-5 were learning to fly B-17 bombers. Any bit of news from the outside flying world always sparked the trainees' imaginations. W-6 graduate, Bonnie Jean Welz, set out to gather more information from previous graduates. "The girls based in Long Beach live in barracks and enjoy the facilities of the officers club," she wrote. The women did their own laundry and had to keep their barracks clean and up to Army standards. They were on duty seven days a week from 8:00 until 5:30, whether they flew or not. Link training proficiency was maintained, as well as other studies. They ended the day with calisthenics or drill practice between 7:00 and 9:00, and marched in review every Saturday. First, they qualified in the new airplanes they would be flying, and before they could fly solo, they had to fly for a while in ferrying groups of from three to five planes.[21]

The 3rd Ferrying Group at Romulus Field, in Michigan, seemed to be living a more exotic life. "Lately they have received target practice with forty-fives," Bonnie Jean wrote. During their orientation training, they carried 25-pound packs that included a pup tent, gas mask and a canteen of warm water, along with the requirement that they know how to use each item. Some of the women were being checked out in AT-6 *Texans* and two extremely "fortunate lassies have been ferrying P-39's," the *Airacobra*, one of the principal fighter aircraft used by the Army during the early war. Two women shared a room in a barracks that included the usual dressers and lockers, but also was equipped with "real beds." Even pets and liquor were OK.

There was also one "mysterious, romantic-sounding job known as the 'special assignment,'" somewhere near Washington, D.C., but Bonnie Jean couldn't get any more information. All she knew was, "Twenty-five girls from the last class were assigned to report there." Of course, the assignment was Camp Davis, North Carolina, and romantic it was not.[22]

In Sweetwater, Aviation Enterprises arranged with the country government to open a club room exclusively for the WASP trainees on the upper floor of the Welfare Building, at the corner of Oak and Fourth streets. The women named it the Avengerette Club. It was similar to a USO Club except that no male soldiers were allowed unless accompanied by a trainee. Women without dates had their own separate room where they could socialize. While Aviation Enterprises paid for most of the interior features and the major renovation work, the trainees contributed to a fund to help furnish the room. Mrs. Deaton took their money, went to Dallas, and bought lounging chairs and sofas, upholstered in blue-gray and maroon material. They matched the color scheme of the walls that were painted blue and yellow. She also brought back a number of thick, white throw rugs. There was a large dance floor in the club, surrounded by tables, a juke box, and a snack bar, featuring non-alcoholic Cokes. Wall lighting sconces gave "a soft glow to the interior of the club—and also to the fliers' suntanned faces." Trainees Clara Jo Marsh and Ellen Santoro, of class 44-W-3, decorated the room with cartoon images of Fifinella in various poses, and an unknown Sweetwater resident donated a used piano. There would never be any final touches as long as trainees were at Avenger, but the basic layout of the room was finished by December 1943.[23]

Even before the club was finished, the women began using the room for special events. One of the first was a Saturday evening Halloween party, dance, and floorshow, where the trainees invited cadets from the Big Spring Bombardier School as special guests. Of course, the event was closely chaperoned. The floorshow featured 43-W-8 class members Dorothy Asbell, dancing in a grass skirt hula, May Ball scratching out a soft-shoe, and Loes Monk singing a few songs. Loes wrote the words and music to what became known as the *WASP Song*. That evening, the men spent the night in special quarters at Avenger Field and the next morning, after breakfast, they returned to their base.[24]

Mary Trebing (43-W-4) was in Dallas at the time, getting ready for her train trip north to Cimarron Field, just west of Oklahoma City, where she and two other WASPs from the 5th Ferrying Group would begin ferrying Fairchild PT-19's trainers back to Love Field.

Mary was born December 31, 1920, in Royalton, near the coalfields of Southern Illinois. She was William and Myrtle Trebing's oldest child. Myrtle was the widow of Harry McLaughlin, who in 1918, at age 33, died with 20 others in a gas explosion at the Franklin Coal & Coke

Company's No. 1 mine. In 1930, when Mary was still in elementary school, William, her coal miner father, moved the family, including Mary's younger brother, William, to the rich Colorado coal fields; first to Lafayette and then Louisville. It was an untimely move. The stock market crash of 1929 and the subsequent depression soon had Colorado's coal industry in steep economic decline. Not long after 1935, the family moved again, this time to Gowen, Oklahoma, where a relative who had an interest in a coal mining company was able to get Mary's father a job.[25]

Here, in the southeastern Oklahoma coal district, Mary finished high school and in 1941 entered Eastern Oklahoma A&M College as a mathematics major. When not in class she worked as a stenographer for the district attorney's office and in her free time she took flying lessons. At the end of 1942, she left to join the WASPs. While she trained at Avenger Field, Mary had a hard time holding on to her gold and black "Eversharp" fountain pen, engraved with an abbreviated form of her name, "Met Trebing." She placed a lost and found ad in an April edition of the Sweetwater newspaper, offering a reward for its return. Apparently, the ad succeeded, because almost exactly a month later, she was advertising the very same pen, as "Lost Again." If she ever again got the pen back and paid another reward, we'll never know. After graduation, in August 1943, and a brief visit home, Mary reported to the 5$^{th}$ Ferrying Group at Love Field.[26]

There are two different versions of how Mary Trebing crashed and died on November 7, 1943. About 20 minutes after taking off from Cimarron Field, near Oklahoma City, there was trouble. Her brother William said he heard that, "her plane ran into difficulties somewhere in the vicinity of Blanchard, Oklahoma. At the time, this was a heavily forested area with only an auxiliary field where there might have been a chance to crash land a plane." With a dead engine, Mary had barely missed crashing into a farmhouse and found herself flying under a power line. "The vertical stabilizer of the plane caught on the high lines," William said, "and nosed her down into the ground. The crash ruptured an artery in her neck and we were told that she died instantly." The major difference between William's account and that reported by the crash investigators is that eyewitnesses on the ground told investigators that Mary had intentionally buzzed the farmhouse. She unexpectedly found herself flying under electric power lines "and the vertical fin snagged a wire, shearing off the top of the fin and tearing the rudder away." She crashed through a fence with the plane coming to rest on its belly, about 200 yards past the power line. The undercarriage of the craft was ripped away. Two months shy of her 23rd birthday, Mary Trebing returned to Boulder, Colorado for her burial.[27]

On November 12, Sweetwater and the Avenger Field trainees celebrated the first anniversary of the WASPs and the graduation of class 43-W-7. At 6 p.m., a parade began snaking its way through the Sweetwater business district. Immediately behind the colors, carried by members of the Texas State Guard, came the Big Spring Field Bombardier Band, leading two flights of Avenger trainees, marching in General's Pants and white shirts. Behind them, the Sweetwater High School band alternated with the Bombardiers, playing rousing marches that kept the women in perfect step. There were mounted cowboys and cowgirls from the Double Heart Ranch, along with Army personnel driving military vehicles, and marching members of the Sweetwater Company of the Texas State Guard.

The parade ended at the entrance to the county courthouse, where a platform was set up in front of the steps. On the steps sat the 59 members of the graduating class. After opening remarks, the graduates received certificates of lifetime Sweetwater citizenship from Acting Mayor Albert Norred. "You have become a part of the town," Norred said. "We are proud of you." Highlight of the event was a gigantic four-layer birthday cake, with a single lit candle on its top. Mrs. Deaton cut out 59 pieces and served them to each graduate. Graduates also received free passes to the Texas Theater for the evening performance of a Paramount Studios short—a WASP documentary recently filmed at Avenger Field. Although the women could stay and watch the feature film, *Five Graves to Cairo*, most left for the graduation dance held in the Avengerette Club.[28]

Winter was coming on fast and, for the first time, women who had spent almost every Thanksgiving of their life at home, surrounded by the warmth of family, were far away from home and lonely. There had been no crackling carpet of fallen leaves to walk on, no smells of roasting turkeys, or pumpkin pies. The war had changed everything. "Thanksgiving," said Mary Strok (44-W-2) "has, by the very dint of war, taken on such a depth and such a new and meaningful aspect that it cannot be compared with the prewar kind." This year the Thanksgiving feast was in the mess hall, not mama's dining room. The trainees had marched through a drowning and chilling downpour that wouldn't stop for long over the next two days. Although dinner might not taste as good as those so fondly remembered, the Army knew how to prepare a traditional meal that, at least made the day seem special. Along with young, roasted turkey, the women could choose from a menu that included, shrimp cocktail, cranberry sauce, candied yams, canned vegetables, traditional dressing, and the sweetest of desserts—pumpkin and apple pies, cakes, and ice cream—as much as they wanted to eat. Thanksgiving was precious now. It had taken on a new and important meaning. As long as the war went on they had their job to do, and they would do it; holding on to their memories and always hoping that soon all would be well again. "The old friends and relatives live in the pleasant memories left behind," Mary Strok said. "Yet, Thanksgiving remains with a new meaning—for it contains a promise of things to come; unfulfilled as yet, but still a dream and a promise."[29]

# [10]

## UNLUCKY 13

It was a father-daughter race for an airplane prize. Dorothy Scott and her father, Guthrie, had challenged each other to a "learn to fly" contest; the prize—a two seat, cabin-style airplane. For two years, Dorothy's attempts to get into a Civilian Pilot Training course at the University of Washington were frustrated, but in February 1941, she finally succeeded. Her father bought a plane and challenged her to a race to find out which of them would be the first to fly solo. The winner would have rights to the plane. With nearly 100 hours of flight training and ground school ahead of her, Dorothy expected to get her license by mid-June. Her father would take flying lessons in the northern part of the state, not far from the Canadian border, near their home in Oroville, Washington. Guthrie bragged to Dorothy that he'd beat her and probably have his license well before June. The race was on. On St. Patrick's Day, 1941, at 10 o'clock in the morning, and just four weeks after she began training, 20-year-old Dorothy soloed in a seaplane over Lake Union in Seattle. As soon as she landed, she rushed to the telegraph office and sent a message to her father in Oroville that told him to hold his airplane for her exclusive use. "I expect to fly to Los Angeles this summer to visit my mother and then continue on to Texas," she told a reporter. "My brother is in the Army there and I want to see him." Seven hours later, at 5 o'clock that afternoon, Dorothy received an excited telephone call from her father. He had soloed and was claiming victory. Apparently, he hadn't yet received Dorothy's telegram. Two weeks later, Guthrie paid up, delivering Dorothy's airplane to his daughter in Seattle.[1]

Now the bet became who could qualify for their pilot's license first.

The loser would have to cook a chicken dinner. Once both finally had their licenses, they planned to share flying time on a flight to El Paso to visit Dorothy's older brother, but Dorothy was skeptical. "I'll bet an old set of plane tires, I do all the flying," she said. "In fact … Oh, there I go, betting again!"[2]

Born a twin with brother, Edward, February 16, 1920, Dorothy was still finishing her studies at the University of Washington. After graduation in December 1941, her father challenged her yet again, this time to try for an instructor's license. It took three months of hard work, but she qualified in August 1943. She accepted a job as a flight instructor in the Civilian Pilot Training program at the Pullman-Moscow Airport, near the Idaho-Washington border. After working less than three months, she left Idaho to join Nancy Love at New Castle Airfield in Delaware, training to become a WAF in the Ferrying Command. At 22, she was one of the youngest women to qualify.[3]

Her father, Guthrie Scott was born in England and came to New York City when he was 4 years old. By the time he was 16, his father had died and Guthrie was helping his widowed mother by working in a dry goods store. By 1913, after a few years spent in Alaska, Guthrie and his mother settled in Washington, where he married Katherine Faeth. In July 1919, he opened his first automobile dealership and began selling cars. By the time Dorothy was studying at the university, he was the largest and best-known Ford dealer in the area. Ten years earlier Guthrie had cleared some of his land and constructed a small airport hoping to have it designated as an international port of entry between Canada and the United States. It would take 21 years before he finally got the OK from the U. S. government.[4]

Dorothy's assignment, after completing WAFS training in January 1943, was the 5th Ferrying Group at Love Field in Dallas. It was a busy year of shuttling aircraft all over the country. Gradually she qualified to fly bigger and more powerful planes and at the end of November she received her dream assignment, pursuit school in Palm Springs, California. By then she had accumulated over 600 hours in the air.[5]

Two years into the war, manufacturers were turning out hundreds of high performance aircraft a month, all of them needing delivery somewhere in the country, for either training or transfer to overseas war zones. Production and ferrying of simple trainers had dropped off sharply, while advanced aircraft, such as the pursuit planes, had taken their place. Faced with the increased delivery burden, the Ferrying Command realized they needed more women pilots capable of flying these demanding planes. "It is, therefore felt," said a memo from

Ferrying Division Headquarters, "that 25 percent of all women who graduate should be trained on pursuit aircraft of the P-39, P-40, P-51, and P-47 types." The Command suggested the women receive 25 hours of specialized instruction and be selected from the very best qualified members of each class. Dorothy Scott was one of the first eight women chosen.[6]

On her second day of pursuit training, December 3, 1943, Dorothy was flying in an AT-6 with her instructor, 2nd Lieutenant Robert Snyder. It was a pleasant winter afternoon over the desert sands of Palm Springs, light winds, and temperatures only reaching into the mid 70s. Dorothy had already flown many takeoffs and landings, and so, at about 5:00 in the evening, she was probably on her final approach of the day. A P-39 flown by 1st Lieutenant Wilson Young followed behind. Both planes were cleared by the tower for landing, but apparently the controller hadn't considered that Young's P-39 was a faster airplane. Coming out of a wide turn on his final approach, Young must not have seen the slower plane. Officials believed the low winter sun might have blinded him. From above and behind he came down, right on top of Dorothy's AT-6, tearing off its tail. Both planes fell, the AT-6 erupting in flames—all all three pilots were dead.[7]

Robert Snyder, Dorothy's instructor, was 23 years old. Born in Edgemont, South Dakota, his parents brought him to Rhinelander, Wisconsin when he was 8. After graduation from Rhineland High School in 1938, he enrolled at the University of Wisconsin to pursue a Law Degree. He learned to fly in the Civilian Pilot Training program at the university. By 1940 he had qualified for his instructor's license. After graduation in 1942, Robert and three of his close friends hopped into a beat up Ford and left Wisconsin for training as civilian flight instructors in Texas. Robert's assignment was Avenger Field, where he would first teach the R.A.F. cadets and then the women of Jackie Cochran's flying detachment. He secured his Army commission in the summer of 1943 and transferred to the 6th Ferrying Group in Long Beach. Two weeks before his final flight with Dorothy, he became an instructor of pursuit pilots at Palm Springs.[8]

The P-39 pilot, 25-year-old Wilson Young, was born in Kansas, where his father, Albert, was a history professor and president of Friends University. Wilson had married Margaret Lord August 25, 1940, in Los Angeles. He was in Palm Springs on a temporary assignment from his home base, the Gore Army Airfield near Great Falls, Montana.[9]

The airport Dorothy's father had started near their home, and the seaplane base on nearby Osoyoos Lake, were renamed for Dorothy. Her father managed the airport and continued to fly until he died in 1954. A year before his death, Washington State Aeronautics Commission records revealed that, at age 69, Guthrie was the oldest active pilot in the state.[10]

Back in Sweetwater, a mini crime wave was striking at Avenger Field. Souvenir hunters were looting the Wishing Well, stealing shiny coins in the middle of the night. The well, rimmed with its low flagstone wall that surrounded a shallow pool, had been a watering hole for thirsty livestock for years before there was an Avenger Field. Now, surrounded by barracks and a sidewalk circle, the Wishing Well was the center of the trainee's most enduring tradition. When a woman first arrived at Avenger, she made a near mandatory pilgrimage to the well, tossing her loose change into the water with a silent prayer, wishing for luck and hoping she would win her wings. Soon, as the training became more difficult, there were times when anxiety was overwhelming and the lure of the well was irresistible. Daily quizzes in ground school might mean just a few pennies lost to the water. An upcoming check ride with an instructor and the threat of elimination from training, required quarters, half-dollars, or maybe even more. "We're not superstitious," they'd tell you. "We're just being careful." But when a trainee finally completed her first solo flight, that's when she knew she was really in for it. Her cheering friends waited for her on the flight line. They carried her to the Wishing Well and threw her in—flying suit and all. It was a dunking everyone devoutly wished for.[11]

The crime wave at the Wishing Well may have begun in April 1943, when the Guinea Pigs, class 43-W-1, were graduating and General Barton K. Yount, head of the training command, was visiting Avenger. As he passed by the Wishing Well, he paused to throw in a silver dollar, "with best wishes for happy landings," he said. The dollar disappeared and the general graciously replaced it—in fact, he replaced it two more times. Finally, they cemented his dollar to the pedestal in the pool and moved the pedestal to the center of the Wishing Well. "Over anxious curio collectors," said the detachments newspaper, "will get damp tootsies if they snitch the lucky buck this time." The general's dollar was safe, and if the looting of other coins continued, it couldn't have amounted to much. By October, monthly collections of the coins in the well for the year had added only $245 to the trainee's welfare fund.[12]

As Wasp training began its second year, days of wearing bulky Zoot Suits and hairnets had some trainees giving up on their personal appearance. An editorial in the detachment newspaper, probably inspired by comments from higher command, urged trainees to shape up and "Look Sharp Sister." A woman couldn't fly an airplane wearing high heels and a ruffled skirt, it said. "That's why the Army lets you fly in Zoot Suits." Nevertheless, the question was, how was a woman supposed to look her best, when she got up at dawn, quickly dressed, and rushed to breakfast, all just to fly through Texas heat and dust all day long? "This Texas dust is really something," one trainee said. "After the first hour you don't even taste the grit." On base, the editorial asked the women to keep their shoes shined, buttons buttoned, and their hair combed. Lt. LaRue, officer in charge of military discipline, reminded trainees that "WASPs are continually being looked over with a critical eye by various Army officials." Lines should be straight, feet kept in step when marching, and hands always out of pockets. When going into town, appearance was even more important. "The townsfolk are among your best friends and, by the same token, are among your severest critics. … Take a few moments to prepare yourself before you saunter into the city." They were the female equivalents of the Army Air Force male cadets, who were known for their sharp appearance. The editorial was positive that the trainees could do even better than the men. "After all," it said. "You've got more to work with."[13]

In November, with word that an official WASP uniform was on its way, the women's morale soared. Measuring all the women of Avenger Field for their new clothes took two days and then the results were sent to a New York City manufacturer. The dress uniform included a white shirt and black tie; a skirt; a belted jacket; and a beret, each made of a wool gabardine material in Santiago blue. "It makes the heretofore General Pantsed trainee look like a movie version of a war heroine," a trainee said. The work uniform consisted of blue slacks; a blue shirt, cotton in summer and flannel in winter; and a waist length "battle jacket," soon to be known as an "Ike jacket," because it was the style preferred by Allied Commander, General "Ike" Eisenhower. When flying, trainees wore blue cotton coveralls. Their trench coat, a putty-colored weatherproof wool gabardine, included a removable dark-blue lining. Their raincoat and rain cover for their beret were made from a black oiled fabric. The WASPs' accessories, all black calfskin, included buckle-style shoes, gloves, and an over the shoulder travel bag. Regulations said the bag must be carried over the left shoulder, unless a WASP was carrying packages. The Army's eight-page book of regulations detailed exactly how, when, and where the uniform must be worn. It included the style and placement of military insignia and pins, as well as the style, material, and color of a woman's hosiery. Makeup must be light and hair should never be shorter than one inch above the collar, but also never touch the collar. It was almost as if trainees were in the real Army. The government also issued the women low cut galoshes, a sweater, a gym suit, socks, two duffle bags, and all WASP insignia. The trainee was responsible for a tie, shirts, shoes, a scarf, stockings, the over the shoulder bag, and, of course, her "unmentionables." Jackie Cochran estimated that each WASP had to put up about "$100 out of her own pocket" to meet the regulations. At least, wrote a reporter, "The Zoot Suit can now be stuffed, mounted, and placed in the Hall of Fame, beside the timeworn armor of Joan of Arc and Annie Oakley's shotgun."[14]

As the weather turned cold, the Army issued the trainees men's winter flying suits. Leather, bulky, and fur lined, they were hardly a favorite with the WASPs. "They're zootier than Zoot Suits," said one trainee. Even the boots were so large they looked like someone had pulled them directly off the feet of a deep-sea diver. The facetious jokes about the winter suits seemed endless. "When do we start for Siberia?" they asked. The women were also sure that wearing the heavy suit while carrying a hefty parachute to the flight line, would soon build up their muscles enough so they would be able to do just about anything. But, on the bright side, there was one plus—the suit had so many zippers and pockets that there was plenty of room to store notebooks, pencils, a toothbrush, pajamas, makeup, and much, much more inside.[15]

When the icy blasts of wind began ripping across the prairie, trainees put on heavy, government issued, knitted cotton sweatshirts and pants to protect them from the cold. The royal blue suits were functional and not glamorous; although, there was a comforting uniformity as the women went through their callisthenic routines and marched to and from the physical training field. A vast undulating sea of blue had replaced the hodgepodge of clothing the women had previously worn while exercising. By early December, temperatures had taken such a deep dip that to ward off the arctic-like chill, one class abandoned their government sweat suits in favor of their own creation. Each pulled on shockingly bright, red long johns, the kind a grandpa and grandma might wear, and covered them over with royal blue shorts and a shirt. Apparently, the new ensemble was warm and also became a big hit.[16]

The newly formed Avenger Women's Chorus was already practicing Christmas carols and planning to lead the trainees in group singing at the upcoming party. There was even talk of performances in Sweetwater and perhaps even a radio concert. On Christmas Eve, snowflakes began to fall and shouts of "it's snowing" brought dozens of excited faces to the windows. "Imagine," said one trainee from Nebraska, "I expected palm trees and it gives me snow." They wondered if there would be a white Christmas after all? The trainees bundled up and sloshed their way to the gym for what would be the only women's Christmas party ever held at Avenger Field. Not only would there be community singing, rollicking skits performed by trainees, a 12-foot Christmas tree, and gifts galore, but also dancing and—men. Over 150 officers and cadets from nearby airfields were coming, and in addition to friends and relatives, trainees could bring a date if they had one. At midnight, Santa Claus, who bore a striking resemblance to the local manager of the Sweetwater Sears store, arrived with bags and bags full of gifts for every trainee and for most of their guests. By Christmas morning, snow had turned to ice, dashing all white Christmas dreams. Still, nearly 100 Avengerettes accepted invitations to Christmas dinners in dozens of Sweetwater homes. Five of the women shared dinner with the on-duty nurses at Sweetwater Municipal Hospital. The highlight of their day was a visit to the nursery where they were allowed to smile and coo at the new babies. Even the women who stayed in the barracks, whether recovering from the night before, reading books, or just writing letters; enjoyed an extra day of quiet away from training, with no need to be anywhere else.[17]

Northerners tended to think that the Texas sun shines nearly 365 days a year, and even the brief fluttering of flakes on Christmas Eve hadn't changed many minds—then came January 12, 1944. There had been some occasional flakes over the prior weeks, and the ice and slush canceled all training flights. Because the roads were frozen and dangerous, even weekend passes into town were cancelled. Then, with icicles dangling precariously from the barracks, a major blizzard struck. Five to seven inches of snow, blown into drifts two feet high, wouldn't have bothered a Midwest farmer, but here in West Texas it was a rarity. The severe conditions and cold temperatures threatened cattle and sheep on the range. The snow got the blame for the deaths of seven passengers in a nearby collision of two trains. At Avenger Field, trainees made the best of this bad situation with snowball attacks on flight instructors and occasionally on each other. A couple of women rolled out a "snow-m'am" against a building, naming her Mae West. Trainees brought out their cameras and the two women happily snapped off winter portraits of the trainees joyfully posing with Mae. When a gas heating line broke one night, the trainees finally found a good use for those bulky winter flying suits. Coupled with layers of gym pants and long johns, the suits kept them toasty and comfortable all night long.[18]

On December 17, 1943, the eighth class of WASPs graduated from training with a chance to spend a few days of Christmas leave with their families. They were the first class to graduate indoors in the gymnasium, and the first class to graduate at night. Jackie Cochran didn't attend. She was recuperating from a recent emergency abdominal operation at Johns Hopkins Hospital in Baltimore. Colonel Norman Olsen, commander of the nation's only Army glider training school, gave the graduation address. He told the graduates to do their best and to always remember, "the record you make will have a distinct bearing on the future of women pilots, not only in the Army, but in the civilian aviation world." The WASPs received their wings and Olsen wished them "clear skies, tail winds, and happy landings." After a farewell party that evening, they scattered to their homes and on to their new flying assignments.[19]

It had been a long and tiresome day of flying. Bertha Mae Hunt (43-W-4) was on her honeymoon. True, it wasn't her first marriage, but she and her husband Roy shared a love of flying and she hoped that she had finally met the man she'd always been looking for. Roy Hunt was chief pilot for the Fain Drilling Company, an oilfield development company based in Oklahoma City. Leslie Fain, president of the company, had asked Roy to fly one of his close friends to Washington, D.C., where the friend's mother-in-law was near death. After her recent wedding, Bertha, still on leave from the WASPs, had decided to fly with them. They were over the Allegheny Mountains, about 275 miles west of Washington, when Roy radioed the Elkins, West Virginia airport tower asking for landing instructions. This would be their final stop for fuel before flying on to the capital city.[20]

Bertha was "Bert" to her fellow WASPs. Born May 31, 1913, near Oklahoma City, she was the eighth child and third daughter of John and Fannie Haggard. After completing one year of high school and before she was 17 years old, Bert married a man named Dodd. In 1931 the couple welcomed a daughter they named Don Rey, but their marriage didn't last and Bert moved back home with her widowed mother.[21]

Another marriage proposal in early 1937 led to a marriage license application by Clifford Giblet. It's unclear whether he and Bert ever married, because by 1940, Bert was still using the last name Dodd and living again with her mother. The most interesting thing about Giblet was that he was a flight instructor, and it's possible that he had helped Bert learn to fly, or at least, managed to pique her interest.[22]

After completing nearly six months of WASP training at Avenger Field in August 1943, Bert reported to the 5th Ferrying Group in Dallas. She may have known Roy Hunt for quite awhile before joining the WASPs, as they lived just two blocks away from each other in Oklahoma City. Bert had been working in department stores and Roy, 16 years her senior, had been flying for the Fain Company for years. Perhaps he had taught Bert to fly.

On February 4, 1944, with just 15 minutes of fuel left in his tank, Roy began circling through the mountainous terrain and a heavy overcast, trying to find his landing approach. Unfamiliar with the area, Roy was flying too low. He slammed through the trees about 200 feet up on Rich Mountain with a wing shearing off, the fuselage shattering on impact, and a spark setting off a small fire. Thrown clear of the plane, bodies of the five onboard were scattered throughout the debris. No one survived.[23]

Although she was still on active duty as a WASP and scheduled to return to her assignment within days, Bertha Hunt is never included in the list of the 38 women who died serving their country during WWII. She had died in a private plane crash and, except for family, friends, and the paperwork in her file, Bert was all but forgotten.

Marian Toevs' (43-W-8) parents, John and Nelle, were at their daughter's graduation, proudly pinning on Marian's silver wings. After the ceremony, they returned to Aberdeen, Idaho, where Marian had a week to relax in her girlhood home. On January 1, 1944, she reported to LeMoore Army Airfield, an Army flight training school in California's Central Valley. Her primary assignment was to test fly BT-13 and BT-15 airplanes, recently repaired by the field's maintenance crew. Early in the morning, Friday, February 18, Marian checked out a parachute, walked to the flight line, and climbed into a BT-13. She fired up the engine, completed her preflight check, then taxied out to the runway. Sources say she was flying to Fresno, California, and perhaps that was her ultimate destination, but Fresno is barely 30 air miles from LeMoore, hardly enough time in the air to fully checkout a previously damaged or faulty airplane. Add the fact that Marian's BT-13 finally wound up nearly 125 miles northwest away from Fresno, in the eastern foothills of San Jose, California, and a simple flight to Fresno just doesn't make any sense. If Fresno was her ultimate destination, she was first flying a longer cross-country flight.[24]

Twenty-six-year old Marian crashed just a block away from where her Uncle Otto Toevs lived in a San Jose, California neighborhood. She had visited with Otto and his wife just two weeks before and it was

Uncle Otto who ultimately identified her body for authorities. "The motor was still going when it hit," Anthony Gullo said. He had been only 75 feet from the crash. Other eyewitnesses said Marian's plane had been flying very low and circling, as if she were looking for a place to land. "I was the second one to reach the spot," Gullo said. "The girl's body was thrown clear of the wreckage. She was blonde and looked about 20 years old. Her face was bloody." At about 11 in the morning, the plane had suddenly nosed up and then plunged to earth. "We watched it disappear behind some houses," one witness said, "then we heard an awful noise and the crash." The BT-13 had fallen into a gully not far from the San Jose Golf Country Club, its wreckage was scattered over a wide area, but luckily had missed nearby homes.[25]

Marian was born May 13, 1917, in Aberdeen, Idaho, where her father, John, owned a grocery store and ran a successful wholesale dry goods business. For a number of years he was also the superintendant of Aberdeen's Agricultural Experiment Station. Marian had four brothers and was her parent's only daughter. Marian graduated from high school in 1935, and that fall began studies at Albion State Normal School, a small teachers college in Albion, Idaho. Two years later, with a teaching certificate in hand, Marian spent the next three years teaching; first at Bickel Elementary School in Twin Falls and then at Hansen Elementary, a few miles east. In 1940, she enrolled in classes at Eastern Washington College that she hoped would improve her abilities as a teacher. The following year, she accepted a position with the elementary school in White Salmon, Washington. It was while teaching here that she became interested in flying and began taking lessons. In March 1943, she took a brief leave of absence from White Salmon so she could finish her Civilian Pilot Training course and earn her pilot's license. Accepted into the WASPs, Marian began training at Avenger Field July 5.[26]

After the Marian's crash, her body was returned to Aberdeen for her funeral. Edgar Toevs, Marian's cousin, was one of the speakers. "She had given everything she had," Edgar said, "and she did all she could."[27]

A week later, as Betty Stine (44-W-2) prepared to leave on her final cross-country flight before graduation, she joined with the excited crowd of trainee's who were cheering a warm welcome to Jackie Cochran. As Jackie began to speak, the enthusiastic WASPs settled down and focused on every word. Wearing the new WASP uniform, Jackie told them that a bill militarizing the WASPs and commissioning graduates as officers in the Army Air Forces was about to be introduced in the House of Representatives. She said she hoped it would pass soon. "I'm proud of the girls who graduate from here, and of you," she said. "Those graduates already at work are making a fine record for women as flyers. It's up to you to uphold it." When she began talking about the ever-larger ships women were beginning to fly, Jackie saw excitement in one petite trainee's eyes. Jackie shook her head. "No," she said, "the big ships are not for the little girls. The minimum height considered is 5 feet 6 inches. The tiny girls can fly pursuit ships, such as the P-47, P-51, and P-39." Then she noticed an unhappy tall girl and Jackie smiled. "The big girls want the pursuits and the little girls want the big ships," she said. But it didn't really matter what they flew. "You must perform your job to the very best of your ability," she said, "for you are making aviation history for women."[28]

Betty Stine had graduated from Santa Barbara High School in June 1939 with dreams of becoming an airline stewardess. Her father, Jake, was born in the oil fields of Oklahoma, but when his mother died when Jake was eight years old in 1909, his father sent him to live with Jake's grandparents, in Castleberry, Texas, near Fort Worth. As he got older he lived a few years in Oklahoma, where he registered for the WWI draft, but eventually, he returned to Fort Worth. There, in late 1920, Jake married Mary Allen. Betty, their only child, was born the following September. Because Jakes uncle was humorist Will Rogers, he named Betty after Will's wife, Betty Blake. For his daughter's middle name he chose Pauline, after Pauline McSpadden, a daughter of one of Will Rogers' sisters.[29]

Perhaps Jake Stine moved his family west because of the discovery of new oil fields around Santa Barbara, California in the late 1920s and early 1930s. By 1935, the Stines were living near the beach in the Californian Hotel on State Street. Jake worked the oil fields, while wife Mary owned and managed a cafe. After her high school graduation, Betty began her studies at Santa Barbara State College and two years later transferred to the University of Arizona. Before reporting to Avenger in September 1943, Betty had returned to Texas to take flying lessons at Fort Worth Municipal Airport.[30]

On February 24, 1944, Betty, along with 12 of her classmates, were returning to Avenger Field from their final cross-country training flight. Graduation was 16 days away. She had just taken off in an AT-6 *Texan* from Blythe Army Airfield in southeastern California, and had crossed over the Colorado River into Arizona. A little after 4:00 in the afternoon, officials believe an exhaust spark set fire to the fabric-covered portion of the *Texan*'s tail assembly. With the tail on fire and about to separate from the plane, Betty bailed out over the mountains surrounding Quartzite, Arizona; less than 25 miles from Blythe. Lewis Aplington, owner of mines around Quartzite, saw the burning plane and Betty's parachute dropping to the ground. It took over 45 minutes for Aplington and two other miners, riding in a truck, to find her in the rugged terrain. Betty was unconscious, but still alive. The high winds had dragged her chute over sharp rocks and boulders and her body was beaten, broken, and bloodied. The men carefully put her onto the bed of the truck and rushed her to Quartzite. Authorities notified Blythe Airfield personnel who dispatched an ambulance that returned her to the base hospital, where she died within hours. The 22-year-old's body was sent home for burial in the Santa Barbara Cemetery.[31]

If only Betty Stine had known how to control her parachute on the ground in strong winds, she never would have died. Officers at Avenger Field hadn't anticipated the need for advanced training in parachute jumps and landings, but Betty's death had changed all of that almost immediately. Lt. Bill LaRue was sent to Randolph Field for a two-week course in parachute jumping. When LaRue returned to Sweetwater in early May, he assured the trainees that while training with him they wouldn't actually have to jump from a plane. As soon as workers constructed training platforms, the women received 12 hours of parachute training. The training was divided into five phases—how to tumble and fall; jumping from a platform; how to manipulate the flight direction of the chute in the air; landing techniques; and finally—what might have saved Betty Stine's life—working in front of a wind machine and learning how to collapse a chute in high winds. LaRue also said he learned that the Army was working on a new parachute harness, specially designed for women.[32]

Verda-Mae Lowe, one of the trainees flying with Betty on that disastrous flight, later had her own fearful moments in the air. Barely 30 miles from a safe landing at the Blythe airfield, Verda-Mae's engine began to sputter and the AT-6 began to shudder. Convinced she was running out of gas, she wasn't sure she could safely make the short distance back to Blythe. She began circling and frantically looked for a place to land. There was something off her wing tip—barracks and a parade ground; a military installation of some kind. Down went her wheels and Verda-Mae lined up for a landing. From the air, the parade ground looked smooth, but she quickly discovered it wasn't. After bounding over a deep ditch, bouncing around holes filled with water from a recent rain storm, and sliding through spots of mud, she was safely on the ground and unharmed—in the middle of Poston,

Arizona's Japanese Internment Camp. Within seconds, curious men, women, and especially children, surrounded the plane. At first, Verda-Mae thought they were Mexican families, but then realized they were Japanese. Unsure of why there were Japanese in Arizona, and a bit afraid, she huddled in the cockpit, trying to decide if she should take off. Then, an Army jeep driven by a lieutenant approached. He stopped, looked up at her, and shouted, "How ya doin'?" The lieutenant drove Verda-Mae to the headquarters building, where she was able to call officials in Blythe. While waiting for help to arrive, she cleaned up, had lunch, and asked and answered dozens of questions. Army officers finally flew in and discovered Verda-Mae's *Texan* wasn't out of gas. After making adjustments to the plane's engine, they watched while Verda-Mae climbed back into the cockpit and took off for Blythe. She made it safely through her time with the WASPs and continued flying after the war, joining the Civil Air Patrol and becoming a flight instructor.[33]

During the chilly winter months at Avenger Field, things were improving for trainees. The long awaited Coffee Shack finally opened. Not far from the flight line, and equipped with six, 12-cup vacuum coffee makers and an endless supply of fresh donuts from the Sunbeam Bakery in Sweetwater, the Shack was open from 6:00 in the morning till midnight. Before and after flights, when the icy wind blew across the Texas plain, trainees, mechanics, and flight instructors could take a few minutes to warm up inside with a hot cup of coffee and a donut, at just five cents each.

Two shuffleboard courts were set up on the concrete edges of the gymnasium, with weighted discs and cue sticks available free to trainees and military personnel. The game, usually played outdoors in the summer or on ocean cruises was becoming a hit. "Avenger folk are waking up to what they missed by not owning a yacht," said a trainee.

When supply received two 35mm motion picture projectors in late March, rumors quickly spread that real movies were finally coming to Avenger. "There seems a fair chance that we might be seeing movies on the post before too many moons," the post newspaper said. But it was not to be. Unfortunately, because Avenger was a civilian contract school and not part of the real Army, the base wasn't eligible for 35mm films distributed by the Army Motion Picture Service. The 35mm projectors stayed dark and the trainees had to find satisfaction in 16mm Army training films and a few feature films provided by the USO.[34]

By mid-March 1944, 18 months after training began, of the 969 women who had started training at New Castle and Avenger Field, 620 had graduated. Thirteen of those women were now dead. In just the next nine months, that number would nearly double.

# [11]

## A SPRING OF DESPAIR

With spring finally blooming in the Sweetwater air, 595 Avenger Fifinellas had survived their training and graduated. Gone were the prewar days when 100 flight instructors, predominately male, were asked their unbiased opinion of women pilots by *Flying and Popular Aviation* magazine. Although there was consensus that women were capable, cautious, more eager to learn than men; and their muscle sense was more acute and better adapted to fly by feel than men's muscles—the men also believed that woman pilots had three major problems. They had a tendency to cry when criticized, lacked an ability to react quickly in an emergency, and required more training than men because "of less early training in coordination, and fewer natural aptitudes." But now the WASPs were finally changing minds. "That slim, straight young woman doesn't look capable of handling a man-sized job of tackling a lone flight mission to the other side of the continent," said a reporter. "She looks as if she ought to be home keeping house—but instead she's off to the Canadian border on a plane delivery, because some guy has to learn to fly a combat formation." Another columnist wrote, "The work of these Army trained women has been so valuable that Army officials are planning to extend their services to a number of other tasks."[1]

Much of the secrecy surrounding the WASP program had disappeared, and overall there was a positive opinion of the WASPs and their abilities, not only from the public, but also from the Army. Their mission details were still classified, as were operational activities and procedures, but the success of this onetime experiment to see if women pilots could contribute to the war effort, had allowed Army officials to gradually discover that publicity for the program was valuable, and that women could do more than just ferry aircraft across the country.

For the moment, publicity was almost always favorable. In January, the War Department announced that a select group of WASPs had successfully completed training in B-26 *Marauder* medium bombers and were now working with the Army Air Force Training Command. The B-26 had a reputation of being one of the most difficult planes to fly, but the women proved that even they could fly it. At Sweetwater, the WASP graduation rate was comparable to men, even though they entered training with an average of 40 hours less flying time. "Quietly and efficiently," said a *Flying* magazine article, "the Womens Airforce Service Pilots are setting an enviable record." *The New York Times*' headlines echoed what many were already thinking. "WASPs Hope Soon to Be Members of the Army Air Forces." Taking the women out of Civil Service and militarizing them with Army commissions and benefits seemed inevitable.[2]

On September 30, 1943, Congressman John Costello of California introduced a bill that allowed appointment "of female pilots in the Air Forces of the Army." It lacked few specifics, other than the fact women pilots would be commissioned, and would "receive the same rights, privileges, and benefits as members of the Army's Officer's Reserve Corps." Referred to the House Military Affairs Committee, the bill never made it to a vote on the House floor. Costello tried again on February 17, 1944, with a bill bearing a similar title, "A bill to provide for the appointment of female pilots and aviation cadets in the Air Forces of the Army." This bill did include more details than the previous effort. Once again, women's commissions would only last for the duration of the war plus six additional months, but depending on their qualifications, some women might be appointed to a higher rank than 2nd lieutenant. However, no woman would have a rank higher than a colonel, and only one woman could hold that rank. If the bill passed, most people assumed that Jackie Cochran would be that colonel. Once commissioned, a woman's ability to command was "specifically limited to the personnel placed under her command." WASPs were not going to be giving orders to male Army officers and enlisted men.[3]

General Arnold offered his full support for the bill on March 22, the Chief of Army Air Forces telling the House Military Affairs Committee that he needed the WASPs because he eventually expected "to have every male army flier sent out of the United States and overseas, fighting. … We must provide fighting men wherever we can," he said, "replacing them with women wherever we can, whether it be in factories, or towing airplane targets, or whatever it may be." Arnold noted that there were already 534 women pilots in the WASP, and that many of them could fly any type of airplane produced. He believed there were even more ways to employ several thousand additional women pilots. He also revealed that the Army was testing the possibility that woman could even replace men as military flight instructors. "We realize that some persons are saying that we are depriving men who have had some training in this program," Arnold said. "But we cannot lower our standards just because a man has had a few hours in the air." To win the war, he said there was a great need for qualified men in combat areas. The best way to relieve as many men as possible from domestic duty was to militarize the WASPs and encourage more women to join. His testimony seemed to work. No sooner had Arnold finished than the committee voted to send the bill out for a House vote, but first, it had to pass through the House Rules Committee for review.[4]

Although there was trouble ahead, for the moment, the future seemed bright for the WASPs, and so, training at Avenger Field intensified. "We are here for the specific purpose of helping each trainee to become the best possible pilot," said Ground School Director Lt. Seaman Winfrey, "and we will do our utmost to be of the greatest possible assistance." But when trainees learned ground school classes were increasing from five to six days a week, and officials announced an additional three more weeks of training, the women groaned. Now it would take 30 weeks to graduate instead of 27, but then again, if it actually increased their skill and better demonstrated their capabilities to the Army and the Congress, the women were all for it.[5]

Believing a pilot would be a better pilot if they knew what it took to keep their aircraft flying, officials added a practical aircraft maintenance course to ground school. The course began with 24 hours of classroom instruction, introducing the trainees to the motors that powered the planes they would fly. The trainees actually had to turn wrenches to discover a motor's internal workings. After completing the indoor course, the women reported for hands on training with a flight line mechanic who supervised their work. Whether it was an engine overhaul or simply gassing up a plane, each trainee did some, if not all of the work. Perhaps the most complicated assignment for the trainees was trying to decipher what their fellow trainees' meant when complaining about an aircraft's performance. Notations such as "Prop missing," "left wing heavy," "falls off right wing in stalls," were bad

**Trainees learned the basics of flight, and everything else related to flying and military procedures, on the ground in ground school. Yet, even after the women graduated and received their duty assignment, there was always something else to learn. Here in 1944, a coeducational class is in session at the Romulus Army Airfield, near Detroit, Michigan. - Air Force photo 110111-D-7991K-003.**

enough, but even more curious was the phrase, "coffee grinder out." The women quickly realized that they all needed to improve their own trouble reporting skills.[6]

Stiffened requirements were also affecting women waiting to join the WASPs. Applicants now had to take and pass the three-hour Aviation Cadet Qualifying Examination, the same test required of male cadets. The women already training at Avenger Field, classes 44-W-6 and 44-W-7, were also required to take the test; however, if they failed to pass, they wouldn't be eliminated from training. The test measured a candidate's mechanical and math comprehension skill, their ability to understand mechanical devices and diagrams, as well as their awareness of new developments in science, aviation, and military affairs. It also tested their judgment in practical situations and, in addition, their leadership qualities. The base newspaper playfully called it, "puzzling over gears, blocks, dots, and lines—topped off by questions concerning the effect of exercise and eating on their respective stomachs."[7]

With militarization of WASPs finally under serious debate, a month of WASP tragedies, could not have come at a worse time. Six women, in quick succession, would die.

Frances Fortune Grimes had begun her training at Houston's Municipal Airport in January 1943, and graduated at Sweetwater with "The Lost Platoon," class 43-W-3. The second of Bushrod and Sada Grimes' three daughters, Frances was born October 7, 1914, in Deer Park, Maryland, just 25 miles west of Keyser, West Virginia. Her father was teaching agriculture there at the Potomac State College and also at the town's high school. Bushrod would go on to social prominence as a professor at the University of West Virginia and as agricultural agent for the university's extension service that served the surrounding counties. In 1933, President Franklin Roosevelt selected him as project manager for Arthurdale, a social experiment during the Great Depression designed to create a community for unemployed West Virginia coal miners. The idea was to move the miners from their filthy mining camps to their own homestead on small plots of farmland. There, they would live in a house with indoor plumbing, especially built for them, and the miner's family could support themselves with livestock and a garden. Arguments still continue over whether Arthurdale was ever a success.[8]

Frances Grimes was an avid sportswoman. "She was very athletic, a real tomboy," her sister told reporters. "And she even played football if mother would allow her." Frances competed in and won many amateur tennis tournaments in the 1930s and early 1940s, including the Maryland and West Virginia championships. She even ranked number one for a while in the Middle Atlantic Lawn Tennis Association. She attended West Virginia University in Morgantown and then the University of Pittsburgh, where she graduated in 1937 with a Bachelors Degree in business administration. She learned to fly in Morgantown as part of the university's Civilian Pilot Training program and not long after obtaining her pilot's license began teaching in the university's pilot training ground school. She joined the Civil Air Patrol and was also a training representative for Tri-State Airlines, in Parkersburg, West Virginia. Just before joining the WASPs, she was again teaching ground school for Southeastern University at the Martinsburg, West Virginia airport. She had fallen in love with flying. "You don't know what it's like to get up there in the blue and fly," she told friends.[9]

After graduation at Avenger Field, Frances had a brief assignment with the 5th Ferrying Group at Love Field in Dallas, but in October 1943, she and 14 of the best and most experienced WASPs received orders to report to Camp Stewart's Liberty Field, about 50 miles southwest of Savannah, Georgia. Camp Stewart was an Army anti-aircraft artillery training center and surrounded by swamps; although, green lawns and lots of trees; willows, persimmons, walnuts, and pecans, covered the base. The women's cover story said they were training to fly tow targets for the artillery, and indeed, they were required to fly some of those missions, but in fact, they actually were part of a highly classified Army experiment—flying aircraft by remote control.

Frances had plenty of off duty time at Liberty Field to pursue her athletic interests. There were tennis courts to play on, but few competitors. As soon as the other woman learned that Frances was a onetime tennis champ, few were willing to challenge her. Once, during one of those frequent WASP softball games, Frances and another WASP outfielder raced to catch a hard hit ball. They smashed into each other, Frances inadvertently biting the other woman's ear so badly that the bleeding required 11 stitches. Frances lost two teeth in the collision. "Frances is practically starved from not being able to eat," said fellow WASP Betty Deuser, "cuz it hurts to eat anything." Frances went to Houston to get dentures made, but had to return to Camp Stewart before they were ready. She was short of the required number of flying hours and if she wanted to graduate with her class, she needed to make them up as quickly as possible. Until her teeth finally arrived, it was an embarrassing two weeks in the cockpit.[10]

Training at Stewart officially ended December 15, 1943, with the rarest of southern snowstorms. The women gathered around the warmth of a headquarters building stove for their graduation exercises. Frances and four other WASPs had orders to report to the 1st Tow Target Squadron on Upper Cape Cod, Massachusetts, at Otis Field on Camp Edwards. Their orders also granted 10 days leave before reporting for duty. Frances celebrated Christmas in Richmond, Virginia with her parents and older sister, Ellen. Only younger sister, Joanna, a Navy officer, was missing.[11]

On Monday, March 27, just five days after the House Military Affairs Committee approved the WASP militarization bill; Frances Grimes was taking off from Otis Field in a Douglas A-24 *Banshee* on another routine target-towing mission. She was still climbing when her engine stalled and the assault bomber spiraled into the ground. Friends believed her carburetor had iced up and caused the crash, but no one was ever sure. "We hadn't seen her since Christmas," her sister, Ellen, later told a reporter. "Frances was killed the day before she was to come home to Richmond for Joanna's wedding. That was a tragic weekend." Three days after her crash, funeral services for the 29-year-old aviator were held at precisely 4:30 in the afternoon, at both Otis Field and at the All Saints Episcopal Church in Richmond.[12]

While her family buried Frances Grimes, the first real rumblings of trouble for the WASPs was coming from Washington, D.C. Robert Ramspeck, Representative from Georgia, a Democrat and House Majority Whip, told reporters on April 3 that "official silence" was blocking his inquiries into charges that the Army was training women pilots at a cost of up to $20,000 each. At the same time, he said the Army was ignoring the potential service of many thousands of male pilots. As chairman of the House Civil Service Investigating Committee, he said he had received many complaints, but had not been able to learn from official sources what the real situation was. If he didn't get the answers soon, he threatened to hold hearings to get them. He said most of the complaints were coming from male pilots who claimed the Army was training "green and inexperienced girls," and leaving untouched the experience of thousands of skilled male pilots now idled.

Two months earlier, in January, the Civil Aeronautics Administration had ended the program that trained flight instructors for the Army Air Forces. The Navy Department said they would do the same thing that summer. CAA officials said the Army no longer needed to rely on civilian flight schools to furnish instructors, because the number of qualified pilots completing combat duty and returning from the theaters of war were more than enough to meet the Army's needs. It wasn't yet time for General Arnold, Jackie Cochran, and the WASP pilots to begin worrying, but a storm was coming and trouble—real trouble, wasn't far away.[13]

On the same day Ramspeck was complaining to the press, the WASPs lost another of their most qualified pilots, a pilot who had overcome every obstacle just to put herself into the air. On April 3, at 10:29 in the morning, Evelyn Genevieve Sharp (WAF) lifted off from the Harrisburg, Pennsylvania airport in a twin-engine fighter, a Lockheed P-38 *Lightning*. She had been flying the fighter all the way across the country, on a delivery flight from the Lockheed plant in Long Beach, California to Liberty Army Airfield in Newark, New Jersey. Following standard takeoff procedure, she immediately retracted her landing gear when she left the ground and almost instantly she noticed black smoke beginning to pour from the plane's left engine. Barely 700 feet in the air, her engine shut down. Evelyn threw the rudder hard right, trying to keep the plane from rolling over. She feathered the left prop and cut its throttle. There wasn't enough power to get higher or stay much longer in the air, so she scanned the countryside, looking for a way to land without hitting any of the homes and buildings below. She veered left, across the Susquehanna River toward Beacon Hill, where the population was scattered. With no time to let down the tricycle landing gear, Evelyn smashed into the ground in an abrupt belly landing, her forward motion only stopped by a forest of trees. The steering column pushed up, forcing Evelyn's head into the canopy. Her neck was broken, and after only a minute in the air, she was dead.[14]

Mounds of flowers were everywhere on April 9, 1944. Although she hadn't lived in her hometown for over four years, the people of Ord, Nebraska and the surrounding countryside came to her Sunday funeral services by the hundreds. Her mother and father came by train from their new home in Nevada, to bury their only child in the town that called Evelyn their "favorite daughter." Fellow WASP and classmate, Nancy Batson, and two servicemen were there to pay their respects. Nancy had accompanied Evelyn's body to Ord, bringing with her $200 donated by the WASPs at New Castle Air Base in Delaware, to help pay for the funeral. From the Methodist Church to the town cemetery, a long procession of cars followed 24-year-old Evelyn to her final rest.[15]

After the ceremony, two women were overheard talking about Evelyn. "It was the saddest thing. I feel so sorry," one woman said. "I don't," her friend said loudly. There was a pause, and then, to the first woman's shocked expression, her friend explained. "Evelyn only lived 20 years or so, but she jammed more fun and adventure into the 10 years she flew all over the country, than I ever will, if I live to be a hundred.—No, I don't feel sorry for her. I envy her."[16]

A few days earlier, delayed by bad weather in Kansas City, Evelyn had written a brief letter to one of the hometown businessmen, Elwin Dunlap, who had encouraged her to fly. "I'm rather proud of flying the P-38," she told him. "It's rather a sporty plane." Dunlap, who had been with Evelyn when she took her first flying lesson, said everyone in town was shocked and saddened. "She was a kid who started the hard way," Dunlap said. "The town thought a lot of her."[17]

Evelyn was adopted, the daughter of Elsie Haeske and Orla Crouse, unmarried or soon to be divorced parents. She was born October 1,

1919, in the railroad town of Melstone, on the central prairies of Montana. A few weeks after her birth, and just before Christmas, Evelyn's mother agreed to give up the baby girl she had named Lois Genevieve Crouse. She would let John and Mary Sharp adopt her as their only child. The Sharps renamed the baby Evelyn and, until she was an adult, they let her believe that Elsie was her aunt and not her real mother. In 1924, after John Sharp's dance hall burned down, the family moved to Hastings, Nebraska, where John opened a grocery store and a small rooming house. When Evelyn was eight, John bought a ranch near Ericson, Nebraska, but two years later, shortly after the stock market crash of 1929, he had to sell the ranch and move to Ord. Here he established a number of businesses, including a roadhouse tavern, a rooming house, a cafe, and an ice cream parlor. When her father began making his ice cream in 1932, Evelyn sold double dip cones throughout the streets of Ord, driving a cart pulled by her horse "Chalky." Two years later, with the depression hitting the family hard, her father had to sell Evelyn's dearly loved pony.[18]

Evelyn soon made her mark in Ord. She was eager and tireless, a bundle of energy who attacked everything in school that interested her, including athletics. Her nickname in her sophomore year of high school was "Tarzan" and, when she graduated, she won the award as the best girl athlete in her class. She captained the girls' soccer team, played competitive tennis, won her letter from the Girls Athletic Association in all four of her high school years, and was a member of the acrobatics team.[19]

She first appeared in the Ord city newspaper in 1930 when she made the honor roll in her sixth grade class. Not only did she carry a full academic load of high school classes, she added two years of typing, two years of shorthand, and during two years of home economics, began designing her own clothes. She played saxophone in the school band, piano at home, sang in the glee club, and in her junior and senior years majored in music. Although she had appeared briefly in other school productions, in her senior year she became active in the Thespian Club and secured a part in the senior play.[20]

After school, besides helping her parents with their businesses, Evelyn took tap dancing lessons, and in the summers had time to go swimming and camping as vice president of the local Camp Fire Girls. She was an outdoor girl who loved to hike and learned to ride horses, hunt, and fish at an early age.[21]

As if all of this wasn't enough to keep this precocious teenager busy, 15-year-old Evelyn wanted to fly. When she asked her adoring father if she could, he quickly said yes. An aviator, Jack Jefford, had arrived in Ord and started a flying school. A week later, Evelyn took her first flight lesson. "February 4, 1935, my father asked me if I would like to fly," Evelyn told a reporter. "I thought he was kidding me. I was so surprised. I said yes." Her father had arranged free flying lessons with Jefford, in exchange for a free room in his rooming house, whenever Jefford was in town. Jefford already had flying schools in three other Nebraska towns, and with nearly 30 students signed up, he'd be frequently in and out of Ord. He had been flying for nine years, had over 2,400 hours in the air without an accident, and had trained 261 pilots. At Ord, he planned to teach every Monday, weather permitting, four miles north of downtown in Joe Gregory's pasture.[22]

Jefford said that Evelyn was a natural pilot, one of the best he had ever seen. "Few among the students I've taught," he said, "have had the touch that enabled them to learn to pilot a plane as quickly as Evelyn has." By the end of May, Evelyn was almost ready to solo, but there were problems. Jefford was often away with his teaching and contract flying, the weather wasn't cooperating, and corn was growing in some pastures, and livestock was grazing in others. Then, in June, it got worse. The airplane used by the Ord trainees had crashed in Colorado, when one of its wings fell off. Jefford had purchased the two-seat, cabin aircraft, equipped with dual controls the previous fall. No one in Ord owned an airplane, and so, Evelyn waited nearly a year to solo.[23]

On March 4, 1936, with only 13 hours of flight time, Evelyn finally flew solo in Jefford's yellow Aeronca C-3. Three days later, she flew the 75 miles to Hastings, Nebraska to pick up her student pilot's license. "I have always been interested in airplanes," she said, "and whenever one came to Ord I wanted to ride in it. But if anyone told me someday I would fly one, I would have thought they were telling fairy tales." That November, after completing the required 50 hours of solo flying, Evelyn took her license examination at Grand Island, Nebraska and easily passed. Although only required to turn four tailspin maneuvers and recover four times, Evelyn, perhaps with youthful exuberance, decided she would complete eight.[24]

After graduation from high school in 1937, 17-year-old Evelyn was still too young to take the transport license exam, but was trying to figure out how she could still get the 200 flight hours required. It seemed all but impossible. She had only been able to grab a few hours in the air, whenever Jack Jefford brought his plane to town, and now he wouldn't be coming. In April, Jefford became airport manager and instructor at the Hastings, Nebraska airport, 90 miles away. Earlier in the year, Evelyn had flown to Omaha, where she became a charter member of the Nebraska 99s organization of women pilots. Even so, by June, she had only accumulated just over 70 hours in the air, well short of the 200 hours she needed. Rather than spend the summer impatiently waiting for someone's airplane to magically appear, Evelyn went to work. The local Red Cross chapter sent her to Colorado Springs to attend classes at the Red Cross school of water safety, where she became a certified swimming instructor. That summer, she taught 125 children to swim in the North Loup River, east of town.[25]

Although Jack Jefford was rarely in town anymore, he still had many friends in the Ord business community and he hadn't forgotten his best pupil. He said if Evelyn had her own plane, she could easily fly her 200 hours before her October birthday. He convinced a group of Ord's prominent businessmen that Evelyn's flying would be great publicity for the town, and if they helped one of the youngest, if not the youngest, women to earn a transport license, the town could benefit even more. The men agreed.

It was late on a hot Tuesday evening, August 17, and Evelyn was cooling herself on her porch. The telephone rang. It was Jack Jefford with a surprise. He told her that the Ord businessmen had bought her an airplane, and if she could meet him at the Grand Island airport, he would fly her to Omaha to pick it up. The next day, Evelyn was at the controls, flying solo in her silver, $2000, two-seat Taylor *Cub*. After landing, she said she had named her plane "The Ord," in honor of her hometown and the people who had helped her fly. Her proud father couldn't resist bragging to reporters. "Evelyn is a quite a girl—never gets excited," he said. "Got her career cut out for her now that she has this plane. She doesn't care much about school or housework. Just interested in flying."[26]

And fly she did. Just a month later she had flown 125 hours, more than doubling all the hours she had flown in the previous two and a half years. On September 24, six days before her birthday, Evelyn landed in Ord, to complete her 200th hour in the air. After hours of hitting the books hard for months, studying meteorology, navigation, airplane engines and their construction, she was eager to take the transport license exam on her birthday. But government officials said that would be impossible. Adding to her frustrations was the sudden departure of her flight instructor and close friend Jack Jefford. Jefford had just signed a contract with Pan American Airways to pilot their planes in Alaska. The two had arranged for Evelyn to visit the Hastings Airport, where Jefford was manager, and get hands-on experience with aircraft motors and equipment under Jefford's guidance, but now, she was on her own. Early in the morning of Tuesday, October 26, Evelyn climbed into her Taylor *Cub* with Kenneth Kearney. Kearney had volunteered to help Evelyn with her studies. They flew the 130 miles from Ord to Lincoln, Nebraska, where Evelyn hoped to begin her three-day ordeal.[27]

When she didn't pass the written examination that afternoon, she had temporarily dashed her hopes of becoming the country's youngest transport pilot. "I flunked it," the surprisingly upbeat 18-year-old told reporters. "But I can take it again in three months." Reporters wondered if she would. "I am!" she said. "I didn't have enough instructions, I guess. But I'll get more."[28]

That Christmas, Evelyn played Santa Claus, renting a larger airplane that could fly the "real" Santa as a passenger along with 200 pounds of gifts. She and St. Nick flew to a half-dozen nearby towns, delighting hundreds of astonished young faces. To the people of Ord she offered her personal Christmas gift of thanks—an advertisement in the local newspaper. Under her high school graduation photograph, she offered: "Yuletide Greetings to You—My Christmas present has already been received in the form of the support you have given me in my flying career. Merry Christmas! Evelyn Sharp."[29]

Once again, the community came to Evelyn's aid. With her next attempt at the transport exam expected to be at the end of February 1938, the town sponsored a benefit dance to raise enough money so that Evelyn could attend the Lincoln Air School. There she could prepare for the license examination. Evelyn flew to Lincoln to take a preliminary test to find out what kind of work she still needed. After the test, Lincoln Air School officials said they were sure that she would be ready to take the transport examination in six weeks or less. It would take a little bit longer, four months longer in fact. On Friday the 13th, 1938, after completing the written examination, demonstrating her flying ability, and parachuting from an airplane, 18-year-old Evelyn received notification that she had passed, and was now the youngest woman pilot in the country to hold a transport pilot's license. Six days later, to commemorate 20 years of airmail flights in the United States, Evelyn received the honor of carrying the first ever airmail between Ord and Grand Island, Nebraska.[30]

Letters poured in from nearly every state in the union, including personal congratulations from the president's wife, Eleanor Roosevelt. Evelyn was accepting requests to fly in many towns in Nebraska and across the Midwest and she carefully weighed each one. She had again planned to teach summer swimming lessons in 1938, but her mounting commitments left little time for swimming. Two weeks after lessons began, she and her father were gone, flying to Greely, Iowa to sell airplane rides. Evelyn had decided to become a barnstormer, selling rides and earning enough money to pay back the Ord businessmen for the cost of her airplane. Before August 1, 1938, she had flown about 700 passengers during her three plus years of flying. After August 1, she had flown over 1,000. "Stunt flying is much more fascinating than safe flying," she said, "but once you get started stunt flying, you can't stop. And then, you're likely to get your neck broken."[31]

Evelyn next passed her examination for a flight instructor's license on June 8, 1940, and left almost immediately for Mitchell, South Dakota, where Evelyn, now 20, took charge of the Civil Aeronautics Authority's flight training program. Within a month she transferred to Spearfish, South Dakota, where she was in the air nearly eight hours a day, earning $300 a month, teaching 14 boys and one girl how to fly. When her students went back to college in September, her contract ended, but she told friends she had an offer to teach in St. Louis.

While she was teaching in South Dakota, she had stored the airplane originally purchased for her by Ord businessmen, back in Nebraska, at the old Grand Island Airport. Early on a Sunday morning, July 28, a suspicious fire destroyed the hangar and Evelyn's Taylor *Cub*.[32]

If Evelyn ever really had an offer to teach in St. Louis, she never took it. By February 1941, the entire family had moved to Bakersfield, California and Evelyn was a CAA flight instructor at the Kern County airport, working for Les Buchner's Flying Service. At the time she was one of only 10 women flight instructors in the United States and was already approaching 1,400 hours in the air. Although there was no war yet, there was a sense that the country would be fighting soon. Evelyn said she would definitely volunteer for war service if hostilities broke out. "There are plenty of things a woman flier can do to help the aviation branches of the service," she said. "I'll do everything I can." When Japan attacked Pearl Harbor, the country feared an invasion of the West Coast could be imminent. The government banned civilian flight training any closer than 150 miles inland from the Pacific Ocean. Evelyn helped Les Buchner move the aviation school from Kern County, over the Sierra Mountains, to Lone Pine, in California's Owens Valley. Here, on a grass airfield, about 10 miles east of Mt. Whitney, Evelyn gave advanced training to men who had previous flying experience, helping them get their commercial pilot's license and to qualify for training as either Army flight instructors or Army glider pilots. It wasn't long before this 117-pound, barely 5 foot 4 inch tall, 22-year-old woman, commanded total respect from the men she trained. Some of the new male trainees would specifically ask that she be their flight instructor, after getting recommendations from friends who already had taken the course. However, if any of the men had romantic intentions, Evelyn could hold her own, and quickly let any amorous young man know they were there to learn aeronautics—and nothing else! By June 1942, she had trained over 350 men.[33]

On October 19, 1942, Evelyn was the 17th woman to join Nancy Love's WAFs at New Castle Air Base, in Delaware. She had flown 2,950 hours at the time and would add an additional 1,165 hours before she died. A new adventure was opening up and Evelyn with her ever-present enthusiasm was enjoying every moment. "I am living in army barracks," she wrote to a friend. "I have been issued all the best army flying equipment, including parachutes, flying suits, goggles— really swell! Also, have a keen gray uniform with all sorts of wings and insignia. We get up at 6:30, drill at 8:00, go to class from 9:00 to 11:30, and 1:00 to 5:00." Her assignment to the 6th Ferrying Group in Long Beach came in February 1943. There, she began an impressive resume of achievements in the powerful airplanes she was able to fly. She was the first woman to fly the Douglas A-20 light bomber, known as the "man killer," and she delivered 12 of them coast to coast. She was one of the very few WASPs who could fly nearly every airplane in the Army's inventory, including C-47 transports, and the P-51 *Mustang* and P-47 *Thunderbolt* pursuit planes. She was also a copilot, and pilot in training, in the B-17 *Flying Fortress*, the B-24 *Liberator*, and the B-25 *Mitchell* bombers. Her final flight, cross-country from Long Beach to Newark, New Jersey had begun on March 30, 1944. Even though the 24-year-old would die during that flight, the flying experience she had gained during that last year of her life, likely saved a number of lives on the ground. Except for fate, she had almost saved herself.[34]

Three years after the war ended, the Ord Municipal Airport was renamed in Evelyn Sharp's honor. Nearly 4,000 people and 1,200 cars swarmed over the area for the dedication ceremonies. James Ramsey, who had worked with Evelyn at Long Beach, described her commitment and dedication. "Often Evelyn would take a fast pursuit plane—with no room for even a change of clothing or a toothbrush—from California in the morning and land it on the east coast that night," he said. "She would take the first airliner back to the west coast and report at the field the next morning, ready for duty. Often she would take off again the same afternoon." Then, Ramsey told the crowd that her accident and death were not her fault. "Investigation proved that the crash was 100 percent mechanical failure," he said. "Evelyn did everything in her power and everything a pilot could do to keep from crashing."

In the midst of these tragedies, influential columnist, Drew Pearson, was turning up the heat and joining in the growing opposition against the WASP program. His syndicated column, "Washington Merry-Go-Round," appeared in over 600 newspapers, and his weekly broadcasts on the NBC radio network reached most of America. "Among the unhappiest, most disillusioned men in the country today," he wrote, "are the thousands of civilian pilot instructors who have built up the great army of U.S.—pilots who have seen thousands of their students commissioned, and who are now discharged without any military standing whatever." When the civilian training program ended in January, Pearson said over 5,000 male flight instructors were fired and "thrown back to draft status." The civilian instructors, "with far more flying time than their students," he said, "are thrown out of work, to start their military service all over again—on the ground." What made it worse, Pearson said, was "the feminine angle"—Jackie Cochran's "inside track" with the Army brass.[35]

On April 10, barely 24 hours after Evelyn Sharp's funeral in Ord, Marie Ethel Sharon, (43-W-4) took off from Rosecrans Army Airfield in St. Joseph, Missouri with her instructor, Lt. Hinton Daniel. This was a navigational training flight in a B-25 *Mitchell* bomber. The Midwest weather that had delayed Evelyn Sharp on her flight across the country had gotten worse. As Marie maneuvered their bomber for over an hour in a thick overcast, passing from point to point and into Nebraska, pelting rain began smashing against the aircraft's skin. The B-25 began to rattle and shudder violently against "extremely hard winds," gusting at 45 mph. Lt. Daniel and Marie frantically fought to maintain altitude and control. Suddenly, the nose wheel door began to twist with a screeching metallic sound. The hinges gave way in the wind and the door flew away, slamming into the right side motor. Sixty-five miles south of Omaha, there was smoke, the engine failed, and the bomber lunged into a nose first dive. It shattered in pieces as it hit the ground and buried itself deep into a farmer's field.[36]

By now, Marie was not a novice flyer. In the eight months since her graduation from Sweetwater, she had quickly moved from a basic Class I Air Transport Command pilot, able to fly the simplest and lightest of Army aircraft, to the more demanding Class III, meaning she was now able to fly two-engine cargo and personnel aircraft. Once her B-25 training ended she would earn a Class IV rating, allowing her to fly two-engine medium bombers and heavy transports. The ultimate goal for all Transport Command pilots, male or female, was a Class V rating that allowed them to fly any type of aircraft, including the four-engine B-24 *Liberator*. Of the 638 WASPs flying for the ATC by the summer of 1944, just 59 had earned a Class IV rate, and only 14 had a Class V.[37]

Marie was born Marie Cihler in Forsyth, Montana, April 21, 1917. She was the youngest child of John Cihler and his wife Pearl Douglas. John and Pearl married in September 1911 and by 1912 were living in Bozeman, Montana, where John was an engineer. When he registered for the draft in 1917, the family was now living in Forsyth and John said he was a farmer. The couple lost their first child, two-year-old Arthur, in 1914, and Marie's sister, Alice, was born four months later.[38]

It was somewhat of a nomadic life for Marie. By 1922 the family had moved west 300 miles and was living in Helena, Montana, where John was now a laborer. Within a few years they were on the move again, this time to Vancouver, Washington, just across the Columbia River from Portland, Oregon. Here, on September 5, 1930, there was a shocking tragedy. "While his little daughter fought in vain to prevent him from taking his life," said the newspaper report, "John Cihler, 44, grocer, swallowed poison at his home last night and died a short time later. His act followed a quarrel with his wife." Although unknown, "his little daughter" could have been 13-year-old Marie or her nearly 16-year-old sister—but it seems likely it was Marie.[39]

Pearl and her daughters moved to Portland where Marie graduated from Jefferson High School. As her sister had done, Marie went to work to help support the family. By 1940, she was a stenographer and cashier for a retail laundry. Before she began training at Avenger Field, February 13, 1943, Marie married Horace Sharon, who shortly after the wedding joined the United States Navy and left for the war. When she arrived in Sweetwater, she listed Bend as her home address. Her mother had remarried and moved there with her new husband.[40]

Marie's flight instructor, Lt. Hinton Daniel, was born in Georgia in January 1913. He graduated in February 1933 from the Academy of Richmond County, a military high school in Augusta, Georgia. After graduation, he attended the Junior College of Augusta. By the end of 1935, he had opened a service station and had asked Martha Harris to marry him. The couple moved to Clearwater, Florida, and opened a ready to wear store. In September 1942, Hinton returned to Georgia to enlist in the Army Air Corps. After eight months of training, he received his instrument flight instructor certification.[41]

Many subsequent reports say that Marie and Hinton were flying a nighttime training mission when they crashed, but in fact, their B-25 went down shortly after 3:00 in the afternoon. Recovery of their bodies wasn't until late in the evening and perhaps that accounts for the discrepancy. Marie Sharon rests near her father in Wilhelm's Memorial Mausoleum in Portland, Oregon. Hinton lies in Augusta's Westover Memorial Park. His wife, Martha, who never remarried, died in 1982 and rests beside him.[42]

Just four days after Marie and Hinton crashed, Jackie Cochran was in Washington, D.C., calling on Congressman Ramspeck. It was an attempt to show the congressman how valuable the WASPs were and what they were still capable of doing for the war effort. Later reports said that she had been concerned that Ramspeck didn't believe there was a place for woman in the Air Force. Ramspeck apparently told her that that wasn't true, and that he based his opinion solely on the cost to train a WASP, which he now estimated at about $6,490 for each trainee. He said he didn't believe such a cost was justifiable, particularly because there were already trained men available who were ready to fly and would hardly cost the government anything.[43]

Ramspeck had no greater supporter than the editorial staff at Washington, D.C.'s *Evening Star* newspaper. "There are a number of things about this WASP program that would stand more examination," they wrote. "The main question is why the Army Air Forces are doing away with the services of literally thousands of experienced civilian male pilots … and is taking on the WASPs—with the thought of increasing their number for duties that these men, in the opinion of competent authorities, are well able to perform. Why should a young woman, after a hundred hours or so of training, be a better or more useful pilot than men with thousands of hours of flying time who have instructors' ratings?" No decision was yet to be made and the newspaper urged the House Rules Committee to conduct a careful inquiry into the issue and, most of all, to "take it's time."[44]

At Avenger Field on April 16, 1944, Elizabeth Erickson (44-W-6), with 111 days still left before graduation, was almost half way through her training. Twenty-five-year-old Mary Howson (44-W-4) was in the homestretch, with just 38 days to go. It was a warm Sunday afternoon with a light, southeasterly breeze—a good day for flying. Mary, flying solo, was the last of her classmates to approach for a landing. They were completing a 530-mile roundtrip training flight around San Antonio. Elizabeth was practicing touch and go landings. Previously, she had made three of these practice landings with her instructor, but now, she was alone in the cockpit and lining up for another landing. Both women were flying AT-6 *Texan* trainers. For some reason, the ground controller didn't notice that the women were both at 800 feet and descending from opposite directions. Both were on their next to the last turn, in preparation for their final approach to the runway. Elizabeth and Mary were on a collision course.

Elizabeth Erickson was eight days shy of her 23rd birthday, the first child of Charles and Lucile Erickson. Charles was the son of Swedish immigrants and was born in Minnesota in 1884. When he was almost five, his father, a trained engineer, took the family to Seattle, Washington. There the senior Erickson helped rebuild the city's business district after a devastating fire had leveled it. After Charles graduated from high school, he attended the University of Washington, and then Cornell. He too graduated with a civil engineering degree. He worked for a number of years in the Bremerton, Washington shipyards and then, in 1935, moved his family to Preston, about 25 miles from Seattle. There he operated his own contracting business and was in charge of road construction and other engineering projects for the Preston Mill.[45]

His daughter, Elizabeth, attended Preston High School for her freshman year and then enrolled at the Issaquah High School, a few miles to the west. "Elizabeth was interested in almost everything," her younger sister, Charlotte, remembered. "She played most sports and had a lot of boyfriends." She was a very busy lady—a cheerleader, editor of the class yearbook, a musician with the band, and a singer in the choir. Mabel Nyberg, a classmate, remembered Elizabeth as a talented artist who was responsible for many of the posters announcing school events. After graduating with honors, Elizabeth enrolled at the University of Washington and majored in art for two years. To help support her studies, she worked part-time as a bookkeeper at the Seattle branch of the National Bank of Commerce. During the summers, the bank let her work full-time.[46]

Here at the bank, she fell in love with Don Smith. Don was a bank clerk and an amateur basketball player who had played high school basketball and had led the bank's basketball team to five consecutive titles, in the Seattle Bank League. Just before he joined the Army, in February 1941, Don asked Elizabeth to marry him. While he left for basic training, they began to plan their wedding by mail and telephone, but with the outbreak of war that December, their plans were postponed. The Army sent Don to further combat training and he eventually received orders to join the North African invasion force.

Elizabeth was left alone, content to receive his frequent letters home. But when no letters came for over two months at the end of 1942, Elizabeth was suddenly worried. A big hole had opened in her life and she began to think of what she could do to help end this war. While driving her sister home one day, Elizabeth admitted that she was tired of just driving a car around. "I'd rather have my hands on the wheel of an airplane," she said. All at once, six letters arrived from Don, and for the moment, Elizabeth was content again.[47]

In the spring of 1943, Elizabeth asked for a transfer to the bank's branch office in Yakima, Washington. She didn't tell her parents that she was going to learn to fly in the Civilian Pilot Training program with the McAllister Flying Service. After 48 hours in the air, Elizabeth returned home to ask her father's permission to join the WASPs. Former high school classmate, Mabel Nyberg, overheard the conversation between father and daughter. They were talking about what pay she would get and about life insurance. Elizabeth told her father that he needn't worry because if something happened she thought the WASPs provided insurance. "I remember,´ Nyberg said, "her Dad suddenly telling her that she didn't need to go because he didn't need the insurance money." Elizabeth's sister, Charlotte, was furious that her father gave in. "I remember being so put out that Dad would allow her to go," she said. "But Dad said she was old enough to make up her own mind. I really tried to talk him out of it." The WASPs accepted Elizabeth's application in October 1943. She left for Sweetwater December 31 and arrived January 5th. Three days later, her training began.[48]

Mary Howson was born into a wealthy family dynasty. Her great grandfather, Henry Howson, an engineer and inventor, arrived in the United States from England in 1851. He settled in Philadelphia and quickly found work with various engineering firms in the area, but soon, became annoyed at how little protection the U.S. Patent Office offered inventors and innovators. By 1853, Henry gave up his engineering career to practice law as a patent attorney, opening an office in 1853, and establishing a firm that has been in business for over 160 years. After graduating from the University of Pennsylvania Law School in 1916, Henry's grandson, Richard Howson, Mary's father, joined the firm. On Christmas Eve the following year, while being called to active duty with the United States Reserve Forces during WWI, Richard married Mary Holmes, daughter of another attorney. Mary Howson, their first child and only daughter, was born February 16, 1919, in Wayne, Pennsylvania, and she grew up in the family home in nearby Ithan.[49]

An old school friend remembered Mary as an outdoor girl, "petite, blond, and pretty." He said she was always willing to take risks and taught herself how to ride a horse and drive a car. Mary graduated from Radnor Township High School in 1936 and that fall left for Smith College in Northampton, Massachusetts. She graduated from Smith in 1940 with a Bachelors Degree in Art. Awarded a teaching fellowship, Mary first taught at Oak Lane Country Day School, a few miles north of Philadelphia. In 1941, after a brief time studying at the University of California at Los Angeles, she returned to Pennsylvania and taught kindergarten at the Booth School in Devon, about 20 miles northwest of Philadelphia. While at Booth, and wanting to find some way to help the war effort, Mary took classes in map-making from photographs, at nearby Bryn Mawr College. By the fall of 1942, she had resigned her teaching position and accepted a job as a photogrammetric technician at the U.S. Geological Survey's Arlington Virginia office. When not analyzing aerial photography for the Army Air Corps, Mary was taking flying lessons. She had decided to become a pilot for the WASPs. "My parents never really understood why Mary wanted to fly," her brother, Arthur, later told a reporter. "But they stood by her decision. Mary was a headstrong person." She began her training with Class 44-W-4 at Avenger Field November 1, 1943.[50]

Just after 1:20 p.m., April 16, 1944, Mary Howson and Elizabeth Erickson's AT-6s slammed into each other. As the planes began tumbling, Mary managed to unfasten her harness, climb out of the cockpit, and jump, but she was too low and her parachute never completely opened. Elizabeth had no chance at all. She was trapped in her cockpit and unable to jump. Both women died instantly just a few yards apart. The following evening, all of the trainees and training staff attended a memorial service for both women in the Avenger Field gymnasium. Classmates took up a collection to send both friends home. Mickie Carmichael (44-W-4) accompanied Mary home for her funeral and burial in the Washington Memorial Chapel Churchyard, Valley Forge, Pennsylvania.[51]

Elinor Fairchild (44-W-6), Elizabeth's friend, accompanied Elizabeth to her burial in Seattle's Lake View Cemetery. As Elinor began her journey, she wrote to a friend. "I am here in Amarillo waiting to take the 10:15 p.m. train to Denver, where I will take the train from Union Station to Seattle Washington—because the day before yesterday, one of my bay mates was killed in a head on collision. … I being her closet friend … have been sent as the escort to take her home. It is going to be so hard for her parents. She was so alive and so young—23—but seemed just a baby."[52]

Mary Howson's mother and father received a kind letter of condolence from Jackie Cochran that did little to quell their anger over a stark and brief telegram they had received from the War Department. "Your daughter was killed this morning," it read. "Where do you want us to ship the body?" Many months later, a government form letter arrived with a $171.50 check "to cover the cost of the funeral." Arthur, Mary's brother, later remembered that his mother "was very bitter about the cold and indifferent way the government handled the matter."[53]

By mid April 1944, the Costello Bill to militarize and commission the WASPs in the Air Corps still wasn't on the House Ways and Means Committee's calendar. The House Military Committee that had already approved the bill, now voted to approve an amendment to Costello's bill, should it eventually make it to the House floor for a vote. It would commission all trainees, not just WASPs, as long as they had completed the Civilian Pilot Training program and could meet all physical and technical requirements.[54]

At Avenger Field, the WASPs were no longer a detachment, but officially designated the 2563rd Army Air Force Base Unit (Contract Pilot School, Women). "Instead of being a detachment, the smallest training unit," said Marjorie Osborne (44-W-9) in a letter home, "we're now a base unit, the largest training unit." The Ground School course had already been extended to 30 weeks in a six-day a week program, and because WASP graduates expected to soon become Army officers, the ground school course now included officer training for the women. The officer training was similar to that offered to the men in OTS, the Officers Training School. The Army had set up OTS to turn college graduates into Army officers. Some of the WASP graduates were already receiving officer training, but military officials believed that including the OTS training within the Avenger Field ground school, would not only save each WASP six weeks schooling after graduation, but more importantly, would save the Army money.[55]

There was just one problem with their thinking. Until now, almost no one in the United States, and above all, hardly anyone in Congress, knew that WASPs were already getting officer training. It was a surprise—and members of Congress don't like surprises.

# [12]

## "IN THE SILENT PLACES OF THE BLUE"

The move to militarize the WASPs and give them commissions in the United States Army Air Corps had taken another hit—a self-inflicted hit caused by the Army itself. Ramspeck and his committee were still pursuing their investigation into the WASPs, and the report on that inquiry was almost ready. No one believed it would be favorable to the women's cause. Thousands of letters from out of work male flight instructors were stuffing mailboxes on Capitol Hill and filling line after line of newspaper and magazine letters to the editor. There was, said one newspaper, "angry and quizzical buzzing—swelling in volume around the WASPs." Yet with all these clues, the Army, so sure that it was winning, decided to send graduated WASPs "for training as prospective officers," to the School of Applied Tactics in Orlando, Florida, The *Washington Daily News* was outraged. "The action literally jumps the gun on Congress," it said, "by anticipating passage of a bill permitting officer status for the WASPs, although enactment of the legislation is unlikely without a fight on the House floor." The opposition couldn't have been happier. "The news sparked new outbursts,′ said *Time* magazine, "in the stalemated battle of the sexes."[1]

Army headquarters in Washington was quick to deny it was training women to be officers and assured the public that the Orlando training did not even resemble officer training. Instead, they said the women were only receiving "physical conditioning and theoretical flight instruction." However, that's not what the women in Sweetwater were hearing. Trainee Marjorie Osborne's father had heard the reports of an officer's training school and asked his daughter about it. Marjorie (44-

W-9) had been at Avenger Field for less than a month, and yet, she had already heard about the post-graduation officer training. "Last night we had a meeting and it looks as though we're pretty close to the Army," she said. "We were told the military discipline would get stricter and also that incorporated into our classes would be everything that we would get in Officer's Training School. OTS is at Orlando, Florida. It is not for flying larger planes, it is for all graduated WASPs, and they're sending them 50 at a time until all those out in the field now will have officer training. … So that's another reason why we think we're practically in the army." Confident they would eventually win; the Army brass ignored the criticism and for months, continued to send women to Orlando.[2]

After 23-year-old Edith Keene (44-W-1) graduated from Sweetwater in February 1944, she quickly moved from her first assignment at Hondo Army Air Field, in Hondo Texas to just north of the Mexican border at the Mission, Texas Army Air Base. Edith had learned to fly in the Pomona Junior College Civilian Pilot Training program, given at Brackett Field, an airfield located between the cities of La Verne and Pomona, California. Edith was born in Canton, Montana, December 19, 1920, the daughter of Newton and Ruth Keene. When she was six years old, her four sisters and their parents moved to Pomona. After graduation from Pomona High School, Edith immediately began studies at the University of California at Los Angeles and graduated in 1942 with a Bachelors Degree in Physical Education. Within a year of her graduation from UCLA, Edith entered the WASP program, beginning her training at Avenger Field August 9, 1943.[3]

Around Moore Field, on the Mission Army Air Base, the thermometer was climbing its way to 90° on April 25, 1944. There had been a trace of rain early in the morning, but the afternoon had cleared to a partly cloudy sky with an occasional light southeast breeze from the Gulf of Mexico. Edith was flying an AT-6 *Texan* with Robert Kuenstler Jr., who had enlisted in the Army a year earlier and had graduated from advanced flight training at Moore Field. Edith was helping Kuenstler with his navigation and instrument flight training. She had traded places with another WASP for the afternoon flight. Kuenstler was at the stick of the AT-6, while Edith observed from the back seat. Just after 2:30, flying about 12 miles northwest of the field, Kuenstler was going through the usual dips, turns, and rolls before dropping into a dive. As he pulled back on the stick to recover, they both could hear the straining scrape of metal as one of the wings separated and fell away. The aircraft began to fall and Kuenstler quickly unfastened his harness and jumped to safety, but Edith could not. Perhaps struck by the wing, her canopy would not open and she went down to her death with the plane. The nineteenth WASP to die, Edith now rests in Pomona Memorial Park beside her mother and father. Dolores Meurer (44-W-1) was the WASP originally scheduled to fly with Kuenstler that day and hadn't heard about the crash until the base chaplain came to her barracks. When answering the knock on her door she saw the shocked and unbelieving look on the chaplain's face. "Meurer," he said. "I was just coming to give you Last Rites."[4]

Early in May, Secretary of War Stimson announced he was in favor of the Army plan to militarize the WASPs by commissioning already trained and qualified women pilots. He was also in favor of setting up a program to do the same for women cadets, once they completed training. "The war department," Stimson said, "proposes to take as full advantage as possible of the contribution which women pilots can make to the war effort." He added that every qualified instructor or partially trained student from the disbanded Civilian Pilot Training program could join the Air Corps, as long as they met basic requirements. Surprisingly, his comments didn't create much of a stir. Cochran and Arnold had already decided that the less they said in defense of the program publicly, the better for the WASPs. There was no point in stirring up the opposition even more; especially with a vote on the Costello bill coming soon. Consequently, most of the press coverage that spring, centered on the very vocal, out of work flight instructors, and the negative rumors leaked from congressional committees. A public defense of the WASPs often came in battles between competing newspaper editorials. The *Boston Herald* printed an editorial strongly supporting Stimson and the WASPs, saying that even if militarization did keep qualified pilots out, "the WASP ought to be retained, if for no other reason than it demonstrates what women can do in military aviation—and sometime that information may be extremely valuable in the nation's defense." They argued that the bill to militarize the WASP was before the House and they believed, "It deserves passage." An *Idaho Statesman* editorial was typical of the opposition, not hesitating to repeat the flight instructors' major complaints. "Jackie Cochran's WASPs are getting a priority of a special kind," it said. "The men are angry about it. WASPs," it continued, could "qualify for transport training with just 35 hours flying time, while men must have 1,000 hours, including 200 in heavy aircraft." Why the discrepancy, they asked. The editorial concluded with the silliest of exaggerated answers. "Probably it is the sentimental softness of American men in regard to their women. In colleges the smooth, good-looking gals get A's without a lick of work; and in the armed services it may be that dimples have a devastating effect even on the generals."[5]

While Stimson was supporting militarization, some members of the House of Representatives and Senate were offering a not so veiled plan that was sure to end any chance of the women becoming Army officers. Representative Overton Brooks, a Democrat from Louisiana, and Senator David Clark, a Democrat from Idaho, had prepared an amendment to the proposed bill that would also commission all 4,500 men who took flight training in 1942. "These men were trained as fliers and should be commissioned as fliers," Brooks said. Other legislators were drafting similar amendments.[6]

General Arnold was again back on Capitol Hill before an executive, closed-door session of the Ramspeck committee to answer questions and defend militarization. Later reports said that Arnold "was emphatic" in his defense of the WASPs and the Army plan to make them part of the Army. He assured the committee that qualified men had every opportunity to fill Air Force jobs, but he added that the WASP training program would expand, only if and when more women fliers were needed to release men for combat. It was obvious that the tide was fast turning against Arnold's plans.[7]

May had been a safe month for the women fliers, although there had been one near miss. Mary Shaw and Laura Rutledge who had both seen their classmate Elizabeth Erickson die at Avenger Field in April, were flying a BT-13 about six miles east of Sweetwater. They were on an instrument training flight and Mary was "under the hood," unable to see outside the aircraft as she practiced instrument navigation. Laura was the safety pilot in the rear seat, watching for any obstacles or other planes that could cause trouble. Just past noon, May 19, they lost control and smashed into a one-room maintenance shack near the highway. The BT-13 was almost completely demolished and one of its engines was thrown nearly 100 yards from where the plane came to rest. Amazingly, both women were still alive. Laura had fractured her left arm and leg and Mary had a broken arm. Both had several minor cuts and bruises. Two ranchers who lived nearby rushed to the scene and took Mary to the Sweetwater Hospital, while an Air Corps officer and his wife who were driving by on the highway followed with Laura. Investigating officers said because Mary and Laura had their safety belts and shoulder strap guards securely fastened, they avoided what likely would have been more serious injuries, if not death. After attending to their wounds, doctors sent both women to recover at the Big Spring Army Air Force hospital. Their WASP careers were over. In December 1944, when the WASP program ended, both women were still recovering from their injuries. "We were still hospitalized in San Antonio when the program deactivated," Laura later explained.[8]

On June 5, Representative Ramspeck submitted his committee's report to the Speaker of the House. There were no surprises in its 13 pages. The report ended with just three recommendations that almost guaranteed an end to the WASP program. Using carefully selected "facts," the majority of committee didn't believe an expansion of the WASP training program was necessary or justified. "Recruiting of inexperienced personnel and their training for the WASPs should be immediately terminated," their report said. They agreed that WASPs already trained and currently in training could still be used, but of course, everyone knew that even that concession was vulnerable to future budgeting decisions. Finally, the report recommended the immediate use of "the several surpluses of experienced pilot personnel available for utilization as service pilots." The minority on the committee voiced their opposition to the report by simply saying the issue of the WASP program was "a matter for the Army Air Forces to determine." The Ramspeck recommendations were of course only recommendations, but were sure to ignite a major battle in Congress over the Costello Bill.[9]

The next day, America discovered that the Allies were invading Europe. D-Day had finally arrived. Trainees in Sweetwater gathered that evening in the Avenger gymnasium to listen to battle reports read to them from United Press dispatches telephoned to the field from the Sweetwater newspaper. At 9:00 o'clock, loudspeakers broadcast President Roosevelt's radio address to the nation and his D-Day prayer.

"Our sons, pride of our Nation, this day have set upon a mighty endeavor, a struggle to preserve our Republic, our religion, and our civilization, and to set free a suffering humanity.

"Lead them straight and true; give strength to their arms, stoutness to their hearts, steadfastness in their faith."

When the speech and prayer were over, the night ended with the women praying for the men who were still fighting on the beaches of Normandy and for those who had already died.[10]

At Avenger Field, training continued and the trainees' off duty time saw even more improvement. The citizens of Sweetwater opened the municipal swimming pool exclusively to the trainees for free swimming three afternoons a week. Now, the old barracks washroom was gone, replaced with a beauty parlor, operated by trained beauticians. No longer would women have to go to town to get their hair done. "Windblown bobs of Avenger's Fifinellas will soon come in for overhaul, right on the post," said the base newspaper. Three tennis courts were under construction, and best of all, the USO was finally bringing the latest Hollywood movies to the base on a regular schedule, "adding a flicker of light and a few secondhand thrills to the off-flight-line lives of trainees."[11]

June 1944 was one of the worst months the WASPs would ever see. Not only was Congress about to terminate the program, but June also marked the beginning of a rapid succession of 19 more deaths in just six months. It had taken eighteen months for the first 19 women to die, but with the ranks of the WASPs swelling, death would now come more frequently. As safely as the women had flown in May, June was a disaster, matching the previous April's record of five deaths in one month. News of the first came just five days after D-Day.

One of the earliest and most experienced WASPs, Dorothy Nichols, was a graduate of Class 43-W-2, training at Houston and graduating at Avenger Field on May 28, 1943. Just two months into her training, Dorothy inadvertently supplied the base newspaper with a humorous story. While on her first cross-country flight, in an open cockpit, an excited Dorothy was joyously waving to her friends who were flying in the group with her. It was what some would call a teaching moment, as the map she held in that waving hand—the map that told her where to go and where to turn—suddenly blew away from her fingers and drifted slowly to earth. "Dottie's face did fall," said the newspaper, "upon retracting her empty digits!" But Dorothy was a good pilot and, after graduation, her assignment was the 6th Ferrying Group in Long Beach. By 1944, she was qualified to fly the Air Force's fastest pursuit planes.[12]

Dorothy was the only daughter of Sheldon and Mabel Nichols, and was born September 26, 1916, on one of Washington's Puget Sound islands. By 1920, the family, including her older brother, Edwin, had moved to a farm in Kern County, California. Trouble was developing in her parent's marriage that eventually led to a separation in the late 1920s and a subsequent divorce. Dorothy and her brother stayed with their mother and the three moved to Van Nuys, California. After graduating from Van Nuys High School, Dorothy enrolled at the University of California at Los Angeles and, in 1938, graduated with a Bachelors Degree in history. Two years later, still at UCLA, she earned her Masters Degree. She left for Baton Rouge, Louisiana, where she began teaching history at Louisiana State University. There, in February 1941, Dorothy was one of only five women who learned to fly as part of the university's Civilian Pilot Training program.[13]

Whether it was her sense that war was likely imminent or she just wanted to be near airplanes, late that summer, Dorothy resigned her professorship and returned to California. She became secretary to the head of public relations at Gardner Field, a recently constructed Army pilot training base in the southern San Joaquin Valley. Two months later, Pearl Harbor was bombed and Dorothy began to wonder what she could do for the war effort. In 1942, after hearing that the Army was going to train women pilots, she wanted to join up right away, but knew she didn't have enough flying hours and had no way to get them. Ever since the Japanese attack, the government had forbidden civilian flying near the coast. Nevertheless, Dorothy was a determined lady.[14]

"Dorothy told me one day that she was going to quit her job and go to Fort Worth," said friend and future fellow trainee, Jary Johnson, "where civilian flying was not restricted. Her goal was to fly until she had enough hours to join Miss Cochran's program." A few days later, in November 1942, they both left for Texas in Jary's car. They had already applied for the women's pilot training program, but because they believed they needed 300 hours to qualify, after they arrived in Texas, they flew every hour they could. They didn't know that the flying requirement had changed to just 200 hours. "Two weeks and a meager number of hours later," Jary said, "we received a telephone call from Miss Cochran's office. Would we like to join the second training class at the Houston Municipal Airport?—Would we?!!"[15]

After graduation in May 1943, Jary received orders for Romulus, Michigan and Dorothy for Long Beach. Later in the year, Dorothy completed pursuit training and received orders to fly a P-39 *Airacobra* fighter from the Bell factory in Niagara Falls, New York to Great Falls, Montana. The P-39s were being sent to the Soviet Union as part of the Lend-Lease agreement. Passed by Congress in early 1941, the Act allowed transfer of military equipment and supplies to any nation whose fighting was vital to the national security of the United States. However, the women couldn't fly out of the country, so once the planes reached Great Falls, men from the Ferrying Division flew the planes on to Fairbanks, Alaska, where they turned them over to Soviet pilots.

At the Bell factory, after a year apart, Dorothy and Jary were reunited. As they flew west, they shared hotel rooms at each stop. When they landed at Bismarck, North Dakota, they couldn't go further.

For days, low-level clouds between them and Great Falls kept their planes on the ground. Dorothy told technicians that she had noticed a rough running engine while coming in to land. Mechanics replaced the carburetor while the women waited. Finally, after church on Sunday, June 11, they heard the weather had cleared. The military took them to the airfield and the WASPs strapped into their planes. As she taxied out for takeoff, Dorothy's engine was still running rough. She told the tower and they said she could return to the flight line if she wanted to, but Dorothy said no, she decided to takeoff. Just as she lifted off, her engine quit, the P-39 crashing into the runway and bursting in a fireball. "Everybody waiting for takeoff taxied back to the flight line," Jary said, "and there we were told that the dead pilot was Dottie."[16]

Jary Johnson accompanied Dorothy's body home to Van Nuys for burial in Forest Lawn Memorial Park in Glendale, California. "After a miserable night in the hotel," Jary said, "I supervised the loading of the coffin in the baggage car and sadly rode the train for three days. The most painful part was meeting Dottie's divorced mother at the station." Seven other WASPs, in dress uniform, acted as pallbearers. Although it was rare, an American flag covered Dorothy's coffin and, at the end of the service; her mother took it home.[17]

In Congress, the anti-WASP militarization foes were finding even more ways to discredit the idea of putting women fliers into the Army. Representative James Morrison, testifying before the Senate Military Affairs Committee, warned the members that an "exclusive Fifth Avenue shop" was responsible for making the new WASP uniforms, each costing $505. Indeed, Jackie Cochran had chosen Neiman-Marcus to fashion the women's blue uniforms. Morrison objected to the uniforms, saying they did not meet Army regulations and, if the Costello bill passed and the women got their commissions, the government would waste over $500,000 of taxpayer money to buy more. He believed commissioning flight instructors made much more sense, because there wouldn't be an added cost of redesigning a uniform. The flight instructors wore uniforms discarded by the Civilian Conversation Corps, and, if militarized, would wear uniforms already in the Army's inventory—there would be no need for any more of those Fifth Avenue styled uniforms. Representative Morrison neglected to mention that the country already had women in regulation uniforms—the Women's Army Corp, the WACs. But then again, Jackie Cochran was opposed to merging the WASPs with WACs.[18]

At the same time, Air Corp headquarters was trying to quiet the growing outrage over unemployed flight instructors, by announcing a proposal to begin letting instructors fly for their country. The proposal was still under consideration in the Senate Military Affairs Committee. If approved, it would allow instructors drafted for active duty, or instructors already serving in some non-flying Air Corp position, the chance to take an Air Corps cadet aviation training course. It also included former instructors still in the United States and currently serving in some other branch of the Army. Applicants would have to be under 27 years of age, meet all physical and mental requirements, but they wouldn't have to take the standard aptitude and classification tests. General Robert Harper, head of Army Air Force training, said he believed that the program would provide commissions for about 90 percent of the 5,000 fired flight instructors. Harper said the Army would continue to train WASPs, but believed the plan to commission the former instructors would remove any objection by the House Civil Service Investigating Committee to the flight training of women. Yet, even this attempt at compromise received a cold reception from the opposition. Flight training students, whose courses had ended before they could graduate, complained that they weren't included in the plan. Representative Morrison argued that the Army Air Force examining boards were actually creating technicalities to "wash out" the instructors who, he said, "had done more than any other single group to give the Air Force the world's finest pilots."[19]

June 12, 1944, the day after Dorothy Nichols died on that Great Falls runway; the House of Representatives was scheduled to begin debate on Representative Costello's WASP militarization bill, but because of other pending legislation, debate was postponed. The following morning, Marjorie Edwards' AT-6 motor began backfiring and belching smoke, near the town of Childress, on the southeast corner of the Texas Panhandle.[20]

Marjorie Edwards (44-W-6) was born not far from her father's Anaheim, California orange groves, September 30, 1918. Frederick Edwards, her father, was born in England and emigrated to the United States in 1913. Three years later, he married Bessie Marie Metz and the couple settled in Huntington Beach, California. Fred worked as a retail oil salesman for Standard Oil, driving a horse drawn oil tank on the roads of Orange County. When the company transferred him to Anaheim a few years later, he found a small family home on a ranch with a walnut tree orchard, just a few miles south of the city. Perhaps inspired by his new job with the Associated Laboratory, Fred eventually replaced his walnuts with orange trees. The laboratory began operation in 1922 as a cooperative amongst the orange growers. Its two primary goals were to analyze and improve fertilizer used in local orange groves and, by using chemical analysis, help orchardists correct soil problems.[21]

The oldest of three Edward's children, Marjorie graduated from Anaheim High School in 1936 and entered into the teacher training program at Santa Barbara State College. In 1940, she graduated with a Bachelors Degree in Junior High Education. Fred Jr., her brother, said it was while she was away at college that she got her first chance to fly. "Her boyfriend had a plane and was a licensed pilot," he said, "and much to the displeasure of her parents, she went flying with him several times and loved it." For the time being, she taught school—first in Baldwin Park, California, and then in Anaheim's John C. Fremont Junior High School, where she taught Home Economics for a semester. During the summers, she took flying lessons and earned her pilot's license. Not long after war broke out, she went to work at the Douglas Aircraft plant in Long Beach, California and sent an application to the WASPs.[22]

Marjorie began training with Elizabeth Erickson and 134 other women on January 6, 1944. Six months later, and barely two months after attending Elizabeth's memorial service, Marjorie herself was in trouble. With black smoke trailing behind and the engine's erratic and explosive backfires snapping over the prairie north of Childress, Texas, Marjorie's AT-6 was rapidly losing altitude. No longer able to stay in the air, Marjorie climbed out of the cockpit and jumped.[23]

The airplane nosed down onto the Campbell family ranch. Within minutes, Frank and Cliff Campbell, along with their 13-year-old nephew, Walter Johnson, were at the crash site. The AT-6 had hit the ground at an 85° angle, squashing down onto itself. Johnson said, "the crumpled engine, wings, canopy, and tail section lay in a flattened mass of metal." In fact, only 6 or 7 feet of the 29-foot-long aircraft was still intact, and still standing above ground. Nearby the crushed plane was a barbed wire fence and on the other side, about 20 yards away, was a white parachute lying on the ground and gently billowing in the wind. Young Walter climbed through the wire and began gathering up the parachute, but suddenly stopped in horror. There, under the nylon, was Marjorie, still attached to the parachute harness. She had been too low for the chute to save her when she jumped. Within an hour, a small convoy, including a truck and a crane, arrived from the Childress Army Airfield, about 18 miles away. They recovered as much of the wreck as possible and then returned to Childress, taking Marjorie's body with them.[24]

One of Marjorie's closest friends at Sweetwater was classmate Elinor Fairchild, the same woman who had accompanied Elizabeth Erickson's body home to Seattle two months before. Now, after that first heartbreaking trip, she was riding the train again, heading for Southern California in full uniform with Marjorie's body. Things were finally changing for the WASPs. Elinor said the Army actually paid for the trip and even gave her flags to give to the family. Arriving in Fullerton, California's Loma Vista Memorial Park, she again would see parents' tears, and watch another best friend and roommate put to rest. How difficult that must have been. Within a few days, she composed a poem for both women; and eventually for all other women fliers who would die. "You have found tomorrow," said one line, "High in the silent places of the blue."[25]

Supporters of the plan to militarize the WASPs did more than just write letters to Congress. Dr. Alice Brues, recent recipient of a PhD in Physical Anthropology from Harvard, had been measuring a small sampling of the women pilots, attempting to determine their average dimensions. She hoped the information would lead aircraft designers to adjust the interiors of military aircraft in a way that would allow WASPs of varying sizes "to operate them safely and efficiently." A major problem was that many of the women were just too short to pilot some types of aircraft, and while flying, needed blocks attached to the floor controls so they could reach them. Dr. Brues' released her report to the press on June 19, 1944. The next day, the WASPs lost another pilot.[26]

Gleanna Roberts (44-W-9) had only been training for nine weeks when she took off from Avenger Field on a solo flight in a PT-17 *Stearman* biplane. Barely 20 miles west of Sweetwater, near Lorraine, Texas, Gleanna was practicing low level flight. Flying downwind, she decided to reverse course and entered into a too steep 180° turn. The plane lost lift, stalled, and began to fall. As the *Stearman* spun in, its left wings struck the ground and the plane began a cartwheel that tore it apart, killing 25-year-old Gleanna. "I knew her very well," classmate, Marjorie Osborne, wrote in a letter home. "She was an awfully nice girl from Iowa City. She was killed instantly. … We aren't allowed to have memorial services for her; they tried it once before and it was very demoralizing."[27]

Born January 11, 1919, Gleanna grew up on her father's farm near Sharon Center, about 10 miles southwest of Iowa City in eastern Iowa. She was the fourth child and second daughter of Robert and Elizabeth Roberts; although, she never really knew her sister, Evaline Joyce, who died when Gleanna had just turned 3 years old in 1922. She attended the new Sharon Center High School and was a key member of the school's speech team. In her senior year, she scored second place for a dramatic reading, in competition against all of the county's schools. It was the third time Sharon High had captured the county's oratorical trophy. Just before graduation in 1936, she was also a cast member in the school's senior play. Then, after nearly four years studying journalism at the University of Iowa, Gleanna was one of only four women invited to join Theta Sigma Phi, the national honorary sorority for women in journalism. Five months later, in June 1941, she graduated from the school of journalism and received her Bachelors Degree.[28]

It didn't take Gleanna long to get her first reporter's job with the *Cedar Rapids Tribune*, where she also was a writer in the editorial department. But, within a few months, her talent quickly found her a new position with even greater responsibility. In February 1942, she accepted a reporter's position with the *Moline Dispatch* newspaper in Illinois, just across the Mississippi River from Davenport, Iowa. By 1944, she was also the paper's Radio Editor and Writer. While living in Moline, she also began taking flying lessons and before she reported to Avenger Field, she had accumulated 65 hours in the air.[29]

Martha Sarager, one of Gleanna's roommates, escorted her body home to Sharon Center and the white, wood-framed First Welsh Congregational Church. In the small churchyard cemetery, Martha stood silently in her dress uniform. There, Gleanna would rest near her grandparents—and the sister she never really knew.[30]

Friends and instructors at Avenger Field collected $75 and sent it to the University of Iowa, asking the school to use it in some significant way as a memorial to Gleanna. Because she was a journalism student who had a fascination with typography, and while studying at the university had worked as a library assistant, there was agreement that some unusual books about typography would be appropriate to add to the university's journalism collection. Each book was dedicated in her name with a special bookplate and would be restricted to use within the library. "We are proud of the contribution which Gleanna made to her country," said University President Virgil Hancher, "and we shall be pleased to have in our library a fitting tribute to her memory."[31]

When Congress approved $6.3 million for the WASP program in June, there was a sigh of relief from WASP supporters. With its passage as part of the Army Air Service appropriation of $12.6 billion, it seemed the women would be flying for at least another year. The people of Sweetwater were elated. "The program has poured millions of dollars into the channels of trade here," wrote a reporter. "Its inception brought hundreds of new families to town, filled up vacant houses, and created a housing shortage." But all of this good news was false hope.[32]

Facing a backlog of appropriation bills that in some cases were critical to the war effort, and with an imminent summer recess just days away for the political conventions in this presidential election year, the debate on the WASP militarization bill finally came to the House floor on June 21. It was a heated, yet surprisingly brief debate. After nearly six months of growing and sometimes vicious opposition, it was all over in just three hours. Minnesota Representative Joseph O'Hara called the WASP program nothing more than a social group and said, "this isn't a time for a glamour war. This bill is society legislation." John Costello, the bill's sponsor, defended the women. "There is no glamour in serving as grease monkeys," he said "or sweating out an overland flight in the face of adverse weather." Congressman Edouard Izac, of California, protested that the bill made Jackie Cochran a colonel in the Army. "We want to make THIS woman a colonel," he said, "while out in California, we have thousands of men, now instructors, who could do this job?" When Izac, a respected WWI Medal of Honor recipient, made a motion for an immediate vote to kill the bill, dreams of militarizing the WASPs were over. On a final tally of 189-169, militarization was dead. Although the women would not become part of the Army, at least it seemed the training program might continue and the women could still fly for the Army. But now, even that was under attack. "The question is," said an editorial in a Washington, D.C. newspaper, "what the War Department proposes to do about the costly training of women pilots already underway." The editorial reminded readers that the Ramspeck Report recommended "the recruiting of inexperienced personnel and training for the WASPs be immediately terminated."[33]

On June 21, while House members were debating the militarization bill, Lea McDonald (44-W-3) was flying in a type of airplane she had never flown before. She had just returned from a three-week leave and planned to resign the following day so she could get married, but because she hadn't yet officially announced her plans, she first had to fly solo in an A-24 dive bomber. In a letter to Mary Martin, her former classmate, Lea said she was afraid to fly this "danger ship" that ever since the deaths of the WASPs in North Carolina the previous year, still had a bad reputation with the women. Gripped by her fears, she asked for someone to fly with her, but superiors denied her request. After flying around the Biggs Army Airfield near El Paso, Texas for a while, she turned toward a landing approach. Martin later said she believed that Lea was so nervous flying the A-24 that she set the unfamiliar flaps incorrectly. Instead of slowing her speed for a landing, she sent the plane into a sudden dive toward the Texas prairie. Her throat mike failed and she was unable to get help from the ground controller. One mile from the end of the runway, at great speed, the A-24 smashed into the ground and immediately erupted in flames.[34]

Lea Ola McDonald was born in Hollywood, Arkansas, October 12, 1921, the third child of Olen and Ada McDonald. The family moved back and forth between Arkansas and Texas for a few years, but after Lea was born, they finally settled on a farm between Gaines and Seagraves, Texas, not far from the New Mexico border. After two years at Wayland Baptist College, a junior college in Plainview, Texas, she took up a business administration course at West Texas State Teachers College in Canyon, Texas. There she took flying lessons in the college's Civilian Pilot Training program and accumulated the 35 hours needed to qualify for the WASPs. After passing the rigid physical and mental examinations, she began training at Avenger Field on October 4, 1943. After graduation on April 15, 1944, she was assigned to the tow target squadron at Biggs Field. Barely two months later, all of her fears were realized. "My best friend was killed in a crash," Mary Martin said, "and we had to collect money to send her home." Four days after that fiery crash, Lea returned to Seagraves for her funeral in the Gaines County Cemetery.[35]

Meanwhile, less than a week after the House vote against militarizing the WASPs, General Arnold, without warning, ordered an end to recruiting and training of any new women pilots. Although there was funding for the program into June of the next year, with no more women arriving at Sweetwater, training would automatically end with the last graduating class, December 7, 1944. "From the debates and committee reports," Arnold said, "the opinion of the majority of the people's representatives was clear. They do not consider that further recruiting and training of WASPs is now necessary." Arnold still believed the women would continue to fly in 1945, but Jackie Cochran soon realized that that was a false and unlikely hope. "This termination of the training program would mean the end of the whole WASP program in due course," she said, "for an organization that has no way to offset attrition through deaths, resignations, and other severances, becomes a shrinking organization."[36]

The fifth WASP to lose her life in June was Bonnie Jean Welz (43-W-6), who crashed into the Texas dust just a week after celebrating her

26th birthday. Born June 22, 1918, in Bridgeport, Washington, redheaded Bonnie was the fourth child and fourth daughter of Lee and Grace Alloway. When she was 4 years old, her father died, and by the time she graduated from high school, her mother had already remarried twice and was about to remarry again. With so many changes in stepfathers, it's not surprising that Bonnie moved quite frequently. From Washington, to Inglewood, and Auburn, California, the family followed along with their newest father. After graduation, Bonnie studied at Coalinga Junior College, on the western edge of California's Central Valley, about 65 miles southwest of Fresno. There she learned to fly as a student in the government's Civilian Pilot Training program. By 1940, she had married Carl Welz, a graduate of San Jose State College and holder of a Masters Degree from Columbia University. The couple moved to New York City, where Carl was an elementary music teacher at a private school in Manhattan and Bonnie was secretary at the school. With the outbreak of war, they returned to California, where Carl enlisted in the Army Air Corps in September 1942. Bonnie was working as assistant superintendant in the request department at the Central Casting Corporation in Hollywood. The company supplied "extra" actors to Hollywood film studios. Bonnie began studies at the University of California at Los Angeles, but in her junior year, she quit and left for Avenger Field, where she began WASP training April 25, 1943.[37]

Bonnie was photo editor for her class graduation book and a reporter for the base newspaper. She published most of her articles without a byline, but in September 1943, about a month before her graduation, she was obviously impatient and ready to finally do what the Army had trained her to do. She began an article about the lives of previously graduated WASPs, including the never-ending questions that gave trainees sleepless nights—the mysteries of what was next. "Out in the Blue," she wrote. "What will we do when we graduate? What kind of planes will we fly? Where will we live? These and many other similar questions are asked daily by Avengerettes, eager to get to work for Uncle Sam."[38]

Bonnie's first assignment was Dodge City Army Airfield in Kansas, where she received transition training in the B-26 *Marauder*, a medium, two-engine bomber. It was 75 hours of flying instruction, 30 as a copilot and 45 hours as first pilot. In addition to ground school and Link training, the flying included nine hours at night, 20 hours on instruments, and 10 hours on navigational flights. The program had two main purposes—teaching the women to fly heavier aircraft, especially for tow target flying, and developing a program to show fearful male pilots that the B-26, known as the "Flying Coffin," was safe.[39]

In January 1944, Bonnie's orders sent her to Harlingen Army Airfield, an Army gunnery school in southern Texas, on the Gulf of Mexico, just across from the U.S.-Mexican border. Harlingen was a Flexible Gunnery training base, where Air Corps gunners learned to shoot various guns, from varying gun positions, within the different Army bombers. Bonnie and her fellow WASPs flew B-26 navigation missions and provided tow targets for the men.[40]

Just past 11 in the morning, June 29, 1944, Bonnie took off in a BT-13 trainer on a "routine administrative cross-country flight" across the West Texas oilfields, bound for Laredo, Texas. Her passenger was Major Robert Stringfellow. Stringfellow had arrived at Harlingen Field shortly after the beginning of the war. A New York native, he was a skilled shooter and had been a shooting champion with his National Guard unit. At Harlingen, he set up a skeet shooting training program, where gunnery trainees could quicken their reflexes and sharpen their aim, by learning the principals of "leading" and "tracking" of aerial targets. Stringfellow had built eight skeet courses at the base and had trained all the instructors.[41]

After about an hour in the air and 40 miles short of Laredo, something happened—and no one was really ever sure what it was. Stringfellow, sitting in the rear cockpit with his canopy open, said they were flying at about 1500 feet when he noticed Bonnie had entered a slow turn to the left and had begun a slow descent. Her cockpit canopy was closed. There seemed to be nothing out of the ordinary and Stringfellow thought she was probably lining up for a normal landing, but there was no conversation between them. On the ground, Lloyd Staggs saw the plane coming down in a wide circle, and to him, it sounded like the throttle was wide open. The plane disappeared behind some trees about a mile away and exploded in a fireball. Staggs raced his truck to the scene and found the BT-13 engulfed in flames and lying on its back. About 50 yards away, a seriously injured and confused passenger was pointing at the wreck and mumbling something about "her" and "she." Trapped inside the flaming cockpit, it was impossible to rescue Bonnie. All Stagg could do was rush Stringfellow to the hospital in Laredo. Bonnie's disturbing Texas death certificate says that Bonnie's cause of death was "a fractured skull and cremation as result of an airplane crash." Her ashes were scattered at an unknown location and there's no known funeral or memorial service.

Some have said carbon monoxide poisoning may have sickened Bonnie as she flew, and perhaps before she passed out she frantically tried to find a safe landing place on the mesquite covered prairie. Others think one wheel on Bonnie's plane rolled through a gopher hole as she was trying an emergency landing, flipping the BT-13 onto its back. The official government accident report said that the plane hit the ground while still in a left turn, concluding that, "the major, minor, and underlying cause of this accident is unknown."[42]

Back at Sweetwater, there was more trouble. Over 100 new women trainees of Class 45-W-1 who had received orders to report to Avenger Field, had already arrived and, with cancellation of their class, they were stranded. They had been traveling from their homes well before General Arnold's sudden and unexpected cancellation of WASP training and hadn't received the telegrams warning them not to come. What were they supposed to do? They had spent most of their money to get here. How were they supposed to get home?

# [13]

## BEGINNING OF THE END

In early June at Avenger Field, Elizabeth Quay was one of over 50 women who received the same telegram.

"Your application for admission to the women's flying training program," it read, "has received favorable consideration.

"You are requested to report at your own expense at 10 a.m., June 30, 1944, to the commanding officer, Two Thousand Five Hundred and Sixty-third Army Air Forces Base Unit, Avenger Field, Sweetwater, Tex. Sufficient allowance should be made for possible delays, as transportation difficulties will not be accepted as an excuse for late arrival.

"Please acknowledge receipt of these instructions and your intention to report as requested. Failure to acknowledge intention to report or to submit, within 10 days after entrance day, valid reason why it was impossible to report, automatically cancels your application for entrance to the women's flying training."[1]

Within a week, Elizabeth sent her letter of acknowledgement, saying she would report for training by the June 30 deadline. She gave herself a week to reach Sweetwater from her Lakeland, Florida home, leaving early in the morning, June 23. Three days later, the telegram canceling her orders arrived at her now vacant residence. "Due to recent recommendations of House Civil Service Committee and unfavorable action of House of Representatives on WASP bill," it said, "your orders to report for WASP training June 30, 1944, are canceled." Driving her own car to Texas, Elizabeth was already halfway to Avenger Field. Near midnight, June 28, while checking in at Sweetwater's Blue Bonnet Hotel, she learned there wasn't going to be a class and that she was stranded over 1,500 miles from home.[2]

They came by bus, train, auto; and some had even hitchhiked. Genevieve Mahre, chosen spokeswoman for the stranded women, said many of them didn't have enough money to get home, even if she still had a home. "Many of the group," she said, "have sold their homes, automobiles, places of business, and given up good jobs" just to become a WASP. She estimated that the women had "spent an average of $500 to get the necessary flying time to qualify," not to mention, additional money to buy related equipment.[3]

Congressman Costello urged General Arnold to continue the training program at least for the women who had faithfully answered their orders to report. "It is unfortunate that these girls cannot go through with the program," Costello said. "The women of America should be offended when they learn that our Congress thinks they cannot qualify to be pilots for the armed forces, as well as our men." Arnold stood firm in his decision and refused. "I deeply regret the inconvenience, hardships, and disappointment occasioned by this decision," he said, "but no other course appears to be open without reconsideration by Congress."[4]

While the Air Force began working on a plan to return the abandoned trainees to their homes, columnist Drew Pearson struck again. He accused Arnold of bypassing Congress by organizing a new and secret plan to commission the WASPs and make them part of the Army Air Corps. "After Congress refused to let the WASPs into the Army," Pearson said, "Arnold and Miss Cochran adopted a backdoor strategy. It was arranged to sign the WASPs up as WACs and then have them reassigned to the Air Forces, this despite Congress' clear ruling that the WASPs should not be taken into the regular Army." Pearson predicted a "cloudburst on Capitol Hill" as soon as Congress was back in session. "The congressmen are up in arms over Arnold's efforts to sidetrack the law, by continuing to use the WASPs," he said. "Thus, the battle of the WASPs continues."[5]

Later, Pearson renewed his nearly constant attack on Jackie Cochran, saying that Washington, D.C. Air Corps officials told him that Cochran "barges into their offices, pounds on their desks, and says, 'I used to work in a factory. I know what the little people want,' then delivers ultimatums about her lady fliers."[6]

The stranded women could go anywhere they wished on the base except for the flight line, and many simply wandered around, imagining what their life could have been. "We want to stay as long as we can," said one disappointed recruit. They were guests in the empty barracks that would have been theirs had their training continued. Beginning in the morning of July 2, one Army transport plane after another began to land and take the women aboard for their return flight home. Once inside most refused to believe that the Army had rejected them, until their plane began to take off. Elizabeth Quay and the other women who had driven their own cars to Sweetwater received gas coupons to help them on their return trip. Later, a few of the women filed claims with the Congress, asking for reimbursement of the expenses they incurred while traveling to Sweetwater. One woman successfully claimed an additional $131 for the wasted travel time, the three weeks of salary she lost while preparing to leave for training, and the expense of securing new employment.[7]

On July 4th, schoolchildren across the country were eagerly anticipating a loud and glittering evening of fireworks, as the nation celebrated its 168th birthday. Just before noon, Susan Parker Clarke (44-W-2), daughter of George Hyde Clarke and Emily Clarke Cooke, had taken off in South Carolina from Columbia Army Air Base. With her in the BT-13 *Valiant* was Lieutenant Harry Thomas, an aviator who had received his wings and commission the previous May. Thomas was on leave and hitching a ride toward his hometown, Pulaski, Virginia, for a visit with his wife and young son. He had been flying with Susan since Atlanta, where she had agreed to let him ride with her on her trip up the East Coast.[8]

Twenty-five-year-old Susan was born the third of four daughters in Cooperstown, New York, August 5, 1918. When her mother was 18, she had survived the sinking of the Titanic. She and George Clarke married three years later. Susan's father was a graduate of Harvard and had inherited his father's estate that had been in the family since the 18th century. After 17 years and seven children, her parent's marriage fell apart. In June 1932, when Susan was 12, her mother went to Reno, Nevada, filed for divorce, and almost immediately married Stephen Beach Cooke, a writer and actor. She and all of her children had to leave the family mansion and move to Cooperstown to live with her new husband. Susan's father remarried a year later.[9]

In her senior year at Cooperstown High School, Susan won the medal as best mathematics student in her class. After graduating in June 1937, she left for New York City to attend the Packard School of Business. In the following years, between trips to Europe and the West Coast, Susan played tennis in local tournaments at the Cooperstown Country Club, capturing a number of championship titles. She also worked as a bank secretary for a time, before moving to Miami, Florida to become secretary for the Embry-Riddle Flying School. In 1940, she enrolled in flight classes at Embry-Riddle and earned her pilot's license.[10]

Susan joined the Women Pilots of America, a private organization determined to make sure every woman who wanted to fly got the chance and the training they needed. With an airport on Long Island, the goal was to have hundreds of women trained to navigate an airplane across the country, in any kind of weather. Much like the WASPs, these non-combat women pilots planned to free up men for military service. Susan quickly became a director of the group and, in April 1942, appeared in a national advertisement for Chesterfield cigarettes, smoking a cigarette and wearing a leather flight helmet and goggles, and standing alongside the organization's founder, Ruth Haviland.[11]

In June 1943, the news that Lieutenant George Hyde Clarke, Jr. was dead, staggered the proud family into agonizing grief. George was Susan's younger brother and only 22. He had joined the Army a year earlier and was in the final days of his navigator training. While on a night training flight over Northern California, he and five others out of a crew of 10 died when their B-24 bomber crashed. Susan was home in Cooperstown when George's body arrived and she watched her tearful mother accept the flag that had covered her oldest son's casket.[12]

By the time she arrived for training at Avenger Field on September 6, 1943, Susan already had over 100 hours of civilian flight time, ranking her second highest in her training class. She rarely made news in the base newspaper, but when she did, it always seemed to revolve around occasional flirting with male trainers and other pilots. Within a month of her arrival, a humorous story in the paper said that her hairnet had somehow snagged onto a visiting pilot's helmet, "complete with the pilot inside," but sadly, "they made her throw him back." When the New Year came around and the trainees gave their New Year's resolutions to the base newspaper, Susan resolved "not to flirt with instructors anymore."[13]

After a visit from her mother and stepfather that spring, Susan received her diploma and silver wings from General Arnold on March 11, 1944. She left for further training at New Castle Air Base in Delaware and then transferred to the 33rd Ferrying Group at Fairfax Field near Kansas City, Kansas. On July 4, 1944, she was flying another ferrying flight up the East Coast of the country.[14]

Flying at 1,500 feet, about three miles out from the Columbia Army Air Base, the South Carolina sky was partly cloudy with a light wind and temperatures in the mid 70s. Some eyewitnesses said they thought a bird or something that wasn't an airplane had struck Susan's BT-13.

Others reported they had seen a B-25 flying nearby, and still others said they hadn't seen anything that could have caused a problem. Almost everyone agreed that the craft suddenly banked left and, with its engine roaring, nosed down at a 45-degree angle into the ground. The left wing struck the earth; the plane began to cartwheel, the shattered body of the craft threw out metal pieces all along the way, and then, the fuel tanks erupted in flame. There was no time to jump—no time to escape.[15]

The next day, Jackie Cochran sent Susan's mother a telegram. "I hope this will convey to you how deeply we all feel about Susan's death," Cochran said. "May God give you strength to find comfort in the fact that when she was called upon to make the supreme sacrifice, she was serving her country in the highest capacity permitted women today."[16]

Susan was buried on the outskirts of Cooperstown in Lakewood Cemetery; her grave just a few feet away from her brother George. Burial for Harry Thomas was in the Oakwood Cemetery in Pulaski, Virginia, Harry's hometown.[17]

While Susan and Harry's funerals were being planned, Paula Loop was flying that BT-13 near Medford, Oregon and crashing into a mountainside, becoming the 26th WASP to die. Authorities had never recorded the location of the crash site and forgot about it for another three years. What was left of Paula's aircraft remained undisturbed on that mountain until a ground party, sent out to find wreckage spotted from the air by a Navy pilot, rediscovered the broken airplane. Even after three years of lying in the open, a searcher was amazed that "the metal parts were as bright as the day it fell and that a part of the fuselage still lay on the ground."[18]

On July 8, the day before Susan Clarke's funeral and the day after Paula Loop's death, another woman was already falling from the sky.

Bettie Mae Scott (44-W-3) was engaged to be married. It had been a whirlwind romance with Lieutenant Frank Cramer, a flight instructor and P-38 pilot stationed at the Waco Army Airbase near Waco, Texas. The two had met not long after Bettie's graduation from Avenger field in mid April and her returned from a ten-day visit home. They planned to marry at the end of July 1944, perhaps on Bettie's 23rd birthday. Bettie was born July 26, 1921, in Monrovia, California, a small town at the base of the San Gabriel Mountains, a few miles east of Pasadena. Her father, Frank, had been police chief in the town since 1926 and had been a city policeman since 1913. Bettie was Frank and Virgel Scott's oldest daughter and the third of their four children.[19]

After graduation from the Monrovia-Arcadia-Duarte High School,

Bettie attended Pasadena Junior College and graduated after two years. Before joining the WASPs she worked as an assistant teller at the Security-First National Bank in Monrovia, a position that helped her pay for private flight lessons offered at a Blythe, California flight school.[20]

Less than three weeks before her 23rd birthday, July 8, 1944, Bettie was walking beside a BT-13 *Valiant* on the flight apron at Blackland Army Airfield in Waco. She had already checked the maintenance sheet on the plane and before taking off was doing her final preflight walk-around. The damaged *Valiant* was now repaired and it was Bettie's job to see if it was airworthy enough for a male trainee pilot to fly. Just before 8:30 that morning, she climbed into the cockpit, continued her preflight checklist, and fired up the motor. As she left the runway, the plane began to climb at too steep of an angle. Reaching 100 feet and no longer able to gather enough wind under its wings, the plane stalled, began to roll, and dropped. It smashed down onto its back, instantly killing Bettie. Later investigation would show that mechanics missed defects in the tail section of the aircraft and Bettie never saw them during her walk-around.[21]

On July 12, Monrovia businesses shut their doors so everyone could attend Bettie's funeral. Her remains had come home in a plain pine box. Pallbearers and honorary pallbearers came from the ranks of the Monrovia fire and police departments. Police Chief Frank Scott and his wife, along with the town's residents, accompanied Bettie to Live Oak Memorial Park for burial. There, Bettie Mae Scott was laid to rest, barely a mile away from her childhood home.[22]

Not all of the women were interested in being militarized and given Army commissions. Some were actually relieved that Congress had axed the bill. Earlier in the year, when it had seemed the militarization bill would inevitably pass, those who preferred civilian status, resigned —something they could do because they were civil service employees—not Army. One of the women wrote briefly in the comment section of her resignation form. "I do not desire to join the Army," she said. Another, a married WASP, already assigned to duty, explained that her husband was coming home soon after a long overseas combat assignment. "It is my desire to be with him upon his return," she said. Another trainee echoed both comments in her resignation letter. "I do not wish to continue in training at the expense of the Government when it is obvious that I would resign if the Women's Airforce Service Pilots became a part of the Army," she said, "or upon the return of my husband from overseas." In late March

1944, Colonel Charles Root, Commanding Officer at Dodge City Army Air Base in Kansas, interviewed the 35 WASPs stationed there. Twenty of the women said they preferred military status as long as it meant they would become commissioned officers. The remaining 15 women wanted to stay in civil service. It wouldn't be long before General Arnold would finally decide the question once and for all.[23]

The crash of Beverly Moses' AT-11 *Kansan* on July 18, 1944, in the Spring Mountains west of Las Vegas, is still one of the most mysterious of all the accidents that claimed 38 WASP lives.

It was a month when the high temperature never dipped below 100 degrees on the ground, and in the cooler air above, winds occasionally swirled around the mountain slopes. Beverly (44-W-5) was flying as co-pilot on the twin engine *Kansan*, used by the Army to train navigators, bombardiers, and gunners. She had drawn straws with her former classmate, Mildred Taylor, to win the right to take the right-hand seat. Lieutenant Frank Smith was the pilot of this instrument training flight, and onboard with him and Beverly were instrument flight instructors, Staff Sergeant James Reagan and Corporal Kenneth Langston. They left Las Vegas Army Airfield late in the morning, flew their practice missions, and then landed to refuel at Indian Springs Army Airfield, about 40 miles northwest of Las Vegas. At Indian Springs, Sergeants Bernard O'Reilly and Herbert Stretton, both gunnery instructors, climbed aboard and moved toward the rear gun positions. Just before 3:00 o'clock, the AT-11 lifted off with her crew of six and began flying over the Nevada desert. About an hour later, Lieutenant Smith received orders to fly toward Charleston Mountain and search the area for a parachute that someone believed they had seen falling in the area. It was the last anyone would hear from the AT-11.[24]

When the plane didn't return that evening and Las Vegas controllers were unable to make contact, a search party was organized. Early the next morning, riding, and at times walking beside their horses, the men set off. Before they finally found the wreck, they had climbed for a grueling 12 hours through the canyons and thin forest on rocky trails. Apparently, Lt. Smith had flown up a canyon toward a treeless slope, covered in gravel and small boulders, close to the top of the mountain. His landing was near perfect as he flopped down like a falling pancake with hardly any forward motion. Everyone would have survived the gentle crash, except for the fire. A rock must have ripped into one of the wing fuel tanks and, with gasoline gushing out, the airplane almost instantly exploded in flame. Two of the crew, probably O'Reilly and Stretton, were partially out of the rear emergency exit before they died, but everyone else was still strapped into their seats, horribly burned. What had happened? Why was Lieutenant Smith flying so low? Accident inspectors could never decide.[25]

Twenty-year-old Beverly Jean Moses was one of the youngest of all the WASPs. Born December 21, 1923, in Des Moines, Iowa, she was the daughter of Alex and Sylvia Moses, and the couple's fourth child. Her father was an automobile mechanic and her mother supplemented the family income with her cooking and catering. Just a few months after Beverly graduated from North Des Moines High School in June 1940, her mother died. Her two older brothers and older sister were already on their own and only Beverly and Eileen, her youngest sister, were still living at home. She did what she could to help the family, working at odd jobs, while attending business school.

Not long after the war broke out, the San Diego based, Solar Aircraft Company bought an old Ford Automobile factory in Des Moines and began making aircraft engines for the war effort. Beverly landed a secretary job with the company. With her extra money, she took flying lessons at the local airport and, after earning her pilot's license, she joined the Civil Air Patrol. Her WASP training began December 7, 1943. Her assignment was the Las Vegas Army Air Base, where three weeks after her June 27, 1944 graduation from Avenger Field, she was dead. She now rests in Oakwood Cemetery in Des Moines with her mother, father, and older brother John.[26]

Ironically, Beverly's plane crashed just 23 miles northwest of where, two and a half years earlier, a Transcontinental & Western Air, DC-3 airliner, flew into Potosi Mountain, killing Clark Gable's movie star wife, Carole Lombard and 21 others.[27]

Despite the looming end to training in Sweetwater for the WASPs, little had changed at Avenger Field. A new course in ground school that was standard for male aviation cadets, now introduced the women to advanced instrument flying and the aviation equipment on the aircraft they would fly in their advanced phase of training. Those WASPs who had already graduated and hadn't received the advanced instrument training began returning to Avenger Field to take the five-week course. A new class of graduates would arrive every five weeks until training completely ended in December.[28]

The tennis courts that had been under construction over the summer were finally completed. The loose net, hastily strung across one of the unfinished courts by some of the eager players, was gone; replaced by regulation nets and backstops. There also seemed to be more time for parties and dances. One day, after hosting a tennis court dance for a few Army aviation cadets from Bruce Field in Ballinger, Texas, some of the women accepted the cadets' return invitation to visit them at the men's graduation dance. At 5 o'clock on a Saturday morning, 54 singing and shouting, wide-awake trainees, merrily climbed onto two cattle trucks for a three-hour trip to Ballinger. After freshening up in a barracks provided for them, the ladies ate in the mess hall with their escorts. The cadets had cleared out a hangar for the dance and a local orchestra provided the music. Early on, a tactical officer decided that the best way to deliver the corsages that the men had purchased for the trainees was to assign one of his cadets to the task. He chose a man who was "walking tours," a military form of punishment, where a soldier marches back and forth in a small area for an hour or more. Because the chosen soldier was in trouble and wouldn't be coming to the dance, the tactical officer explained that it made perfect sense for him to march the flowers to the ladies. "He wasn't accomplishing anything out there (on the flight line)," the sergeant said. "Somebody had to deliver the flowers and, after all, there's a manpower shortage." Later that evening, with the dance over, the exhausted women sleepily climbed aboard the cattle trucks for the three-hour ride home. The chaos of the morning was all gone, and while the truck rocked and rattled its way home, the women silently did their best to sleep. Arriving home at Avenger at 4 a.m., they quickly rushed to their beds in the barracks. They had been awake for over 24 hours, but not one of the women complained—it was worth every single minute.[29]

Anthropologist Dr. Alice Brues was still trying to influence the design of airplanes so women could fly them more safely and easily. She was back in the news again; this time with more details of her studies. After completing her measurements of the majority of the WASPs, Dr. Brues returned to the Army Air Corps Aero Medical Laboratory at Wright Field, just east of Dayton, Ohio. After calculating the average of 35 measurements, taken on each woman, she had three types of mannequins constructed out of transparent plastic. One newspaper called these averaged women pilots, "custom made ghosts," because you could see right through them. Type A mannequins were 5 feet 4.9 inches tall, with a 35-inch bust, and a thigh circumference of 38.1 inches. Type B measured 5 feet 2.5 inches tall, with a 34.4-inch bust, and a thigh of 37.4 inches. Type C was the tallest at 5 feet 9 inches, and carried a bust of 35.8 inches and a thigh of 39 inches. To help with studies of space requirements for the various women, each mannequin could wear a helmet and flight gear and was equipped with replica human joints, the joint action controlled by artificial elastic tendons. Dr. Brues said she believed that after the war, similar mannequins could help design automobiles, furniture, and any sort of personal equipment.[30]

By the beginning of August 1944, there were 699 active WASP pilots. Three hundred were flying for the Training Command, towing targets, engineering flying, and instructing. The Transport Command had absorbed 299 women. They flew the ferrying missions originally envisioned for the women. The Weather Wing had 12 women flying liaison missions between the various commands. There were two women testing flight clothing and making engineering test flights for the Material Command, and five women towing targets for the Proving Ground Command. The final 81 pilots were flying with various units of the stateside Air Force.[31]

On August 1, Jackie Cochran sent a report to General Arnold saying that either the women be given military status, or the entire WASP organization should be discontinued entirely. "Under a civilian status," she said, "so many elements of the experimental project are lost or weakened." Because the women were civilian employees, there was no way to keep them from quitting at anytime, at the expense of the cost of training them. "Serious consideration should be given to inactivation of the WASP program," she said, "if militarization is not soon authorized." If deactivated, Cochran said she believed the women should receive the rank of 2nd Lieutenant for at least one day, so they would be eligible for veteran's benefits when the program ended. "Twenty-eight WASPs, performing the same functions as the male Air Corps officers, have given their lives for their country," she said. "WASPs already have demonstrated that carefully selected women can fly all military aircraft skillfully and safely." Perhaps hoping Cochran's report might turn the tide back into support for WASP militarization, General Arnold released a summary of her comments to the press—and waited.[32]

The day after Christmas, 1911, 25-year-old Paul Hartson married Isabel Blanche in Kootenai, Idaho, about 40 miles east of Spokane, Washington. Paul had landed a traveling salesman's job with the J. I. Case Threshing Machine Company, working out of the company's Spokane and Walla Walla offices. In 1912, he set up residence in Portland, Oregon, but continued to travel until about 1920, when he secured a cashier-auditor position with the company. The couple's first child, Henry, was born in 1913 and Mary, his only sister arrived January 11, 1917.[33]

Mary Hartson (43-W-5) graduated from Washington High School in Portland and soon moved to Washington, D.C., where she worked as a clerk in the Federal Security Agency's General Consul Office. The agency was in charge of food and drug safety, education funding, public health programs, and the Social Security pension program.

In the spring of 1941, the Civil Aeronautics Administration awarded Mary a scholarship that gave her enough time and money to earn her private pilot's license in the Civilian Pilot Training program. A year later, Mary applied to the WASP. On March 26, 1943, she began the six months of training, receiving her wings from Jackie Cochran at graduation ceremonies September 11. Although her first assignment was the Air Transport Command at New Castle Air Base, within a few weeks orders began quickly sending her from one Army air base to another. She was the first WASP ever assigned to the Coffeyville Army Airfield in southeastern Kansas, one of the Army's newest basic flight training schools. There, she flew as a utility pilot. By the late summer of 1944, she was at her fifth base, flying as an engineering test pilot and flight instructor out of Perrin Army Air Base, near Sherman, Texas.[34]

On August 14, the sky was clear, winds from the south were light, and temperatures were simmering toward 103 degrees. Mary took off in a BT-13 from the Perrin Airfield with Staff Sergeant Orville Eitzen in the rear seat. This was a basic test flight just to check out the plane's recently repaired radio. About 15 miles north of the runway, the aircraft suddenly stalled and spun into the ground. There were no witnesses and the cause of the crash that killed both Mary and Orville was never determined. When found, both had their harnesses unfastened as if preparing to jump, but for some reason, they never got the chance.[35]

WASP Starley Grona (44-W-3), also stationed at Perrin Field, told an Army interviewer that because Mary Hartson had crashed, "many members of the male flying personnel at this field refused to go up with a WASP again." She conceded that, "This attitude is stupid and prejudiced, but it still casts an unfavorable light on the organization [the WASPs] as a whole, and is due in large part to discrimination against our sex." She believed most men who worked closely with the WASPs were in favor of keeping the organization, but the attitude of the others worked against what the women were trying to do.[36]

Mary Hartson came home to Portland for a funeral service and the placing of her ashes in Wilhelm's Portland Memorial Mausoleum. She was 27 years old. Orville Eitzen, also 27, who had married just two years earlier, returned to his wife's hometown of Shenandoah, Iowa and was buried in the Elmwood Cemetery, about 11 miles southeast of town.[37]

In the last weeks of August, Jackie Cochran's demand of militarization or elimination of the WASP program was generating a surge of support. Perhaps there was still hope for the WASPs. "The WASPs have not yet lost their sting," predicted columnist Helen Essary. Sweetwater city officials appointed a "Committee on WASP Legislation" to support efforts to keep the women flying and Avenger Field in business. In the pamphlet the committee prepared, they asked, "why should Congress discriminate against women in the Air Force?" After all, they said, the Army already had WACS, the Navy had WAVES, SPARS served in the Coast Guard, and there were even "lady Marines." The committee recommended that everyone in the area write to all of the congressmen and senators, telling them to support the WASPs and demanding to know what each legislator's position on militarization was, and, if opposed, to explain why. There was immediate support from Mrs. Jane Perry, chairwoman of the Texas Federation of Women's Clubs. "Women will appear at the world peace table, as well as having a hand in post war reconstruction," Perry said. "A program for women fliers will be set up after the war somewhere in the nation and Sweetwater is the strategic point—it could be made the women's West Point of the Air."[38]

On August 20, a contingent of women fliers from the Texas Chapter of the 99 Club brought their annual session to Sweetwater for a three-day weekend conference. They met to protest the defeat of the WASP militarization bill and discuss what they could do to help. They took a tour of Avenger Field and held study sessions downtown at the Blue Bonnet Hotel. "A great deal of misinformation has been circulated concerning the WASP program," said Ziggy Hunter, a veteran flier and chair of the club. "Accusation has been made by certain groups that women are taking jobs away from men pilots. That statement does not take into account that the jobs belong to no one except those with the training and ability to perform them."[39]

Meanwhile, the trainees at Avenger were experiencing a wave of invading crickets. Women were sweeping them out of their lockers, while other chirping hordes gathered outside their windows. Evelyn Brier (44-W-9) dumped a cup of hot coffee on them, but it didn't seem to bother the pesky intruders. They were everywhere and underfoot wherever the trainees went. Sarah Allshouse (44-W-9) even discovered one in her shoe, but only after feeling a deadly crunch on the inside of her shoe, as she answered the command to "Forward! March!" Old timers in the area said you could forecast the weather by measuring how far a cricket jumped. No one could explain how that would work, and the weather professionals just ignored them.[40]

A couple of announcements at the end of August were welcome news for the women at Avenger Field. With the presidential election just a few months away and the trainees so far from home, some were worried that because they weren't members of the Army, they wouldn't be able to vote. Captain Stovall, voting officer for the Army, assured them that they were designated "attached civilians serving with the armed forces of the United States," and included under provisions of the Soldier Voting Law. Stovall gave them notarized postcards that allowed them to request an absentee ballot from their home state. As long as their state law allowed the ballot, the women could vote.[41]

Of course, the most welcomed news for the women that month was that they were finally getting a summer uniform. Even though the scorching Texas summer was beginning to fade into a more moderate range of temperatures, the news had everyone excited. The three-piece uniform included a beret, a jacket, and a short sleeve dress, all in blue chambray. It wasn't government issue, and, as always, the women would have to buy their own, but it was a flattering look and quite a step up from those early white shirts and General's Pants. There were also rumors that a new lightweight overcoat and new dress shoes would be coming soon.[42]

On September 13, 1944, a month after Mary Hartson's accident, classmate Alice Lovejoy (43-W-5) was flying over the Port Isabel Channel, near Brownsville, Texas in the rear seat of an AT-6 *Texan* fighter. She had just celebrated her 29th birthday and her first anniversary as a WASP pilot. Her first duty station had been the Romulus Army Airfield near Detroit, Michigan. There, for a year, she learned to fly heavier aircraft, including B-17, B-24, and B-25 bombers. Delivery flights took her all over the country and even into Canada. As one of the more qualified WASP pilots, Alice got orders for Pursuit School at the Brownsville Army Airfield, where she would fly some of the country's best and fastest fighter aircraft.[43]

Born August 15, 1915, in Scarsdale, New York, Alice was the second of four daughters born to Frank and Emma Lovejoy. Frank worked for a number of years as publication manager for the Curtis Publishing Company's distribution office in Scarsdale, New York. The Curtis Company published the *Saturday Evening Post* magazine. In 1924, he left Curtis for a sales executive job with the Socony Vacuum Oil Company, where he would spend the rest of his career, overseeing sales and offering frequent lectures about sales and advertising techniques.[44]

September 8, 1944, just five days before Alice Lovejoy fell near Brownsville, Texas, Class 44-W-7 marched the Avenger Field flight line as part of their graduation ceremony. This was one of the few classes to not lose a classmate – *Air Force photo.*

Even as early as seven years old, Alice was performing at piano recitals in Scarsdale, winning a number of ribbons and awards. By the time she reached high school, she had become a dedicated and essential team player on the Scarsdale High School women's field hockey team. She was one of their better players. After one unexpected loss to the New Rochelle team, when Alice was ill and couldn't play, the local newspaper noted that the team did quite well, "all things considered," especially because "the varsity had to play without the services of its competent goalkeeper, Alice Lovejoy." She was quite the athlete, even a member of the girl's tumbling team.[45]

Alice graduated in June 1933, unsure of which college she should attend, but her final choice was the Pace Institute in New York City. Two years later, in 1936, she graduated. After a two-week cruise in the Caribbean and two more years at Syracuse University, Alice began working as a script editor and an assistant scriptwriter for NBC Radio's Blue Network. In early 1942, with the country now at war, she became a clearance officer for the Piper Aviation Company in Lock Haven, Pennsylvania. There she earned her pilot license and a year later, March 26, 1943, she began her WASP training in Sweetwater.[46]

Just after noon, September 13, 1944, three planes were on a training exercise in a V Formation. Alice and her instructor were flying back behind the leading AT-6 as one of the wingmen. Descriptions of the accident are vague, but it appears that one of the wingmen was moving into either a Right or Left Echelon Formation—where the planes change from a triangular formation into a diagonal line formation with one plane following the other. If it were a Right Echelon Formation, the left wingman would drop down and then back off a few feet, slowly skid right until he was outside and behind the right wingman, and then, move back up and forward into position. A Left Echelon would be the reverse. Because news reports say there was a collision between the two wingmen when the "wing planes were changing position," and because of the final crash results, it's possible that Alice was piloting the plane that was moving, right or left, and she collided with the other plane when she was moving up into position. Alice was unconscious. She must have struck her head somehow. Her slightly injured instructor, who was flying with her, said he tried to get her out, but couldn't. He jumped to safety, landing at the mouth of the Port Isabel Channel, and was rescued from the water by the crew of an Army engineering dredge. Alice crashed and died in the AT-6. The other pilot made it back to Brownsville Field safely. He was uninjured.[47]

Mary Louise Bowden (43-W-4), who had roomed with Alice at

Avenger Field and was also stationed at Romulus, said she heard Alice was flying in the lead plane when the collision occurred. Mary and another WASP traveled from Michigan to Brownsville, where they picked up Alice's body and escorted it home to Scarsdale. "That was the worst thing in my entire time as a WASP," she said. She remembered facing Alice's parents and how sad they were as they buried their daughter in the Ferncliff Mausoleum in Hartsdale, New York. Less than three months later, Mary Bowden's plane crashed and she narrowly missed joining Alice in death.[48]

At Avenger Field, the first class of previously graduated WASPs had completed the advanced instrument flying course and a new wave of post-grad women wearing Santiago blue had arrived to take their place. They would be flying many hours "under the hood," unable to see around them. Because there would be so many of them in the air at one time, as a warning to other pilots, they flew in trainers that were prominently marked with large red stripes.[49]

On September 15, WASP Helen Fremd (43-W-5) had a narrow escape at Dayton, Ohio's Patterson Field, when her pursuit plane collided with a twin-engine cargo plane, while both planes were taxiing for takeoff. Three Army men on the cargo plane died, but Fremd was uninjured.[50]

Out on Long Island, New York, at Republic Aviation's Farmingdale plant, Jackie Cochran was smashing a bottle of champagne on the nose of the 10,000th P-47 *Thunderbolt*, while 10,000 workers cheered her on. She christened the fighter, "Ten Grand," as Assistant Secretary of War Robert Patterson looked on.[51]

Then—on October 3—General Arnold said the WASPs were shutting down.

# [14]

## NOT ALWAYS HAPPY LANDINGS

It was a secret wedding—no one knew—not until her casket came home.

Marie Michell (44-W-2) wasn't even ten years old when her father, Roy, and her mother, Ruth, divorced. Roy Michell would one day own his own company, but at the time of the divorce he was manager for a tool making plant in Detroit. Not long after, Marie's mother married Maurice Zetterholm a corporate attorney and an advertising manager for General Motors. Zetterholm headed up the division that produced and distributed short advertisements that were regularly shown in as many as 9,000 movie theaters across the country.[1]

Zetterholm had been an Army officer during WWI and, after the war, Congressional legislation placed his name on the Army's retired list; subject to recall into the service whenever the Army needed him. Late in 1940, with the possibility of war looming, the Army activated Zetterholm as a Major in the regular Infantry. By early 1942, he moved his family to Washington, D.C.[2]

Marie was born May 23, 1924, in Detroit, Michigan and by 1933 she and her brother Roy lived with their mother and stepfather in Chicago. While in high school, Marie worked for a short time on the Lake Michigan shores as a professional dancer at the Edgewater Beach resort hotel. She was also a professional ballet dancer. After the move to Washington, D.C., Marie attended National Park Junior College in Forest Glen, Maryland, about eight miles north of the Capital. The building was a former seminary, converted in the late 1930s into an all girls, private preparatory school. Luckily, Marie graduated before the Army purchased the school in late 1943 to use as an annex of Walter Reed hospital. It was while studying at National Park that Marie took flying lessons, and at her graduation, she surprised the family by taking off and landing an airplane.[3]

"To Marie, flying was just a natural thing," said her brother Roy. "She loved it." Marie's inspiration for flying was Jack Hayward, a young man who went to school with Roy. "Jack was already a pilot while still in high school," Roy said. "Marie decided to impress him by becoming a pilot, too." Marie's skill as a pilot got her a job in Chicago as a Link flying instructor at the American Airlines Pilot Training School. On September 6, 1943, she began training at Avenger Field. That same month, Jack Hayward, now a Navy pilot, died when his airplane crashed.[4]

After graduation from Avenger in March 1944, Marie reported to the 5th Ferrying Group at Love Field in Dallas. There, Marie met an Army flight surgeon, Captain Hampton Robinson, who had recently returned from duty on Gilbert Island in the South Pacific. Whenever Marie's busy ferrying schedule allowed, they went on dates and it seemed to be another case of love at first sight. In late September, Marie transferred to Victorville Army Air Field in the California desert, about 65 miles northeast of Los Angeles. She was going to learn how to fly bombers. Capt. Hampton was already at his new assignment, Reno Army Airfield. Somehow, the couple found enough time together that they decided to marry. Late in September, in a ceremony kept secret from relatives, Hampton and Marie tied the knot. In letters home, she hinted to relatives that she was just thinking of getting married someday. She and Hampton had already agreed that they would have a formal ceremony in front of all the relatives, whenever they could make the arrangements.[5]

In the afternoon of October 2, 1944, at about 1:15, 20-year-old Marie was taking off as copilot in a B-25 *Mitchell* bomber. Earlier that morning her roommate, originally scheduled to fly that day, awoke with a toothache and without hesitation Marie agreed to take the roommates place. With her in the plane were the pilot, Lieutenant George Rosado, and the crew chief, Staff Sergeant Gordon Walker. A San Diego radio announcer in civilian life, Rosado, 27, joined the Air Corps in April 1942. He was married and the father of two sons, ages 6 and 2. Walker, 24, enlisted from San Bernardino County, California in October 1940. He was also married and father of a 2-year-old son.[6]

Less than a half hour after takeoff, the bomber had crashed and Marie and the crew were all dead. The only witness was an Army aviator flying nearby. He said the bomber was flying at a low altitude, had stalled, and began to spin as it fell. It was a flat spin—the aircraft rotating completely around with the nose remaining nearly level with the horizon all the way down. Perhaps because the plane was spinning too fast, there was no time for anyone to bail out. The bomber hit the desert floor about 25 miles west of Victorville at 1:40 and erupted in a blazing fire.[7]

After the bodies were recovered, WASP Elizabeth MacKethan (44-W-2) was at Cochran Field, in Georgia, waiting to catch a hop on a transport plane to Michigan so she could be at Marie's funeral. Marie and Elizabeth were classmates at Avenger and had become fast friends. They had promised each other that if anything ever happened to either one of them, the survivor would go and comfort the heartbroken mother. Of course, neither one believed it could, or would, ever happen to them. As Elizabeth continued to wait in the operations room for her flight, she replayed in her mind that first flight after hearing the news that Marie was dead. High in the air, flying through the drifting clouds, she later said she had felt Marie was with her in the sky. She took out a pencil and began to write. She said the words to her poem came easily; almost as if someone were dictating them to her. When she was done, she had written "Celestial Flight," a tribute to Marie Robinson. The poem begins:

"She is not dead
But only flying higher,
Higher than she's flown before,
And earthly limitations
Will hinder her no more."

Elizabeth caught her flight to Michigan and shared her poem with Marie's mother.[8]

Captain Hampton Robinson accompanied Marie home to her mother and stepfather, the first time either had known that she was married. The funeral at White Chapel Memorial Park, north of Detroit in Troy, Michigan, was small and solemn. "It was very subdued," her brother Roy said. Hampton Robinson married twice after Marie's death. He returned to Houston, Texas after the war, where he became a successful physician and chairman of the Texas Board of Health. He died at age 73 in February 1982.[9]

George Rosado's final resting place was Fort Rosecrans National Cemetery, San Diego. Gordon Walker found his final rest in Stockton, California's San Joaquin Catholic Cemetery. His wife would lie beside him 22 years later.

A day after Marie's crash it was Peggy Martin (44-W-4) falling from the sky. At 32, Peggy was one of the oldest WASPs, and yet, the details of her life have all but disappeared. Even as late as 1993, the WASP Association's file on Peggy was "empty," and the women were asking for contributions. Peggy was born February 8, 1912, in Seattle, Washington, to Carl and Edith Wilson. Her brother Willard, her only sibling, was also born in Seattle seven years earlier. Her father worked at the Ames Shipyard in Seattle and her mother managed the apartment house where they lived. Sometime after 1918, before Peggy was 8 years old, her parents divorced. Peggy and Willard stayed with their mother while her father moved to a rooming house in Seattle. Within a few years, her mother married Myron Hopper and she and the children moved to his Southern California home. Hopper died in 1934 and within a year, mother and her children were back living with Peggy's father. Edith kept her married name of Hopper and listed her occupation on the 1940 census as maid in her ex-husband Carl Wilson's home. Although she and Carl had reconciled enough to live together, it appears they never remarried.[10]

The 1940 census record tells us that Peggy was also living in her father's home and was divorced from a man named Martin who she had married sometime between 1935 and 1940. Who that man was and how long they were married is a mystery. The 1940 census also shows that she was a high school graduate and was working as a waitress in a restaurant, but until she entered WASP training three years later, details of her life are missing.

Peggy began training at Avenger Field November 1, 1943, and graduated May 23, 1944. Her first duty assignment after graduation was the pilot training base at Gardner Army Airfield near Taft, California. She was only there a short time before she received orders for Arizona's Marana Army Airfield, about 30 miles northwest of Tucson. It was another Army training facility and Peggy's primary assignment was engineering test pilot, flying recently repaired aircraft to be sure they were airworthy. With a population lingering around 250 people, there really wasn't much to do in the town of Marana, and so, the few WASPs assigned there usually stayed on base.[11]

On October 3, 1944, Peggy climbed into a BT-13 *Valiant* with Marion Hagan (44-W-6). Marion had graduated from Sweetwater two months before, and Marana Air Base was her first assignment. She was riding as an observer as Peggy gunned the plane's engine for takeoff. There was something sluggish in the way the engine struggled to get the *Valiant* into the air. About 11 miles from the field, the engine suddenly lost all of its oil. Peggy tried to turn the airplane toward a nearby auxiliary airfield, but with no power to keep the craft flying, it stalled and crashed to earth. Peggy and Marion were still alive when the rescue team arrived and rushed them to the base hospital. Marion survived, but had severe injuries and suffered for weeks in hospitals before recovery. Peggy only lived for an hour after arriving at the hospital. She was returned to Southern California for burial in Whittier's Rose Hills Memorial Park.[12]

**Engineering test pilots were stationed across the country. Their hazardous job was to test repaired aircraft before returning them to regular service. Here, three WASP test pilots, ready, to fly their assigned mission, walk beside two Martin B-26 bombers at Laredo Army Airfield. Laredo was a flexible and aerial gunnery school for male cadets. - *National Archives photo 342-FH-4A-05360-40124AC.***

That same day, October 3, the press reported that General Arnold had decided to shut down the entire WASP program by December 20. Two days earlier, in a memo to Jackie Cochran, he explained his decision. "The reduction in the flying training program and the changing war situations bearing on availability and deployment of pilots, make it evident that the WASP will soon become pilot material in excess of need." He said that although he was proud of what the women had done, he emphasized that, "they are serving to release male pilots for other work and not to replace them." Arnold also prepared a letter of thanks and ordered it sent to every WASP and WASP trainee. "I am very proud of you young women and the outstanding job you have done as members of the Air Force team," he said. "When we needed you, you came through and have served most commendably under very difficult circumstances. … but now the war situation has changed and the time has come when your volunteered services are no longer needed. … if you continue in service, you will be replacing instead of releasing our young men. I know that the WASP wouldn't want that. … My sincerest thanks and Happy Landings always."[13]

Jackie Cochran wrote her own letter to the women, concluding with her thanks and her best wishes. "Each of you has made an important contribution to your country at war, and has aided immeasurably in establishing women's place in aviation. It has been a great honor to have been the Director of this program and a pleasure to have known most of you individually. My very best wishes for your future success and happiness."[14]

A few days later, responding to a letter from WASPs stationed at Biggs Field in El Paso, Texas, Jackie said she was proud of the outstanding record they had made, "in a field which was untried and in which few placed sufficient confidence in your ability. … It is with deep regret that I found it necessary to recommend inactivation of the entire program, for I know how sorry you girls will be to have to divorce yourselves from Army flying."[15]

Overall, the WASP women were angry that everything was ending; especially the WASPs who barely had a chance to fly. "Do I want the WASP to continue?" Mary Hillberg (44-W-6) said to an interviewer. "By all means. I was terribly disappointed when I heard they were closing the whole WASP program." Hillberg blamed bad publicity, "Like the false and misleading letters written by civilian pilots," she said. "The 'men' we were supposed to be releasing to fight a war didn't want to; they just wanted our non-combatant flying jobs." WASP Dolores Lamb (44-W-10) was also frustrated. "These young women like to fly," she said, "and I think most of them regard it as a serious job." There was a consensus that militarization would have provided the discipline and feeling of permanency needed for the program's best results. "The lack of it," Lamb said, "brought about much criticism and the girls themselves were at a loss with their 'half-in-half-out' status." Ann Brothers (44-W-3) felt militarization would have made the WASPs better and would have improved relationships with the regular Army staff. "My feeling as a WASP," she said, "has sometimes been that of an unwanted child—tolerantly adopted by the Army Air Forces, but never accepted or claimed as a relative. In spite of this—militarization or not—wanted or not wanted—I know American women pilots will be ready always to tackle any job that the Army Air Forces cared to hand them."[16]

Even with the limited number of days and hours left to fly before the program ended, there was still plenty of danger for the women pilots. Just 23 days before her graduation, October 16, 1944, Margie Davis (44-W-9) was in advanced training, flying solo on a 2,000-mile cross-country flight from Avenger Field in an AT-6 *Texan*. The destination for the flight of 13 aircraft was Courtland Army Airfield in north central Alabama. Their first refueling stop was the Stuttgart, Arkansas Army Airfield, where the women and Lieutenant Leonard Gonye, their instructor and flight leader, took a break and ate a meal before flying on.[17]

When Margie had graduated from Hollywood High School in 1941, Stuttgart, Arkansas was probably one of the last places she expected to be visiting. She told her high school yearbook committee that she planned to be a teacher. That fall, she entered UCLA in pursuit of a physical education major, but just two weeks before her 19th birthday, the Japanese bombed Pearl Harbor and Margie's education plans turned toward aviation. Without telling her parents, she left UCLA in 1943 and headed for Sparks, Nevada, just south of Reno. There, she shared a room and expenses with another woman and learned to fly at Gus Gustavson's Flying Service School that he called the Reno Sky Ranch. "Uncle Sam is training all the pilots he possibly can," read Gustavson's newspaper advertisement. "You can help by learning to fly." Margie did learn to fly and in a few months applied to the WASPs. On April 13, 1944, she began training at Avenger Field as part of what would become the next to the last class at Sweetwater.[18]

Born Marjorie Laverne Davis, December 20, 1922, in Hollywood, California, Margie was the second of five children and the first daughter of Clinton and Margaret Davis. Their third child, Robert had died before Margie was three. Born in Iowa, her father came to California with his family and worked on his father's farm near Hemet, about 70 miles southeast of Los Angeles. In 1920, Clinton married Margaret Anderson, left the farm, and moved to Los Angeles. By 1940, the family was living in West Hollywood and Clinton was the owner of an automobile painting business. When war broke out, he took a job at the Vega Aircraft plant, north of town, in Burbank. Margie was still going to college and hadn't told them about her dreams of flying.[19]

In Stuttgart, after they finished eating, Margie and the rest of the flight climbed into their planes and took off. At about 7:30 in the evening, Margie was about 90 miles from Courtland Field in Alabama and just over the Tennessee state line, a few miles south of Walnut, Mississippi. The sky was clear and temperatures were slowly dropping into the upper 40s. Except for the stars sparkling in a cloudless sky, it was dark. The sun had set over two hours earlier and the moon had disappeared nine minutes later. Flying by instruments, Margie was lost and already overdue at Courtland Field. Investigators found one witness who said Margie's plane had been flying in circles for nearly an hour. Apparently, she had tried to land in a field, but on her approach, she snagged a power line, snapping it in two. She accelerated and went around for another try. Crash investigators believed she had loosened her harness and opened the canopy to lean out in the dark and try to find the fast approaching ground. When her wheels touched down the impact forced her head against the edge of the cockpit canopy—hard enough to kill her. The plane slid to a stop just a few feet from an irrigation ditch.[20]

As flight leader and trainer, Lieutenant Gonye was with the women during the entire flight. When he landed in Alabama, he quickly realized that Margie had strayed and was missing. As he began the process of searching for her, word came that she had crashed and that Margie was dead—the last WASP to die in training. Hallie Stires (44-W-4), WASP and also Staff Advisor at Avenger Field, escorted Margie home to California for her burial in the Hollywood Forever Cemetery.[21]

At nearly the same moment that Margie was about to crash in Mississippi, a telegram was arriving at Darcy Lewellen's Columbus, Indiana home. His daughter's plane had crashed and Jeanne Marcille Lewellen Norbeck (44-W-3) was dead.

Late in the afternoon, October 16, 1944, Jeanne and Marybelle Lyall [44-W-4] flipped a coin to see which of two planes they would fly. A month before her 32$^{nd}$ birthday, Jeanne had just returned from a weekend visit with her parents in Columbus, Indiana. Jeanne won the flight line coin toss and chose the BT-13 that had just been released by mechanics. The previous pilot had said the plane had a "heavy wing," rolling slightly to the left. It was Jeanne's job to test it and make sure everything was now in working order.

Jeanne graduated from training at Avenger Field in April 1944 and was assigned to Shaw Army Airbase in South Carolina, about 8 miles northwest of Sumter. Before she reported to Shaw, she attended the controversial School of Applied Tactics in Orlando, Florida, what some believed was actually officer training for the women. A month later, with the course completed, she reported to Shaw as an engineering test pilot of repaired airplanes.

Just before 4 o'clock, Jeanne and Marybelle in separate airplanes were in the air and flying south toward the Shaw Field testing area, about 15 miles away. They were in constant radio contact and when they reached the test area, both agreed that their airplanes were flying well. They separated, flying in opposite directions. That was the last Marybelle ever heard from Jeanne. At 4:15, flying through a clear sky with little wind, Jeanne was heading back to base, flying at 500 feet, and entering the landing pattern. The plane slammed into the ground, upside down, canopy first. Jeanne never had a chance.[22]

Jeanne Lewellen was born November 14, 1912, in Columbus, Indiana, the daughter of Darcy Lewellen and Mayme Emmons. Her father was the founder and president of Lewellen Manufacturing, a company he set up just after WWI that specialized in transmissions and machinery. Not long after forming the company there was trouble at home. In 1921, Jeanne's mother filed for divorce, but within a month withdrew her suit. Two and a half years later, she filed again and the couple went to court, offering what one newspaper described as three days of "unusual testimony." Husband and wife carried on a scandalous series of accusations against each other, including infidelity and threats of physical violence. That spring, page one headlines and lengthy stories detailing their battles were plastered across many newspaper pages. Jeanne's father won his countersuit, receiving custody of 11-year-old Jeanne, while his wife received nothing, not even alimony support after 27 years of marriage.[23]

Jeanne graduated from Columbus High School in 1929, where she was junior and senior class secretary, senior yearbook editor, and a member of the Honor Society. "She was not afraid to be a leader," said classmate Dorothea Brandt, "and to do things that others of us would be too shy to do." She took a few flying lessons in her senior year, but didn't get her pilot's license until she was in college. Jeanne was an English major at the State College of Washington, today's Washington State University, in Pullman, Washington. She graduated with honors in 1933.[24]

While studying at State, Jeanne met Edward Norbeck who was finishing his degree. Edward had applied for a job with the Federal Land Bank, and taking the advice of one of his teachers, added five years to his age on his application. It must have worked. He was hired as secretary to the treasurer and was quickly promoted to head of the department. Between 1934 and 1938, with one year away to complete his studies at Washington State, Edward worked as assistant personnel manager and then as manager of the Mason City Hospital. The company hospital was set up by the contractors who were building the Grand Coulee Dam across the Columbia River in Washington. Edward was able to get Jeanne hired as a receptionist and secretary to the chief surgeon at the hospital, a position she held for four years.[25]

In Victoria, British Columbia, on April 13, 1938, Edward boarded the passenger liner *Aorangi*, for what was supposed to be a six-day vacation cruise to Hawaii. Once again, he had lied about his age, but this time only adding two years. Two months later, Jeanne was aboard the same ship and arriving in Honolulu. She found that Edward had decided to stay in Hawaii. He accepted a job as manager of the Libby, McNeil & Libby pineapple plantation in the Waipio Valley northwest of Honolulu. A week after Jeanne arrived in Hawaii, she returned to Washington and her job at the Mason City Hospital. Perhaps there had been a romance between her and Edward, or perhaps just a friendly visit between friends. Nevertheless, in the spring of the following year Jeanne's parents announced her engagement to Donald Paxton, a construction worker in Mason City. The engagement didn't last. During the summer of 1940, Jeanne returned to her Indiana home for a visit with the family and to tell her father that she and Edward Norbeck were going to marry. Shortly after her return to Honolulu in late September, Edward in a white, three-button, double breasted suit and Jeanne in a simple bridal gown were married.[26]

Edward Norbeck was born to Swedish immigrants, March 18, 1915, in Prince Albert, Saskatchewan, Canada. When he was 8 years old, he, his brother, and three sisters moved with their parents to Idaho and then Washington, where his father labored in the forest. Edward graduated from high school when he was 16 and then took on the challenge of a business college course, rushing through to completion in just five months. Then he entered the State College of Washington, where he met Jeanne.[27]

Jeanne and Edward lived about eight miles from the naval base at Pearl Harbor and could see the Japanese planes flying over during the December 7, 1941, attack. For nearly a year and a half, they suffered through food shortages, nighttime curfews, and martial law. Tens of thousands of civilians were anxious to return to the mainland, but the U.S. government wasn't sure of Japan's military strength east of Hawaii, and the possibility of an attack on the Pacific Coast, so they delayed evacuations for weeks.

In early 1943, with the threat of invasion eased, Jeanne and Edward returned to the mainland. In May, while in Los Angeles, Edward enlisted in the Army and Jeanne briefly returned to Indiana. Edward entered Army intelligence and began studying Japanese, eventually translating Japanese wartime transmissions. Jeanne was also anxious to join the war effort. She had flown some in high school and college and decided to apply to the WASPs, but she didn't have enough flight time to qualify. She went to Dallas and took more flying lessons at Love Field, and with just over the minimum of 35 hours, the WASPs accepted her as a pilot trainee. She began training October 4, 1943, and six months later, she was on her way to South Carolina.[28]

No one could remember a WASP's body ever receiving a military escort home; nevertheless, not only was an Army officer escorting Jeanne's body to Indiana; he also brought a flag to cover her casket. Now an Army corporal, Edward was studying at Fort Leonard Wood in Missouri and got a mere, one-day leave to attend the funeral. Jeanne's body arrived in Columbus late in the afternoon, October 19, and rested in her father's home. The next morning, after the closed casket funeral service ended, a procession followed Jeanne on the one-mile trip to the Garland Brook Cemetery. Edward returned to Fort Leonard Wood the next morning.[29]

Edward remarried in February 1950 and although he and his wife were parents of three children, Edward always carried a photograph of Jeanne with him. After his Army discharge in January 1947, he entered the University of Michigan, where he completed his Bachelor, Masters, and PhD degrees in anthropology. He was on the teaching staffs of the University of Utah and the University of California, Berkeley, before joining the staff at Rice University as an assistant professor of anthropology in 1960. Two years later, he took over as chairman of the department and remained there until he retired, ten years before his death in 1991 at age 76.[30]

A hush was echoing throughout Avenger Field. Fewer than 125 trainees still walked the flight line and lived in the barracks. After Class 44-W-9 graduated, November 8, there would be fewer than 70 of the women left. So far, 34 women had crashed and died, but for them, at least their remains had made it home to relatives and friends for burial. Now, with less than seven weeks to go before the last class graduated at Sweetwater, and two months before the end of the entire WASP program, there was genuine hope and a little bit of prayer, that no one else would have to die.

Gertrude Vreeland Tomkins (43-W-7) had stuttered all of her life. Even after a year tending goats in the tranquil country, the shy New Jersey girl couldn't help herself through one embarrassing conversation after another. She had graduated from the prestigious Kent Place, a girl's private school in Summit, New Jersey, but years of teasing from other students had only made things worse, and a year in the countryside just wasn't enough.[31]

Gertrude was the third and youngest daughter of Vreeland and Laura Tompkins, born October 16, 1912. Vreeland was a graduate of Rutgers and an expert chemist. Soon after graduation from college, he found a way to manufacture concrete that could "withstand red heat, steam, water, or oil, and expand and contract like steel." He called it "Iron Cement," and in 1895 set up the Smooth-On factory in Jersey City, New Jersey. It was a grand success. The family lived quite comfortably and his daughters had the pick of all the finest colleges, but perhaps, because of her shyness, Gertrude modestly chose the Pennsylvania School of Horticulture for Women in Ambler, Pennsylvania, just north of Philadelphia. There, her interest in farm animals blossomed. She had found her calling, at least for the moment. For the next decade, when she wasn't home helping her father at his factory, Gertrude made frequent trips to all parts of the world, sometimes with family, but usually alone. She wanted to see the world's farms and gardens. She traveled to England, Italy, Spain, and France. Her family remembers that during her trip to New Zealand and Australia in the winter of 1935-1936, Gertrude tried diligently to convince Australian government officials to encourage more people to raise goats instead of cattle, because, as she said, goats were better for the environment and also more nutritious.[32]

Gertrude's sister, Elizabeth Whittall, told a reporter that when Gertrude was young, she fell in love with a young pilot who was teaching her to fly at a Long Island airfield. No one remembers his name. Gertrude loved to fly and she soon found that aviation had a major advantage. "She didn't stutter when she was in a plane, or the whole time she was in the WASP," Whittall said. Probably inspired in part by thoughts of her young man, airplanes had become Gertrude's newest calling, replacing her farm animals. Sadly for her, the young man felt a sense of duty, and rather than wait for the United States to enter the war, he joined the RAF as a fighter pilot. Not long after his arrival in England he died when German pilots shot him down.[33]

Gertrude entered training at Avenger Field on May 23, 1943, and was one of 59 out of 101 trainees to successfully graduate on

November 13. Her assignment was with the 5th Ferrying Group at Love Field in Dallas. For nearly a year she flew almost every type of plane produced for the Army, and after a month's worth of training at the Palm Springs Army Airfield, she qualified to fly the P-51 *Mustang* and other pursuit aircraft. Perhaps it was at Dallas where she met Technical Sergeant Henry Mann Silver.

Henry was the son of Dr. Lewis Silver and his wife, Roberta. Born November 6, 1904, Henry was named after his uncle, who was also a physician. In 1918, Henry entered the Classical Studies Department at the Phillips Academy in Andover, Massachusetts. It was a private boarding high school for boys. After four years studying at Phillips, he entered Yale, where he graduated in 1926. The Columbia University Press hired Henry, and by 1942 he was manager of their subsidiary, King's Crown Press. In June 1942, he took a leave of absence from the company and joined the Army.[34]

Gertrude and Henry announced their plans to marry at the end of November 1943. Henry's 46-year-old sister, Marguerite, had passed away in late September, shortly after giving birth to a girl. Her husband had died in 1939 and there were rumors that she had been having an affair with a Boston physician. Henry was determined to adopt the now orphaned baby; something Gertrude must have known about and agreed to before their engagement. Ten months later, September 22, 1944, Gertrude and Henry, both in uniforms, married at the Tompkins' summer home in Bridgehampton, New York. There wasn't much time for a honeymoon as Gertrude and Henry returned to their duty assignments.[35]

Returning to Love Field, Gertrude received orders to report to the North American Aviation factory alongside Mines Field (now part of the Los Angeles International Airport). She and 40 other women would fly brand new P-51 fighters from Los Angeles to Newark, New Jersey. Once they reached Newark, the planes were partially disassembled, put on ships, and then sent on to England and the European war. Because WASPs could only fly during daylight hours and had orders to spend nights at an Army airfield, the cross-country hop would take at least four days.

On October 26, 1944, Gertrude reported to Mines Field at about 2:00 in the afternoon. She had already flown over 753 hours and 46 of those hours were in P-51s. There was a lingering fog at about 2,500 feet. Temperatures were cool, hovering in the mid to lower 60s. Trouble with a canopy that wouldn't lock and its subsequent repair, delayed her takeoff until sometime around 4:00 that afternoon. Leaving the runway, she flew west over Santa Monica Bay, disappearing into the fog. Because night was approaching and it would be too dark for her to fly all the way to the first scheduled overnight stay at Coolidge Airfield, Arizona, she would have to land and spend the night at Palm Springs. She never made it. Gertrude Silver had disappeared, but no one noticed for another four days, not until the 5th Ferrying Group officials in Dallas realized they had not received any reports from Gertrude. They contacted Los Angeles to ask where she was. The next day an extensive search began from Santa Monica Bay in the west all the way east into Arizona. They didn't find a thing. On November 1, the Army finally notified Henry Silver and Gertrude's father that Gertrude was missing. She had vanished just 10 days after her 32nd birthday. Although there have been many subsequent search attempts over the years, Gertrude has never been found.[36]

Henry never remarried and continued to raise his adopted daughter as his own, telling the world that Gertrude was her mother. He took over as president of the Smooth-On Manufacturing Company in 1953, just two years before Gertrude's father died. In 1964, Henry gave his daughter away in marriage. Six months later—he died at age 60.[37]

# [15]

## CHINA-GAL AND THE HANDWRITING EXPERT

No one was afraid of "The Flying Coffin" anymore. The now accepted theory said, if the women could do it, so could the men.

When first introduced, the Martin B-26 *Marauder* bomber was a very difficult airplane for Army trainees to fly. Early on, there were so many training accidents that the twin-engine bomber probably earned more negative nicknames than any other aircraft ever. To the male pilots she was the "Widow Maker," "The B-Dash Crash," "The One-Way Ticket," "The Martin Murderer," "The Coffin without Handles," and many, many more. In Florida, the trainees at MacDill Army Airfield had so many takeoff accidents and "water landings," they began to put their frustration into rhyme—"One a day into Tampa Bay" they chanted.

In early November 1944, the Command pilot training school near Dodge City, Kansas, announced that the "Widow Maker" was now "tenderly regarded by qualified airmen as a plane to be feared by its enemies," not its pilots. In the previous six months of training, with flights totaling a distance equal to a trip around the moon, there had not been a single fatal accident. "This," said an Air Force spokesman, "along with reports of combat successes, has blasted the accusation that the lethal bullet-shaped medium bomber is a temperamental 'baby.'" Credit for the success went to a 10-week intensive transition course that replaced the original on-the-job training. It was the same B-26 transitional training that WASP Bonnie Welz and others had helped pioneer with other male pilots. The Army had cashed in on their bet that training a few WASPs to fly the "Coffin" would shame any hesitant male and overcome their fears. In the world of 1944, when men were men and women were "girls," a female at the controls of a huge aircraft was a not so subtle push against a man's ego.[1]

On November 4, tears were flowing at the Avengerette Club in downtown Sweetwater. Class 44-W-9, the 17th and next to the last class of Avenger trainees, were saying goodbye to each other. Of course it was sad to leave friends who had shared the joys and pains, struggling to become a WASP, but even more devastating was realizing they had less than two months to fly before everything ended. Music from the Big Spring Bombardier Band and dancing with their invited young men, helped ease emotions and cheer their spirits, but never far away were thoughts of their vanishing dreams and going home.[2]

"I am sorry your future in the Air Forces is not brighter," said Colonel Edward Suarez, principal speaker at Monday's graduation ceremonies. As an assistant to the chief of staff at the Army Air Force Training Command, Suarez offered a personal message. "I wish you could serve with us for the rest of your lives." As they handed out diplomas and pinned on silver wings, Jackie Cochran stood beside Col. Suarez. This was the first graduation Jackie had attended since the deactivation announcement. Her comments were brief, simply telling the women how proud she was of them and wishing them the best.[3]

The following day, November 7, was Election Day, and although the final tally would take days to compute, there was little doubt that President Franklin Delano Roosevelt would overwhelmingly be reelected to a fourth term. The president ultimately won by 3.5 million votes and captured 432 electoral votes against Republican Thomas Dewey's 99.

On November 19, Jackie Cochran was in Oklahoma City addressing the National Aviation Clinic. It was a meeting of leaders in the aviation industry who were discussing how to expand civil aviation after the war. Jackie warned them not to think that flying was just a "man's game." She told them that women had been "overlooked or discounted to the great disadvantage of our aviation industry." She reminded them that women greatly outnumbered men in the country and that women controlled a higher percentage of the nation's wealth. "If the airline companies, the aviation schools, and the plane manufacturers wish to broaden their customer lists," she said, "the industry is going to have to cater to 'petticoat pilots.' … American women are just as susceptible to the lure of flying as are American men." In conclusion, she said women were "the major hope for expanded aviation activity."[4]

Meanwhile, in Sweetwater, the city commissioners and officials of the Chamber of Commerce were scrambling to find a revenue stream to support the postwar utilization of Avenger Field, before it once again became the city's municipal airport. They hoped that once the

WASP trainees were gone, the Army would still be using Avenger, but they wondered how to pay for maintenance on the airfield when the Army no longer needed it. At a commissioners meeting, City Manager Robert Hoppe said negotiations were ongoing to secure a proposed Air Force installation larger than the WASP program, with perhaps 1,000 military personnel on base. "Sweetwater is being considered," Hoppe said, "conditions look very favorable."[5]

At the same meeting, WASP Hally Stires (44-W-4), Staff Advisor at Avenger, asked the city to reduce rent on the Avengerette Club, because there was only one class of women left to train and, before Avenger Field closed, the women would only use the club one more time. The commission agreed.[6]

Meanwhile, Peggy Nispel (44-W-5) became a very lucky WASP. At 9,000 feet, parachuting in the middle of the night into Arizona's Huachuca Mountains from a BT-13 sputtering through a turbulent thunderstorm, her name could easily been added to the growing list of dead WASPs. Graduating from Avenger Field, June 27, 1944, Peggy's assignment was as an engineering test pilot at Marana Air Base in Arizona. It was the same base where Peggy Martin had lost her life in a repaired BT-13 just a month earlier. High winds and a killing frost that lasted nearly every night for a month, had warned area residents that a hard winter was coming.

Peggy's plane had gone dark in the sky—an electrical failure. It was Peggy's first jump and a terrifying leap into the blackness below. There were the occasional lightning flashes and those agonizing minutes of falling down onto an unknown rock and tree covered landscape, but the jump was surprisingly trouble free. She gathered her parachute into a bundle and began walking. After two hours of stumbling around in the dark, falling down and bruising her cheek, Peggy worried that she might drop into a crevice or walk off a cliff. She stopped and climbed onto the low branches of a tree, wrapped herself in her parachute, and tried to sleep until dawn. All night, strange sounds would suddenly wake her from her restless sleep. Later, she'd say the sound of howling coyotes didn't bother her, but she did admit she worried about meeting a rattlesnake. Thankfully, she hadn't known that hunters had been out in the mountains with their dogs for days, hunting mountain lions.[7]

In the morning she began walking, still clutching her parachute bundle. For three days, she followed a creek downhill until she found a road. She began walking down, hoping she would find some sort of civilization. A couple, driving by in a car, saw ahead what they thought was a "Mexican or black man or woman." The person was carrying what looked like a large sheet in their arms. "We weren't going to pick up someone and their laundry," they said in a letter to Peggy's hometown newspaper, "and we didn't slow down." However, as they passed by, they realized they were wrong. "Imagine our surprise," they said, "we had passed a sunburned young girl in a blue military costume, holding of all things, an open parachute. We stopped and backed up in a hurry." Peggy asked them to take her to the nearest Army Post, worried that by now her parents thought she was dead. When they reached Fort Huachuca, near Sierra Vista, Arizona, they discovered the commanding officer and his assistants hadn't yet arrived for duty. The couple took Peggy to the post cafe for breakfast, her first meal since breakfast four days earlier. She returned to her base and continued to fly for the next few weeks. When the WASP program ended in December, she and the 16 other WASPs stationed at Marana Airfield returned home. Peggy lived until 1974, dying in Dallas when she was 53.[8]

Only two native born Americans of Chinese ancestry became WASPs—Maggie Gee (44-W-9) who was born in Berkeley, California; and Hazel Ying Lee Louie (43-W-4), born in Portland, Oregon. Maggie survived the war, but Hazel did not.

Hazel was lost and running out of fuel somewhere in Kansas. Still in training, she and three other women were flying BT-13s cross-country. They finally realized they were lost. They didn't even know what part of Texas they were looking at and had no idea of which direction to take home. "Nobody, absolutely nobody, gets lost on cross-country," said one of the WASP trainees. She anonymously wrote their story for the base newspaper. "You may meander about a bit looking for jack rabbits," she said, "or get off course while you repair your lipstick; but you blithely tell your instructor, 'I was hitting every checkpoint right on the nose.'" The nameless author had landed safely at the Cisco, Texas airport, and although she wanted to remain anonymous in her story, she didn't hesitate to name her directionally clueless WASP partners. Kathleen Kelly had landed at the military aviation school in Brady, Texas, and Hazel landed in a recently plowed cotton field.[9]

After climbing out of the cockpit, Hazel looked over the plane to see if there was any damage, but didn't have much time to figure it out. A green sedan, trailing a dust cloud, came clattering across the field and slid into a rocky stop beside Hazel and the BT-13. A farmer and his wife stepped out. The woman held tightly to her baby as her husband spoke. "Are you a China-gal or Japanee?" the farmer asked. "I'm a China-gal, sir," Hazel said, pointing to her nametag. "Well dag gum it,"

Flying cross-country was challenging and required careful planning and complete attention to detail when in the air. You have to "hit every checkpoint right on the nose", said one trainee. Otherwise, you'll be lost. – *Air Force photo 080717-F-1234P-004.*

he said. "You sure made a purty landing."[10]

Hazel told the farmer she needed to call Avenger Field and let them know about her trouble. The farmer, Mr. Doty, told her to get in the car and he would take her to his phone. It was a slow 10-mile trip for Doty's stubborn sedan, equipped with a radiator that was boiling over most of the time. When they got to Doty's home, steam was gushing. The long distance telephone connection with Avenger was poor, both sides shouting at each other to get the story across. It was already getting dark and no one was coming to Hazel's rescue until the next day. The Dotys invited her to sit with them for a supper of fried eggs and bacon. They had an evening chat, and then they showed her to their spare bedroom and wished her a good night's rest. "I slept restlessly," Hazel said, "and was up early for a breakfast of more fried eggs and bacon."

About mid-morning, she heard a plane overhead and went outside to see it circling in the distance above her downed BT-13. Lunch was a helping of fried eggs and bacon, followed by Mr. Doty rocking his chair like an agitated oil derrick, holding his baby son, and singing cowboy songs. Late in the afternoon, as Mrs. Doty began another fried egg and bacon supper, five soldiers arrived in an Army car. "Boy. Am I glad to see you!" Hazel said. They told her they were glad to see her too. To them, it seemed that they had opened just about every gate in West Texas trying to find the Doty farmhouse.

As she was leaving and saying her thanks and goodbyes to the Dotys, Mr. Doty got a serious look on his face. "Miss Lee," he said. "What they goin' to do to you—put you in the cooler, or whut? Le'me hear from you—dag gum it."[11]

Hazel Ying Lee was born in Portland, Oregon, August 24 1912. Her father, Yuet Lee, came to the United States in 1880, eventually returning to China, where he married Ssiu Lan, 20 years his junior. In 1910, he brought his wife and their two children to Portland. The rest of their eight children, including Hazel, were born in Portland. The family lived on NW 4th Avenue in Portland's Chinatown, where Yuet also owned a store and was a partner in some Chinese restaurants.[12]

Hazel took ballet lessons at the local YWCA and during her early years, she danced in a number of different venues. One of her earliest performances was in 1921, when Hazel was 8 years old. The YWCA was hosting a "Fairyland" at a nearby church; featuring dancers from the Y. There was a crowning of a fairy queen and dancing by over 40 young girls. Little Hazel's dance received a positive review in the newspaper. "Hazel Lee, a Chinese girl who was dressed in a rose-red ballet costume, danced a solo dance called *A Red, Red, Rose.* This proved a popular number." If she wasn't dancing, playing, or helping in her father's store, she was selling Girl Scout cookies. Except for the many occasions when she was asked to wear traditional Chinese clothing for parties and special events, she was just a typical girl growing up in a big city. Her friends and fellow performers were never just Chinese.[13]

After finishing studies at the old Atkinson Grammar School, where a majority of the students were Chinese, Hazel attended the High School of Commerce. After graduation, she got a job in the stockroom of H. Liebes & Company, a women's furnishing store. It was less than 10 blocks from her home. Soon she became the company's smiling elevator operator.[14]

In September 1931, the Japanese Army invaded Manchuria. When American-Chinese heard about the bombing of civilians in Chinese cities, they were outraged. Chinese patriots worldwide quickly contributed over $20,000 to fund flight training in the United States for pilots who would fly and fight for China. The newly formed Chinese Flying Club of Portland began accepting memberships late that November, and by May 1932, flight instructor Al Greenwood was teaching 36 students in two classes, including Hazel Lee, one of only two women to sign up. Students came from as far away as Chicago and New York. Lessons commenced on Swan Island, in the Columbia River, from Portland's first airport. While learning to fly, trainees lived in barracks built and funded by the Chinese Aeronautical Association of America. They were required to sign a pledge that, if needed, they would forfeit their life for China. Without hesitation, they all signed.[15]

On one day, instructor Greenwood and an assistant would fly nine hours with half of the Chinese trainees, and the next day fly nine hours with the remaining 18. "I was surprised," Greenwood said, "at the ease with which they picked up the elements, and advanced rapidly into the more intricate phases of flying. They were fine students, they worked hard, and they really knew what flying was all about." Other local pilots told Greenwood that he would have nothing but trouble with the Chinese pilots because they believed the Chinese couldn't fly and would crash all of his airplanes. "Well Sir," a proud Greenwood told a reporter, "we flew 1,600 hours, including 30 to 40 hours of solo for each student, in two airplanes without an accident—without breaking a wing!"

In six months, all but four of the trainees soloed and earned their pilot's license. Each had accumulated at least 45 hours in the air, including 10 hours of spins, loops, rolls, and other aerial maneuvers. Fifteen of Greenwood's students left in August for Canton, China, enlisting in the Cantonese air force. The second group of 17, including Hazel, who had earned her pilot's license in October, left for Shanghai in March 1933. There they joined the national government's air force.[16]

"My ambition," 20-year-old Hazel said, "is to stimulate interest in aviation and flying among the women in China." She was taking a short break from running the department store elevator to answer reporters' questions. "I have no elaborate plans," she said. "I am going over to see what's what, and to do what I can to interest others in aviation." She had gotten the urge to fly during her first ride in an airplane. "That was at the Christofferson Airport on the Columbia River Highway," she said. "The instructor of a group of Chinese boys took me up for a ride. … It appealed to me. It was a distinct thrill." Reporters asked her how long she planned to stay in China. "It's an indefinite stay," she said. "Of course, I will come back sometime to see how things are moving in Portland." Before she left, 40 of the women who also worked at the store gave her a goodbye dinner.[17]

When she arrived in China, Hazel learned that the Chinese wouldn't allow her to fly combat missions, but she could fly cargo and passengers that were important to the war effort. The Chinese Commission on Aeronautical Affairs gave her the rank of 2nd lieutenant and sent her for further training. "Thanks to the Chinese government," she said, "I was able to continue flying. They gave me my own plane." She met and occasionally flew with Madame Chiang Kai-Shek, China's Secretary General of the Commission on Aeronautical Affairs and wife of the military and political leader of the Chinese Republic. Hazel knew her well and admired her. By the spring of 1935, Hazel was teaching flying at the Nanchang air base and dropping propaganda leaflets over the countryside. Hazel was in Canton on Easter Sunday, April 17, 1938, when 27 Japanese aviators, flying in three squadrons, bombed several of the poorest sections of the city, killing over 250 civilians. "The Chinese anti-aircraft guns kept the bombers pretty high," she said, "some 6,000 or 8,000 feet, I judged—and at last scattered them."[18]

In late November 1938, Hazel returned home after nearly six years of war in China. She praised the effort of the Chinese-American fliers who had gone with her to China and those who were still alive continuing to fight. "I was told that the boys who were shot down gave excellent accounts of themselves before they were killed," Hazel said. How long would the war last, reporters asked. "Until the Japanese say they will stop," she said, "until they give China back all her territory they have taken. … I think the Chinese were never more united than they are now."[19]

Hazel had seen terrible devastation in what seemed like an endless war. Just before leaving China, she had visited a refugee camp for mothers of young babies, and now she was asking Americans to help them. "They don't need money," she said, "but they are very much in need of clothing, food, and medical supplies." When she and three of her friends learned that scrap metal bound for Japan was about to leave Portland on a ship, the four of them formed a small waterfront demonstration. "America must stop these shipments to Japan in the interest of humanity," Hazel said. "We've seen pieces of scrap metal burst from bombs and kill or wound everyone in range." The young women made their point and got the publicity they sought, but the ship still sailed on.[20]

Hazel left for New York City to live with her older sister Rose and her family. "Between 1938 and 1942, I did very little flying," Hazel told a reporter. Instead, she first became a lecturer at Ripley's Odditorium in New York City, a museum of weird and unusual stories and artifacts collected by Robert Ripley, creator of the "Ripley's Believe It or Not!" newspaper feature. Then she began working for the Chinese government at the Universal Trading Corporation, supporting the Chinese war effort by finding and buying necessary war materials.[21]

When WASP recruitment began in late 1942, Hazel didn't have enough flying hours to qualify. It was a disappointment, but there was a bright side. "In the meantime, I met my future husband," she said. While working for Universal Trading, Hazel was reunited with Clifford Yim-Qun Louie, now a major in the Chinese air force. In Portland, when they were younger, Clifford and Hazel took those flying lessons with Al Greenwood and then left for China together. Clifford entered combat, where he rose to the rank of squadron leader and shot down at least three Japanese enemy aircraft, receiving decorations from the Chinese government for his distinguished service. Wounded in the war that was still ravaging the Chinese mainland, Clifford returned to United States for recovery and some military training with the Army. While in New York, he and Hazel had met again and apparently began or rekindled a romance.[22]

When the Air Corps reduced the required flight hours needed to apply for the WASP program, Hazel almost immediately applied. Her training at Sweetwater began in February 1943. Clifford managed to get a brief visit with her at Avenger Field, just as training began and returned a few more times in the following months. Hazel quickly became a favorite with her classmates. They voted her one of the best-liked pilots on all of Avenger Field. When a reporter asked about her popularity, she modestly told him, "Everyone is just as popular as any other. The climate is hot, the wind blows all the time, but all the people are nice." After graduation in August 1943, Hazel returned to New York City, before taking up her assignment with the 3rd Ferrying Group at Romulus Air Base in Michigan. New York's Chinatown mayor, Shavey Lee, invited Hazel and Clifford to a dinner in her honor and presented a scroll that celebrated Hazel as the first woman of Chinese heritage to become a WASP. On October 9, Hazel and Clifford married. They had just nine days together before he returned to the Japanese front in China and she returned to ferrying planes.[23]

That December, Hazel was once again on her way to Canada with two other WASPs, flying on what they called the "icicle lane." They were delivering Fairchild PT-26 *Cornells* to the Royal Canadian Air Force. The RCAF used the plane as a trainer for their aviation cadets. Although it featured two cockpits and room for two pilots, the women flew the planes alone. The flight began in Minneapolis, Minnesota from a snow packed field with temperatures lingering at zero on a bright sunny day. Because a recent blizzard had already kept the planes on the ground for days, a ground crew worker said he was sure that no matter who the pilots were, "They'll never get those crates off today. It'll take a week just to thaw them out." When the man saw that the pilots were women, he was doubly sure the planes were staying right where they were.[24]

Looking like overinflated, puffy-blue snowmen in their winter flying suits, the women waddled to their planes. The temperature at flying altitude was likely 20 degrees below zero, and although the cockpit was equipped with a heater and a sliding canopy, it was best to be prepared for any trouble. Besides wearing their normal flying outfits, the women had also put on the heavy fleece-lined flight suits, helmets, boots, furry gloves, and chamois facemasks. It all weighed about 60 pounds, and that didn't include their 26-pound parachute. The Army said their winter flight outfits would keep them safe in an unheated cockpit all the way down to a temperature of 35 degrees below zero.

Even with the warming rays of the sun, it took close to five hours for the women and ground crew, to broom the snow off the airplanes, chip ice off the wings, clean and unstick the transparent canopies with alcohol soaked rags, and then try to coax the reluctant engines back to life. With the runway cleared ahead, they were off on what was one of their shorter winter flights—12 ½ hours. Nevertheless, there were

"They're zootier than Zoot Suits," said one WASP trainee. The Army said these bulky men's winter flying suits would keep the women safe all the way down to 35 degrees below zero. - *Air Force photo 140307 F XX000 010.*

more weather delays. In the end, it took another full week to get to Canada. Sometimes the weather would be so bad it would take 18 or more days to complete a delivery.

Hazel graduated in June 1944 from the School of Applied Tactics in Orlando, Florida, what some were saying was actually officer training. By October, she was almost finished with pursuit training in Brownsville, Texas, and had already mastered the P-39 *Airacobra*, the P-63 *Kingcobra*, the P-51 *Mustang*, and the P-47 *Thunderbolt* fighters. Because she was so short, it was hard to believe she was even able to fly something as big as the P-47. When she was sitting in the cockpit, the only thing showing was her head. She was excited to fly some of the country's most powerful aircraft. "It's a great thrill to lift one of these thundering fighters into the air," she said. A reporter wanted to know if flying for the WASP was fun. "No," she said. "It's work. I've known girls who have been away from their home base for as many as seven weeks. We ferry a plane from Detroit to Chicago. Orders may then take us to somewhere in Pennsylvania, and before getting back to our home base, we may have gone to California, Nebraska, Texas, and New Jersey." She praised the training she was getting. "We're watched very carefully," she said. "After every landing our instructor comes and talks it over with us and points out any mistakes we may have made. When we graduate, we will be returned to our home bases to carry on with ferrying fighter and other type of aircraft."[25]

After graduation from pursuit school, on October 2, Hazel returned to her ferrying duties at Romulus. Late in November, she received orders to report to the Bell Aircraft factory in Niagara Falls, New York. There she would pick up a P-63 *Kingcobra* and fly it from the assembly line to Great Falls, Montana. From Montana, male pilots would ferry the airplane to Alaska, where Russian allies would pick it up and fly it back to the Soviet Union.

Hazel and the women she was flying with managed to get as far as the Fargo, North Dakota Airfield before bad weather and low clouds kept them on the ground for a few days. Finally, there was a brief clearing in the sub-zero sky and they were off again.

On Thanksgiving Day, November 23, just after 2:00 in the afternoon, Hazel was on final approach to Great Falls Army Airfield. It was a busy day for air controllers with many airplanes taking off and landing. While Hazel was on final approach, Lieutenant Charles Russell was making an emergency landing in his P-63 without control from the tower. His radio wasn't working and he didn't see Hazel below him. When the controller saw the impending collision between the two aircraft, he ordered both pilots to pull up and abort their landings. Russell never heard the order, but Hazel did immediately pull up and smashed into the belly of Russell's descending plane. There was a loud explosion and a huge fireball as the aircraft fell to the runway. Russell managed to get out and run to safety with minor injuries, but Hazel, knocked unconscious and trapped in the burning plane, had to wait for the rescue crew to arrive. They pulled her from the plane and removed her smoldering flight suit as they rushed her to the base hospital. Severely burned and in critical condition, she regained consciousness and suffered terribly for two days before she died—but she never complained.[26]

Three days later, while Hazel's sister, Florence Chung, was planning Hazel's funeral, their brother, Corporal Victor Ling Lee died in France. After landing on Utah Beach shortly after the D-Day invasion, Victor's unit, Company C of the 607th Tank Destroyer Battalion, fought across France and eventually into Germany. On November 28, the day Victor died; Company C was defending the French town of Falck, near the German border in the Saar Valley. German forces opened a barrage of artillery and mortars from the nearby hills and followed with several unsuccessful infantry attempts to take the town. The battle was costly to both sides and Victor's family never found out exactly how Victor died.[27]

Officials at Portland's Riverview Cemetery at first opposed Hazel's burial because she was Chinese, but her sister Florence Chung convinced them that refusal would bring them bad publicity. On December 1, 1944, after a morning memorial service, Hazel Ying Lee Louie's family buried her in a vaulted gravesite overlooking the Willamette River.[28]

Her brother Victor rested in France until after the war, when Portland veterans remembered him by organizing the Victor Ying Lee, all Chinese American Legion Post. Two and a half years later, in September 1948, Victor finally came home to a military burial beside his sister at Riverview Cemetery. Members of the Victor Ying Lee Legion Post conducted the ceremonies.[29]

The day after Hazel died; 39-year-old Kay Dussaq (44-W-1) was in trouble over Western Ohio. Perhaps it was the freezing rain, the fog, or ice, but at about 8:45 in the evening Kay's AT-6 was going down near New Carlisle, Ohio. For some reason, Kay was not wearing her safety harness, and when the plane crashed, she struck her head on the control stick and died instantly.[30]

Katherine Applegate was born in Dayton, Washington, March 14,

1905. Hers was an Oregon pioneer family. In 1846, her great uncle, Jesse Applegate, had blazed the Applegate Trail into the Oregon Territory. Her Father, Arthur McClellan Applegate, had risen from laboring in a flourmill to manager of several flour mills in Oregon and Washington. He had married Kay's mother, Clare Moritz, in November 1898. Kay was their third daughter and grew up in Dayton with her three sisters and two brothers. After graduation from Harrington High School, she attended Whitman College in Walla Walla, Washington, and then the State College of Washington in Pullman. In 1924, she was one of 70 students out of 700 applicants accepted by Stanford University, in Palo Alto, California. She graduated in 1927 with a degree in Psychology.[31]

After graduation, Kay and a female student from the University of California, Berkeley, snuck aboard the passenger liner *Maui* in San Francisco and stowed away until the ship was well on its way to Honolulu. They had mailed suitcases of clothing ahead by parcel post, intending to get to Hawaii without paying for a ticket. Two days out on the Pacific, a *Maui* crewmember discovered the girls and took them to the ship's captain. The captain told them they could freely roam the ship until the liner *Matsonia* passed by on its way back east to the mainland. Then, he said he would transfer them to the *Matsonia* and send them home. Amazingly, just before the *Matsonia* appeared on the horizon, Kay and her friend both suddenly developed symptoms of seasickness that steadily grew worse as the *Matsonia* approached. The ship's surgeon decided that the women were just too sick to risk a transfer and the crew watched as the *Matsonia's* smoke disappeared on the eastern horizon. On May 5th, 1927, the ship docked in Honolulu Harbor and the two stowaways, identically dressed, walked down the gangplank without paying a cent for their ocean voyage or any of its services. They smiled at the captain and then rushed off the pier to the post office, where they picked up their luggage.[32]

Kay got a supervisor's job in a pineapple cannery, drove a sightseeing bus, and learned to fly in her spare time. Six months after she arrived, she returned to the mainland, this time with a ticket in hand. She settled for a while in Portland, Oregon, writing advertising copy for a department store. But in 1929, she and one of her friends from Stanford, Leonarde Keeler, went to Chicago and began working at Northwestern University in the Scientific Crime Detection Laboratory. Created in July 1929, after the shocking St. Valentine's Day Massacre, law enforcement believed the laboratory would improve collection of evidence and solve more crimes. "I followed Mr. Keeler to

Chicago," Kay told reporters. Kay and Leonarde married, August 14, 1930.[33]

Keeler continued his experiments that had begun at the University of California on what would become the modern lie detector. Kay immersed herself in forensic sciences. With eyes in a microscope, she studied fingerprints and handwriting, soon becoming the country's first female handwriting expert and an expert witness in criminal and civil trials. "Her eloquence on the witness stand," one reporter said, "has helped to lodge many a kidnaper and forger behind bars." She said she didn't like parties and preferred to spend her free time training her German Shepherd puppy, watching wrestling, and following the latest developments in aircraft engineering. She hired a housekeeper to take care of the couple's high-rise apartment, because, "I don't have time for anything but work."[34]

When Northwestern sold the criminal laboratory in 1938, Keeler became a private polygraph consultant and opened a polygraph school, while Kay, along with three of her assistants, set up her own private laboratory. Perhaps this is when the marriage began to fall apart. There were rumors that they both engaged in extracurricular affairs and that tensions between them grew quite heated at times. In April 1941, the couple officially separated, although the actual separation likely occurred much earlier. In May, Kay filed for divorce, ending their nearly 10-year marriage, Kay saying Keeler had abandoned her.[35]

By December, the divorce was final and Kay married Rene Dussaq. Dussaq was a popular lecturer, particularly with women. Born in Argentina, he graduated from the Sorbonne in Paris and was fluent in a number of languages. He had an international athletic reputation, having held tennis championships in Switzerland and Cuba, and had competed as a rower and coxswain in the Olympics twice. Within days of their marriage, the Japanese bombed Pearl Harbor and in March 1942, Dussaq enlisted. Besides wanting to be a part of the war effort, Dussaq had another reason for his enlistment. Because he spoke with an accent, suspicious citizens often reported him to the FBI, and during the three months after his marriage, he had been arrested four times as a potential spy. He trained as a paratrooper in the United States and then left for Europe. Because of his language ability and familiarity with Europe, the Army sent him on a secret mission. On May 22, 1944, just days before D-Day, Dussaq, wearing civilian clothes, parachuted behind German lines and began organizing and training resistance forces. He taught sabotage and guerilla warfare, and led raids against enemy forces and installations. After the war, he received the Distinguished Service

Cross for "the courage and skill with which he planned and executed his operations against the enemy."[36]

Kay closed her consulting business and went to work for the Piper Aircraft Cooperation in Lock Haven, Pennsylvania. She had already been flying whenever she could, but as an employee at Piper, she joined with other women who were all encouraged to fly as part of the company's "Cub Flyers" program. Kay applied to the WASPs and began training at Avenger Field, August 9, 1943. By graduation the following February, she had raised her total flying time to over 400 hours. Her assignment was Sioux Falls Army Base in South Dakota, but soon she transferred to Randolph Field, near San Antonio, Texas. Because of her flying hours, and the recognition she had attained during her decade of scientific crime fighting, at age 39, Kay moved quickly from staff pilot to Coordinator of WASP activities. She now had a greater say in operational activities. Just before her fatal flight, Kay had received another promotion. She moved to Training Command Headquarters in Houston as WASP Executive for all three training commands.[37]

After her crash on November 26, Kay returned home for burial between her mother and father in the Dayton, Washington City Cemetery. Her ex-husband, Leonarde Keeler, died of heart trouble on September 20, 1949. Rene Dussaq, remarried, continued to lecture, and became an executive with the Prudential Insurance Company. He died June 5, 1996 at age 85.[38]

Kay Dussaq had been in on the discussions with Jackie Cochran and Army staff over what to do for the WASPs after deactivation. With her help, the Army agreed that each WASP would be issued a card listing her aircraft horsepower qualification and designating her as a rated pilot of military aircraft. There would also be a certificate of honorable service and discharge, similar to those issued to Army officers when relieved from active duty. Should a WASP wish to pursue a civilian aviation career, the card would help her acquire a commercial aviation license from the Civil Aeronautics Authority. She would still have to pass a written examination on air commerce rules, but no flight check was required. The pathway to a commercial license was quite an incentive and Army officials realized it would tempt some of the women to leave the program immediately. To avoid a mass exodus of pilots, the plan required a WASP to continue working as a WASP until November 20, 1944. Not many left, but a few did, and that arbitrary date would mean sudden death for two former WASPs and a WASP trainee.[39]

# [16]

## STARDUST IN OUR EYES

Sixty-eight women in Santiago blue uniforms walked across the gymnasium stage to receive their graduation diploma from General Barton Yount, head of the Army Air Force Training Command. General Arnold handed each woman their silver wings and then the graduates formed ranks at the side of the stage. Three years after Pearl Harbor, the very last WASP class was graduating.

"Frankly," General Arnold said, "I didn't know in 1941 whether a slip of a young girl could fight the controls of a B-17 in the heavy weather they would naturally encounter in operational flying. Those of us who had been flying for 20 or 30 years knew that flying an airplane was something you do not learn overnight. … You, and more than 900 of your sisters, have shown that you can fly wingtip to wingtip with your brothers. If ever there was a doubt in anyone's mind that women can become skillful pilots, the WASP have dispelled that doubt."

General Yount paid tribute to the 37 WASPs who had lost their lives. "Those who were killed," Yount said, "died courageously in the performance of arduous and exacting duties, without being able to see and feel the final results of their work. … We shall always keep and remember the brave heritage of the women who gave their lives. It is the heritage of faith in victory and in the ultimate freedom of humanity."[1]

Jackie Cochran spoke briefly, telling the graduates how proud she was of the 1,000 women who had learned to fly the Army way. "You can exert a great deal of influence on women concerning aviation," she said, "and you can be of much help to national aeronautics after the war."[2]

"At the end of the ceremony, we all marched down," said Mary

General Hap Arnold attended two WASP graduations at Avenger Field, in March 1944 and the final graduation on December 7, of the same year. *– National Archives photo 342-FH-05481-A36488.*

Martin Wyall (44-W-10). "Of course, we all had our hair up. We were looking real nice. And then we sang the song, *We're the last, last class of Avenger Field...* Because we ain't gonna be here much longer." They celebrated for the rest of the day, she said, "slept overnight in the Avenger Field barracks, and then, we all packed and left the field and went home."[3]

After the ceremony and before the graduates left, Jackie Cochran spoke to the women with words of encouragement. She said she was trying to get each WASP eligible for the G.I. Bill of Rights and urged them to write their congressman. Over 100,000 service women would receive benefits and Jackie saw no reason her WASPs shouldn't be included. She also said she was trying to get them put on reserve status so they could fly government aircraft for four hours a month. Nothing ever came of the idea, but the women found it just one more reason to love her for what she had done for their lives.[4]

That same morning, while the trainees were preparing for graduation, two regular Army fliers and 15 civilian ferry pilots gathered at the Omaha Municipal Airport. Each had delivered a surplus military aircraft to various airfields in the area and now were returning to their base near Oklahoma City. Among the 17 were two former Sweetwater flight instructors, two former WASPs, and a former WASP trainee. All three of the women had been members of Class 43-W-7 and all three had secured civilian employment with the Defense Plant Corporation. The company's employees transported surplus military aircraft to scrap yards, holding depots, and aircraft buyers across the country. The trainee, Verna Turner, had "washed out," either unable or unwilling to finish the course to graduation. WASPs Virginia Hope and Margaret Isbill had resigned, within a week of the Air Corps' arbitrary resignation date of November 20, waiting just long enough to get the government-promised pilot rating card.[5]

Verna Turner was born March 24, 1912 in Mississippi. At a very young age, she became a virtual orphan. Her father was gone and her mother remarried; quickly having two children by her new husband. By 1930, Verna was left in Michigan, living with her aunt and uncle, while her mother was living in Montana with her new husband and their children.

Verna left home for Cleveland, Ohio when she was barely 18 and got a job as a waitress at a downtown hotel. She set her sights on becoming a delayed parachute jumper, a competition few women ever attempted. Much like today's freefall jumpers, contestants dropped a few thousand feet from a plane, before they opened their parachute.

They competed for prize money, trying to be the closest to a target marked out on the ground. In 1934, when she was just 22, Verna dropped off a plane's wing at the Cleveland National Air Races, falling for a few seconds before pulling her ripcord. She didn't win any prize money, but had gained the respect of her male competitors. "She is as coolheaded as they come," one of them said. "She leaves nothing to chance." Verna was already a licensed parachute packer and was learning to fly. By the time war came in December 1941, she was still jumping and had turned professional. She entered WASP training at Avenger Field in May 1943, but never completed the course.[6]

Virginia Hope, the only child of Robert and Addaline Hope, was born August 17, 1921, in Winnebago, Minnesota. She grew up on her father's farm helping with chores and harvests, but still had time to enjoy riding horses and to join in on an occasional pheasant hunt. She was well versed in the cooking, sewing, and cleaning chores expected of a young girl, but she also loved to drive—and to drive fast. Her family remembered that she was mechanically inclined and could take apart and reassemble an automobile engine. She began studying at Gustavus Adolphus College, a private Lutheran College in St. Peter, Minnesota, but soon left for Northwestern University in Evanston, Illinois. There, Virginia learned to fly in the Civilian Pilot Training program. She earned her pilot and commercial licenses in 1941 and began working as an air traffic controller at the Minneapolis airport. Loving to fly, and accepted by the WASPs, she rode the train to Texas and began training on May 23, 1943. Virginia was the first in her class to solo and to receive the traditional dunking in the Avenger Field wishing well. After graduation, and a 10-day visit home, Virginia was one of 10 women, including Margaret Isbill, assigned to the Army Air Force Weather Wing.[7]

Upon their arrival at Wing headquarters in Asheville, North Carolina, the women received a two-week orientation to Weather Wing operations, including a refresher course in meteorology. They had to prove they could fly the various aircraft assigned to the Wing before beginning their duties. They were required to fly a minimum of 25 hours each month, half of which had to be cross-country, away from base.[8]

Virginia was assigned to the 2nd Weather Region Squadron based at Patterson Army Airfield in Ohio and reported for duty on December 20, 1943. Her primary assignment was ferrying military personnel to and from various airports in the region. During her time with the squadron, she compiled 650 hours in the air. She flew 16 aircraft, most often the UC-78 *Bobcat*, a twin-engine, light personnel transport. But the most powerful aircraft she flew was the C-47 *Skytrain*, a militarily improved version of the DC-3 civilian passenger liner. In addition to her Patterson Field flights, Virginia received temporary duty orders for over 45 other Army facilities, including a four-week stay at the "officer training school" in Orlando, Florida.

When 23-year-old Virginia resigned from the WASPs in November 1944, her commanding officers gave her a commendation and thanked her for her service. "Miss Hope has proven to be a very fine pilot," wrote the Base Operations Officer Major Parkerson. "She possesses an excellent temperament and an unusual pilot instinct. ... Miss Hope is pleasant, cooperative, and aggressive. This officer highly recommends Miss Hope for any position involving aircraft piloting." Major Jacoby, the Assistant Regional Control Officer, agreed. "The performance of WASP Hope on this assignment has been outstanding from the standpoint of devotion to duty and consistent dependability," he said. "Her sincere interest in flying and everything pertaining thereto; and her constant effort to maintain the highest possible degree of proficiency, are highly commendable and a credit to the WASP organization."

When asked in March 1944 if she wanted to be militarized and to become a part of the Army Air Corps, Virginia had said yes. Later in the year, when it became clear that the program was ending, Virginia decided to resign and fly as a civilian. She left for Oklahoma City and the Defense Plant Corporation.[9]

Classmate Margaret Isbill was born in McGregor Texas, February 16, 1921. Her father, Grady, had married Carrie Sanderford in 1918. Margaret was their first child. Grady had been a good student and a star guard on the Baylor University football team, graduating in 1911 with a Liberal Arts degree. He spent the next few years as a farm and ranch hand, but eventually became principal of the McGregor grammar school. When Margaret was 11 years old, her mother died when a flu turned into pneumonia. The oldest of three children, Margaret's only brother was just two years old. A year and a half later, her father married one of the school district's teachers.[10]

After graduation from high school, Margaret moved to Austin, Texas, working as a stenographer for the Texas State Liquor Control Board. While in the state capital she got her pilot's license, flew with the Civil Air Patrol, and joined the women fliers in the Texas wing of the 99s organization. When she began training at Avenger Field, she had logged 60 hours of flying time.[11]

From Avenger Field, Margaret accompanied Virginia Hope and eight other WASPs to the Army Air Force Weather Wing headquarters in Asheville. When she completed the course, she left for the Atlanta Army Airbase and her assignment with the 4th Weather Region Squadron. Margaret's commanding officer, Captain Ogness, didn't offer much detail or enthusiasm when he reported on her service with the squadron. "The WASP was readily able to adapt herself to assigned duties," he said. "Her conduct was exemplary, and her personal record was excellent." He noted that she had attended the WASP Military Course in Orlando and during her last month as a WASP had attended the advanced instrument flying course at Avenger Field. "Miss Isbill was quartered in the city of Atlanta," Ogness said, "at a location of her own choosing. She purchased her meals at places to her liking." Twenty-three-year-old Margaret resigned as a WASP November 28, 1944, a week after Virginia Hope.[12]

Classmates Verna, Virginia, and Margaret must have kept in touch after going their separate ways. On December 7, 1944, all three were together in Omaha, waiting for takeoff along with 14 other employees of the Defense Plant Corporation. The previous Saturday, 13 of the men had delivered planes to Omaha for a public sale, but for five days, foggy weather had delayed their return to Cimarron Field in Oklahoma City. The Lockheed Model 18 *Lodestar* that would take them home arrived in Omaha early that morning. In the late afternoon, the employees and pilot, Lieutenant Dick Tate, climbed aboard. Tate was a former flight instructor at Sweetwater. His brother, Nathan, and Lieutenant Roman Torkelson, another former Avenger Field instructor, were also on board.[13]

The twin-engine transport rolled down the runway and easily rolled into a takeoff attitude. With wheels still down Tate angled the plane sharply up until it reached an altitude of 500 feet and was about to leave the edge of the airport. The steep angle had slowed the airplane too much and it stalled, with no forward motion at all. The nose dipped down, the *Lodestar* rolled on its side, and dropped straight to the ground. The airport fire crews rushed to the raging blaze, but until units from the Omaha Fire Department joined the fight, the fire was out of control. All 17 onboard the plane died instantly.[14]

Verna Turner, Virginia Hope, and Marion Isbill are never included in the list of WASPs killed during the life of the program. Verna, of course, had washed out as a trainee, but other trainees had crashed and died and were still included in the 38 fallen WASPs. It also seems likely that if the WASP program had continued, Virginia Hope and Margaret

Isbill, after already flying for a year as WASPs, would have proudly remained in the program. The only difference was that these women were no longer active WASPs. That wasn't good enough for WASP veterans who had formed their own association after the war. "Three WASP from our class were not included in the group of WASP who died in service," said a 1989 article in the association's newsletter. "Therefore they were not registered in the memorial to Women in the Military Service for America. There is strong sentiment that we should get these women registered." The call went out for information about the three women and a request for donations to cover the $75 registration fee. In January 1990, all three women were finally recognized and their names added to the memorial that stands at the entrance gate to Arlington National Cemetery, directly across from Memorial Bridge.[15]

With barely two weeks before the WASP program would end, 37 women had officially lost their lives in service to the Air Corp and their country. No one would have expected another woman to fall, but 24 hours after the crash in Omaha, freezing winter clouds drifted over Oklahoma.

Mary Webster (44-W-8) and a two-man crew were flying into a cold front with intermittent snow and rain and temperatures dropping. Their UC-78 *Bobcat*, nicknamed "the bamboo bomber," was taking them on a cross-country training flight to Chicago from Frederick Army Airfield in southwestern Oklahoma. Following her graduation that October, Mary had reported to Frederick for advanced training in B-24 *Liberator* bombers. With only 11 days remaining until WASP deactivation, it should have seemed ridiculous to continue training; yet, there she was, flying between Tulsa and Claremore, Oklahoma.[16]

Born June 30, 1919, Mary was the seventh of eight children and the second daughter. Her father, William Webster, was born in Canada and immigrated to the United States in 1895. He settled southeast of Seattle in Ellensburg, Washington, where he met and married Mary Pott. He worked as a railroad engineer for the Northern Pacific until 1909 and that same year he became a U.S. citizen. He quit the railroad and went into business for himself, opening the Webster Smokehouse, a cigar store. By 1920, he was successful enough to not only own his own business, but also his home. He added candy and other goods to his inventory and in 1932 opened the Webster Cafe and Poolroom. He followed in 1937 with the major purchase of a three-story, brick hotel that he renamed The Webster.[17]

Mary graduated from the Holy Names Academy, a private Catholic all-girls high school in Seattle. After graduation, she studied for two years at the Seattle Business College and earned her diploma. Although believing business was her best career choice, Mary had always dreamed of flying, and when Central Washington State College announced a Civilian Pilot Training course in May 1940, Mary leaped at the chance. It wasn't easy being one of only three women accepted in the program. "I knew Mary and I liked her," a fellow student later told a reporter. "But there was a reluctant acceptance about her being in the program with the men. There were jokes that she should be home raising kids." Mary had nearly completed the aviation course in late 1941, but before she could take the test for her pilot's license, war broke out and the government banned recreational and commercial flying near the West Coast. She drove to Yakima, where flying was still allowed, to get additional training, and there she passed the test. She applied to the WASP program and waited. For the next year she worked as a private secretary with A. M. Castle & Company, a steel distributor based in Seattle.[18]

After graduation from Avenger on October 18, 1944, and following her 10-day furlough, Mary reported to Frederick Army Airbase to begin her advanced training. A month later she was riding in the *Bobcat* with Lieutenant George Crowe at the controls. Crowe was from Wisconsin and had turned 21 just a few days earlier. He joined the Army in July 1942 and by November 1943 had earned his Air Corps wings. Also with them was 22-year-old Sergeant Melvin Clark, a married Oklahoma native who had been assigned to Frederick when the base opened in September 1942.[19]

An hour out from Frederick on December 9, the UC-78 was flying at 9,000 feet above the clouds, when Crowe noticed ice forming on the wings. He radioed the air controller and received permission to descend, hoping warmer air would keep more ice from forming. Now, deep in the clouds, the aircraft began to fall and Crowe lost control. The UC-78 fell straight down and crashed, killing everyone aboard.[20]

WASP and former classmate Nettie Winfield (44-W-8), who had come to Frederick Field with Mary, was Mary's escort back to Ellensburg for burial in Holy Cross Cemetery.[21]

Mary Webster was the last of the 38 official WASP deaths before the program ended, but another woman almost joined her.

Based at Romulus Air Base in Michigan, Louise Bowden (43-W-4) had graduated over a year earlier. On December 9, flying a P-51 *Mustang* to New Jersey from the North American aircraft plant near Dallas, her engine began sputtering and backfiring near Greensboro,

North Carolina. Louise immediately descended to 1,500 feet, trying to find a place to land. Suddenly the engine caught on fire. Realizing it was hopeless and that she had little time to escape, she radioed the Greensboro Airport tower to say she was jumping. Louise opened her canopy, pulled sharply back on the stick, threw off her safety belt and shoulder harness, stood up, and hit the silk, jumping out toward the wing of the plane. Moments after her chute opened; the *Mustang* nosed over and dove toward the ground. As she floated down, she saw the plane bury itself in a plowed field and erupt in a fireball. Moments later, she landed just 20 yards away. The *Mustang* had missed a house by only 40 yards. Louise survived the war, earned her instructors license, and taught flying. She passed away at age 96 in January 2013.[22]

The WASP experiment was rapidly winding down now and none of the woman were happy about it. Nancy Love told reporters that the WASPs were "sad and mad." Silver haired and only 30 years old, Nancy said the women had been calling her "at all hours of the night, from all parts of the country; to insist 'they can't do this!'"[23]

Desperate to fly, a few of the women said they were more than willing to continue flying for only one dollar a year, but Army Air Force headquarters turned them down. "Your offer to serve is appreciated," said General Arnold, "but I must advise that available combat returnees and others in the pilot pool meet all current requirements and do not occasion retention of women pilots." Nancy Love had little to say when asked about the government's refusal. "Some of the women don't need the money," she said—but then added, "a lot of them do."[24]

Barbara Poole, one of the original 25 WAFs chosen by Nancy Love, wrote a provocative story denouncing the decision to deactivate the WASP. Published in the December 1944 edition of *Flying* magazine, she called her story "Requiem for the WASP." The government had spent a lot of money to train the WASP, she wrote. "Now we are throwing this money away at the demand of a few thousand male pilots who were employed, until recently, in a civilian capacity, on government flight programs. The curtailment of these programs has thrown these pilots out of work and now they are to get the WASP jobs." Unemployed pilots were afraid of the draft, she wrote. "This state of affairs is very sad for the pilot, but after all, we're running a war, not an employment bureau for disgruntled flyers." Poole addressed one of the chief complaints against the women by the male pilots—why women only needed 35 hours to receive flight training. "The training school first required the girls to have 200 hours and a private license," Poole said. "Eventually the entrance hours were lowered to 35 with no license.

This became one of the principal gripes of our friends, the CAA pilots. They demanded to know why the girls only had to have 35 hours." Poole answered their question with her own question. "If young men going into flight training with the Army Air Forces are not required to have any previous flight experience, why should the girls have to have 35 hours? The training is supposedly the same." To Poole, the issue was nothing more than "a barrage of innuendoes and blurred facts ...an egotistic battle of the sexes."[25]

The following February, *Flying* printed a rebuttal letter from Robert Barrett, a former flight instructor who opposed much of Poole's story. "The author was mistaken," Barrett said, "in her repeated assertions that male pilots opposed the WASP organization because of jealousy or a fancied superman complex." Barrett thought that the majority, if not all of the men, realized "that these fighting girls were motivated by a high sense of patriotism." He resented the assertion that the now unemployed flight instructors were afraid of the draft. "To accuse men in this situation of being draft dodgers is a pretty foul blow. I wonder if all the girls discharged from the WASP are seriously considering enlistment in the WAC, WAVE, or SPAR." Then he struck a definite blow in Poole's battle of the sexes. "If the women had better safety records than the men," Barrett said, "I strongly suspect that it was due to gallantry of operations officers rather than to the superior ability of the women." Although he admitted there were many outstanding women pilots, as a flight instructor of both sexes, he was sure "the average woman has far less flying aptitude then the average man." He ended his letter with a peace offering to the women. "Here's an orchid to them for their fight and spirit," he said, "and a very sour lemon to whoever is responsible for the Army's double deal, perpetrated against both the WASP and the War Training Service boys."[26]

As the final day drew near, Jackie Cochran tried to rationalize General Arnold's decision to disband the WASPs. "Personally, I was disappointed that all the WASPs could not continue to fly in the war effort," she said. "But there is nothing that would hurt the cause of women pilots so much as to keep them on when really no longer needed. The rumble that had already started to the effect that they were getting air hours at the expense of men would have gradually grown into a roar with no logical comeback."[27]

The Central Flying Command ordered that, as much as possible, the last two graduating classes of trainees should receive assignments to a station near their home, or to a location near where they planned to live after deactivation. The final graduating class wasn't so lucky. With no assignment to report to, they were left to wander around Avenger Field with little to do, their Army flying days over. Those few remaining Avenger Field WASPs had to be off the base by midnight, December 20. As Christmas approached, the remaining WASPs did receive a homecoming present of sorts. Headquarters said that each would have the opportunity to ride a military aircraft to their homes or to choose a final destination. There were only two exceptions. There had to be space available on an aircraft and there could be no additional expense for the government.[28]

After deactivation, the women were still allowed to wear their uniforms; however, the official Air Corps insignia had to be removed by midnight, December 20th. From then on, the women could only wear WASP wings on their Santiago Blues. While no woman would fly again for the Army Air Force, the Command said it was desirable that qualified WASPs "be considered for any available civilian clerical, professional, or technical ground position." Duty station commanders were directed to report any of their WASP who were "worthy of commendation because of outstanding performance." Finally, before they left for home, each WASP received an exit physical examination.[29]

Avenger Field was nearly silent now—at least for the next month. In January, the roar of airplane engines would once again rattle the skies over Sweetwater as male Air Force cadets arrived at the old WASP nest for combat flight training.

In Sweetwater, city officials bought the upstairs of the building on Oak Street that had been the Avengerette Club, hoping to convert it into a youth center. Aviation Enterprises, the government contractor that had trained the women and equipped the club, agreed to sell Sweetwater the nearly $2,500 worth of equipment inside the building for just $600.

The city's Board of Commercial Development presented a Stetson hat to Colonel Roy Ward, Avenger Field commander, and because of how he had cemented relations between the WASPs and the town's residents, they proclaimed him an honorary citizen of Sweetwater. The women would be gone, but their memory would endure.[30]

Returning home, there was a surge in marriage and engagement announcements from the WASPs. "Engagements are really in vogue," said an article in a WASP produced newsletter. There had always been rules that there would be no social contact allowed between instructors and trainees, and that any instructor found dating a trainee would be fired immediately—and yet—it was amazing how many women wound up married to those very same instructors.[31]

Some of the women returned to their pre-WASP employers. Vergie Bryant (44-W-3) was back in Georgia as an assistant sales manager for a hardware business. Phyllis Ryder (44-W-1) was off to New York to study drama, while Marjorie Logan (43-W-6) was helping her father run an airport in Montana. Five women were off to Alaska as Air Traffic Controllers for the Civil Aeronautics Authority. Some joined the Red Cross for an overseas assignment and others just took a few weeks off to enjoy a vacation. A very few managed to find work in the air, but the vast majority just returned to the everyday life they had known before.[32]

A colorful chapter in the country's military history had ended. More than a thousand women had stepped out of Army Air Force planes for the very last time. It would be decades before women would fly again for the Air Force, this time as regular commissioned officers, not civilians. As the year ended, the editor of the final edition of the *WASP Newsletter* before disbandment, wished each WASP a Merry Christmas and closed with a hopeful prayer. "May the New Year bring us nearer to the time when all mankind will fly together on wings of peace."[33]

The WASPs achievements were impressive. In the ferrying division alone, Nancy Love said the women had flown over 9 million domestic miles, "in fair weather and foul," and, since June 1944, they had delivered a quarter of all pursuit airplanes ferried by that division. "It hasn't been an easy job, or highly paid—or glamorous," Nancy said with a smile. "You can't be glamorous when you're on a one or two week trip away from base and you have room in your fighter plane for only one clean shirt, a toothbrush, and maybe a pair of pajamas."[34]

Just a month before deactivation, a group of WASPs stationed at Maxwell Air Field, near Montgomery, Alabama, started a newsletter and began to distribute it to every WASP they could find. It began as a way to share information about employment opportunities for the women after the WASP program ended, but quickly became a way for the women to keep in touch with each other. The Army didn't support the idea and it took negotiations by Kay Dussaq, as administrator of WASP activities, to get the Training Command's approval. She completed her negotiations just days before her fatal November plane crash. The Army agreed to pay for the paper and postage for the first few issues of the newsletter, but told the women that after deactivation they would be on their own. The women began planning an organization that could help keep them together in spirit and help them influence legislation for their benefit. A small $5 annual membership fee would provide enough money to continue the newsletter and perhaps fund other projects. The result was the Order of the Fifinella. By December 20, over 300 women had joined and, five months later, the Order boasted over 700 members, nearly 75 per cent of all women who had flown as WASPs.[35]

When the war ended in 1945, the officers of the Fifinella Order began planning their first reunion and convention. Held in August 1946, nearly 200 WASPs from 25 states came to Lock Haven, Pennsylvania, eager to reunite with their friends and fellow pilots. The three-day affair included landing and bomb dropping contests at the airport and ended in the crowning of a "Champion Fifinella." Festivities closed with 150 airplanes flying from Piper's Lock Haven factory to the National Air Show in Cleveland. The women said it was the largest peacetime flight of its kind in aviation history.

Many issues had filled the convention's business discussions, but one of the highest items on the women's list was how to establish a memorial in tribute to the 41 WASPs who died while the program was still active. They believed that Virginia Hope, Marion Isbill, and Verna Turner, who had all died together in that December 1944 Omaha plane crash, were Fifinella sisters. It seemed only right that they be included in the list of fallen women pilots. It took two years to organize a memorial, but by then, the Order of the Fifinella had changed its mind.[36]

A National Memorial Service was the highlight of the Fifinella's third convention, in mid September 1948. Headquartered at the Hollywood, Roosevelt Hotel, over 300 former WASPs attended. At 11 in the morning, September 16, they gathered in the Church of the Recessional at Forest Lawn Memorial Park, a few miles northeast of Hollywood. Fletcher Bowron, mayor of Los Angeles, had declared this day, "WASP Memorial Day." The ceremony centered on a floral arrangement in the shape of a broken propeller with the word "WASP" written diagonally across it. Following the posting of the flags, singing of the *Star Spangled Banner*, and the invocation, letters from General Arnold and Jackie Cochran were read. Redheaded Irish tenor, Jimmy O'Brien, followed with a solo performance of *There Is No Death*, a song written in 1919 in remembrance of WWI's fallen soldiers.

Featured speaker was retired General Ralph Cousins, former commander of the Western Flying Training Command who had commanded many WASPs during the war. General Cousins' memorial address, "Women with Wings," brought tears to some eyes. "These gallant women were soldiers," he said, "and they kept the soldiers' faith. Theirs was a far greater sacrifice. Men have always gone to war, but these fliers gave up the comfort and protection of their homes for daring feats of war. They gave up their lives in defense of their country."

Hollywood movie star and soprano, Rhonda Fleming sang *Ave Maria* in preparation for the "In Memoriam Ritual." As Betty Jane Williams (44-W-6), president of the Order of Fifinella, read the 38 names of the fallen women, four WASPs took turns lighting a candle for each name. Overhead, fighter jets from California's Air National Guard roared past, dipping their wings in a salute of honor, their rumblings clearly heard and felt within the church. It was all over in less than an hour.[37]

Over the coming years, as the WASPs began to pass on, a list of their names appeared in WASP newsletters. The names of the 38 were always included.

In her final report to General Arnold, Jackie Cochran said that of the 25,000 women who applied to become a WASP, 1,830 were accepted and 1,074 graduated. Nine hundred of those women were still flying when the program ended. Of the original 25 WAFS, 16 still flew. The WASPs, Jackie said, had flown over 60 million miles for the Army Air Force, and although 38 women had died, about one death for every 16,000 hours of flying, she said that that figure compared "favorably with the rates of male pilots in similar work."[38]

Ultimately unable to get officer commissions or veteran benefits for her women, Jackie Cochran added a paragraph to her final report's recommendations. Should the Air Force ever consider women pilots in the future, and the Congress grant veteran's rights and benefits to civilians who had served with the armed forces; she believed that all WASPs should be included. Further, "the next of kin of WASPs who died in the line of duty should receive compensation comparable to that which would have been received if the WASP had been on military status with insurance privileges and benefits." Congress and the Air Force weren't ready to act and Jackie would have to wait until 1977, three years before she died. That was the year when Congress finally passed and President Carter signed the bill giving WASPs veteran benefits.[39]

Though they had been disappointed, the women didn't fight termination of their Army flying. Early in 1973, when the fight for veteran benefits was just heating up, former WASP, Mary Ellen Keil (44-W-2) told a reporter that the women were proud and delighted by what they had done.

"Everyone was just kind of elated back then," she said. "We had such stardust in our eyes that we were given a chance to serve. We were happy just for the chance to fly.

"There wasn't such a thing as a women's liberation movement in 1944," she said. "So we all just took our pride—and went away."[40]

# APPENDICES

# WASP CASUALTIES

| WASP | DEATH DATE | CLASS | DEATH LOCATION |
|---|---|---|---|
| Champlin, Jane Dolores | June 7, 1943 | 43-4**t** | Westbrook, TX |
| Clarke, Susan Parker | July 4, 1944 | 44-2 | Columbia, SC |
| Davis, Marjorie Laverne | October 16, 1944 | 44-9**t** | Walnut, MS |
| Dussaq, Katherine (Applegate) | November 26, 1944 | 44-1 | New Carlisle, OH |
| Edwards, Marjorie Doris | June 13, 1944 | 44-6**t** | Childress, TX |
| Erickson, Jayne Elizabeth | April 16, 1944 | 44-6**t** | Sweetwater, TX |
| Fort, Cornelia | March 21, 1943 | WAFS | Abilene, TX |
| Grimes, Frances Fortune | March 27, 1944 | 43-3 | Otis Field, MA |
| Hartson, Mary P. | August 14, 1944 | 43-5 | Sherman, TX |
| Howson, Mary Holmes | April 16, 1944 | 44-4**t** | Sweetwater, TX |
| Keene, Edith Clayton | April 25, 1944 | 44-1 | Mission, TX |
| Lawrence, Kathryn Barbara | August 4, 1943 | 43-8**t** | Sweetwater, TX |
| Loop, Paula R. | July 7, 1944 | 43-2 | Medford, OR |
| Louie, Hazel Ying (Lee) | November 23, 1944 | 43-4 | Great Falls, MT |
| Lovejoy, Alice E. | September 13, 1944 | 43-5 | Brownsville, TX |
| Martin, Peggy (Wilson) | October 3, 1944 | 44-4 | Marana, AZ |
| McDonald, Lea Ola | June 21, 1944 | 44-3 | El Paso, TX |
| Moffatt, Virginia C. | October 5, 1943 | 43-2 | Ontario, CA |
| Moses, Beverly Jean | July 18, 1944 | 44-5 | Las Vegas, NV |
| Nichols, Dorothy Mae | June 11, 1944 | 43-2 | Bismarck, ND |
| Norbeck, Jeanne (Lewellen) | October 16, 1944 | 44-3 | Shaw Field, SC |
| Oldenburg, Margaret (Sanford) | March 7, 1943 | 43-4**t** | Houston, TX |
| Rawlinson, Mabel Virginia | August 23, 1943 | 43-3 | Camp Davis, NC |
| Roberts, Gleanna | June 20, 1944 | 44-9**t** | Lorraine, TX |
| Robinson, Marie N. (Michell) | October 2, 1944 | 44-2 | Victorville, CA |
| Scott, Dorothy F. | December 3, 1943 | WAFS | Palm Springs, CA |
| Scott, Elizabeth Mae | July 8, 1944 | 44-3 | Waco, TX |
| Seip, Margaret June | August 30, 1943 | 43-5**t** | Big Spring, TX |
| Severson, Helen Jo (Anderson) | August 30, 1943 | 43-5**t** | Big Spring, TX |
| Sharon, Marie Ethel (Cihler) | April 10, 1944 | 43-4 | Tecumseh, NE |
| Sharp, Evelyn | April 3, 1944 | WAFS | New Cumberland, PA |
| Silver, Gertrude Vreeland | October 26, 1944 | 43-7 | Southern California ? |
| Stine, Betty Pauline | February 25, 1944 | 44-2**t** | Tucson, AZ |
| Toevs, Marian J. | February 18, 1944 | 43-8 | San Jose, CA |
| Trebing, Mary Elizabeth | November 7, 1943 | 43-4 | Blanchard, OK |
| Webster, Mary Louise | December 9, 1944 | 44-8 | Claremore, OK |
| Welz, Bonnie Jean (Alloway) | June 29, 1944 | 43-6 | Randado, TX |
| Wood, Betty L. (Taylor) | September 23, 1943 | 43-4 | Camp Davis, NC |

(*maiden name*)
**t** = died in training

# WASP DEATHS BY DATE

| WASP | DEATH DATE | CLASS | DEATH LOCATION |
|---|---|---|---|
| Margaret Oldenburg (Sanford) | March 7, 1943 | 43-4**t** | Houston, TX |
| Cornelia Fort | March 21, 1943 | WAFS | Abilene, TX |
| Jane Dolores Champlin | June 7, 1943 | 43-4**t** | Westbrook, TX |
| Kathryn Barbara Lawrence | August 4, 1943 | 43-8**t** | Sweetwater, TX |
| Mabel Virginia Rawlinson | August 23, 1943 | 43-3 | Camp Davis, NC |
| Margaret June Seip | August 30, 1943 | 43-5**t** | Big Spring, TX |
| Helen Jo Severson (Anderson) | August 30, 1943 | 43-5**t** | Big Spring, TX |
| Betty L. Wood (Taylor) | September 23, 1943 | 43-4 | Camp Davis, NC |
| Virginia C. Moffatt | October 5, 1943 | 43-2 | Ontario, CA |
| Mary Elizabeth Trebing | November 7, 1943 | 43-4 | Blanchard, OK |
| Dorothy F. Scott | December 3, 1943 | WAFS | Palm Springs, CA |
| Marian J. Toevs | February 18, 1944 | 43-8 | San Jose, CA |
| Betty Pauline Stine | February 25, 1944 | 44-2**t** | Tucson, AZ |
| Frances Fortune Grimes | March 27, 1944 | 43-3 | Otis Field, MA |
| Evelyn Sharp | April 3, 1944 | WAFS | New Cumberland, PA |
| Marie Ethel Sharon (Cihler) | April 10, 1944 | 43-4 | Tecumseh, NE |
| Jayne Elizabeth Erickson | April 16, 1944 | 44-6**t** | Sweetwater, TX |
| Mary Holmes Howson | April 16, 1944 | 44-4**t** | Sweetwater, TX |
| Edith Clayton Keene | April 25, 1944 | 44-1 | Mission, TX |
| Dorothy Mae Nichols | June 11, 1944 | 43-2 | Bismarck, ND |
| Marjorie Doris Edwards | June 13, 1944 | 44-6**t** | Childress, TX |
| Gleanna Roberts | June 20, 1944 | 44-9**t** | Lorraine, TX |
| Lea Ola McDonald | June 21, 1944 | 44-3 | El Paso, TX |
| Bonnie Jean Welz (Alloway) | June 29, 1944 | 43-6 | Randado, TX |
| Susan Parker Clarke | July 4, 1944 | 44-2 | Columbia, SC |
| Paula R. Loop | July 7, 1944 | 43-2 | Medford, OR |
| Elizabeth Mae Scott | July 8, 1944 | 44-3 | Waco, TX |
| Beverly Jean Moses | July 18, 1944 | 44-5 | Las Vegas, NV |
| Mary P. Hartson | August 14, 1944 | 43-5 | Sherman, TX |
| Alice E. Lovejoy | September 13, 1944 | 43-5 | Brownsville, TX |
| Marie N. Robinson (Michell) | October 2, 1944 | 44-2 | Victorville, CA |
| Peggy Martin (Wilson) | October 3, 1944 | 44-4 | Marana, AZ |
| Marjorie Laverne Davis | October 16, 1944 | 44-9**t** | Walnut, MS |
| Jeanne Norbeck (Lewellen) | October 16, 1944 | 44-3 | Shaw Field, SC |
| Gertrude Vreeland Silver | October 26, 1944 | 43-7 | Southern California? |
| Hazel Ying Louie (Lee) | November 23, 1944 | 43-4 | Great Falls, MT |
| Katherine Dussaq (Applegate) | November 26, 1944 | 44-1 | New Carlisle, OH |
| Mary Louise Webster | December 9, 1944 | 44-8 | Claremore, OK |

(*maiden name*)
**t** = died in training

# WASP DEATHS BY CLASS

| WASP | DEATH DATE | CLASS | DEATH LOCATION |
|---|---|---|---|
| Loop, Paula R. | July 7, 1944 | 43-2 | Medford, OR |
| Moffatt, Virginia C. | October 5, 1943 | 43-2 | Ontario, CA |
| Nichols, Dorothy Mae | June 11, 1944 | 43-2 | Bismarck, ND |
| Grimes, Frances Fortune | March 27, 1944 | 43-3 | Otis Field, MA |
| Rawlinson, Mabel Virginia | August 23, 1943 | 43-3 | Camp Davis, NC |
| Louie, Hazel Ying (Lee) | November 23, 1944 | 43-4 | Great Falls, MT |
| Sharon, Marie Ethel (Cihler) | April 10, 1944 | 43-4 | Tecumseh, NE |
| Trebing, Mary Elizabeth | November 7, 1943 | 43-4 | Blanchard, OK |
| Wood, Betty L. (Taylor) | September 23, 1943 | 43-4 | Camp Davis, NC |
| Champlin, Jane Dolores | June 7, 1943 | 43-4**t** | Westbrook, TX |
| Oldenburg, Margaret (Sanford) | March 7, 1943 | 43-4**t** | Houston, TX |
| Hartson, Mary P. | August 14, 1944 | 43-5 | Sherman, TX |
| Lovejoy, Alice E. | September 13, 1944 | 43-5 | Brownsville, TX |
| Seip, Margaret June | August 30, 1943 | 43-5**t** | Big Spring, TX |
| Severson, Helen Jo (Anderson) | August 30, 1943 | 43-5**t** | Big Spring, TX |
| Welz, Bonnie Jean (Alloway) | June 29, 1944 | 43-6 | Randado, TX |
| Silver, Gertrude Vreeland | October 26, 1944 (never | 43-7 | Southern California |
| Toevs, Marian J. | February 18, 1944 | 43-8 | San Jose, CA |
| Lawrence, Kathryn Barbara | August 4, 1943 | 43-8**t** | Sweetwater, TX |
| Dussaq, Katherine (Applegate) | November 26, 1944 | 44-1 | New Carlisle, OH |
| Keene, Edith Clayton | April 25, 1944 | 44-1 | Mission, TX |
| Clarke, Susan Parker | July 4, 1944 | 44-2 | Columbia, SC |
| Robinson, Marie N. (Michell) | October 2, 1944 | 44-2 | Victorville, CA |
| Stine, Betty Pauline | February 25, 1944 | 44-2**t** | Tucson, AZ |
| McDonald, Lea Ola | June 21, 1944 | 44-3 | El Paso, TX |
| Norbeck, Jeanne (Lewellen) | October 16, 1944 | 44-3 | Shaw Field, SC |
| Scott, Elizabeth Mae | July 8, 1944 | 44-3 | Waco, TX |
| Martin, Peggy (Wilson) | October 3, 1944 | 44-4 | Marana, AZ |
| Howson, Mary Holmes | April 16, 1944 | 44-4**t** | Sweetwater, TX |
| Moses, Beverly Jean | July 18, 1944 | 44-5 | Las Vegas, NV |
| Edwards, Marjorie Doris | June 13, 1944 | 44-6**t** | Childress, TX |
| Erickson, Jayne Elizabeth | April 16, 1944 | 44-6**t** | Sweetwater, TX |
| Webster, Mary Louise | December 9, 1944 | 44-8 | Claremore, OK |
| Davis, Marjorie Laverne | October 16, 1944 | 44-9**t** | Walnut, MS |
| Roberts, Gleanna | June 20, 1944 | 44-9**t** | Lorraine, TX |
| Fort, Cornelia | March 21, 1943 | WAFS | Abilene, TX |
| Scott, Dorothy F. | December 3, 1943 | WAFS | Palm Springs, CA |
| Sharp, Evelyn | April 3, 1944 | WAFS | New Cumberland, PA |

(*maiden name*)
**t** = died in training

# WASP BURIAL LOCATIONS

| WASP | CEMETERY | LOCATION |
|---|---|---|
| Champlin, Jane Dolores | Calvary Cemetery and Mausoleum | St. Louis, MO |
| Clarke, Susan Parker | Lakewood Cemetery | Cooperstown, NY |
| Davis, Marjorie Laverne | Hollywood Forever Cemetery | Hollywood, CA |
| Dussaq, Katherine (Applegate) | Dayton City Cemetery | Dayton, WA |
| Edwards, Marjorie Doris | Loma Vista Memorial Park | Fullerton, CA |
| Erickson, Jayne Elizabeth | Lake View Cemetery | Seattle, WA |
| Fort, Cornelia | Mount Olivet Cemetery | Nashville, TN |
| Grimes, Frances Fortune | South Side Cemetery | Pittsburgh, PA |
| Hartson, Mary P. | Wilhelm's Portland Memorial | Portland, OR |
| Hope, Virginia ** | Riverside Cemetery | Winnebago, MN |
| Howson, Mary Holmes | Washington Memorial Chapel Cemetery | Valley Forge, PA |
| Hunt, Bertha Mae (Haggard) * | Memorial Park Cemetery | Oklahoma City, OK |
| Isbill, Margaret ** | McGregor Cemetery | McGregor Cemetery |
| Keene, Edith Clayton | Pomona Cemetery | Pomona, , TX |
| Lawrence, Kathryn Barbara | Memorial Park Cemetery | Grand Forks, ND |
| Loop, Paula R. | Wakita Cemetery | Wakita, OK |
| Louie, Hazel Ying (Lee) | River View Cemetery | Portland, OR |
| Lovejoy, Alice E. | Ferncliff Mausoleum | Hartsdale, NY |
| Martin, Peggy (Wilson) | Rose Hills Memorial Park | Whittier, CA |
| McDonald, Lea Ola | Gaines County Cemetery at Seagraves | Seagraves, TX |
| Moffatt, Virginia C. | Inglewood Park Cemetery | Inglewood, CA |
| Moses, Beverly Jean | Oakwood Cemetery | Pleasant Hill, IA |
| Nichols, Dorothy Mae | Forest Lawn Memorial Park | Glendale, CA |
| Norbeck, Jeanne (Lewellen) | Garland Brook Cemetery | Columbus, IN |
| Oldenburg, Margaret (Sanford) | Mountain View Cemetery | Oakland, CA |
| Rawlinson, Mabel Virginia | Mount Ever-Rest Memorial Park South | Kalamazoo, MI |
| Roberts, Gleanna | Welsh Pioneer Cemetery | Union Twp., IA |
| Robinson, Marie N. (Michell) | White Chapel Memorial Park Cemetery | Troy, MI |
| Scott, Dorothy F. | Pierce Brothers Valhalla Memorial Park | North Hollywood, CA |
| Scott, Elizabeth Mae | Live Oak Memorial Park | Monrovia, CA |
| Seip, Margaret June | Forest Home Cemetery | Milwaukee, WI |
| Severson, Helen Jo (Anderson) | Greenwood Cemetery | Brookings County, SD |
| Sharon, Marie Ethel (Cihler) | Wilhelm's Portland Memorial | Portland, OR |
| Sharp, Evelyn | Ord Cemetery | Ord, NE |
| Silver, Gertrude (Tompkins) | *Remains never found* | *Southern California?* |
| Stine, Betty Pauline | Santa Barbara Cemetery | Santa Barbara, CA |
| Toevs, Marian J. | Aberdeen Cemetery | Aberdeen, ID |
| Trebing, Mary Elizabeth | Green Mountain Cemetery | Boulder, CO |
| Turner, Verna ** | Mount Hope Cemetery | Pontiac, MI |
| Webster, Mary Louise | Holy Cross Cemetery | Ellensburg, WA |
| Welz, Bonnie Jean (Alloway) | *Ashes scattered* | *Unknown* |
| Wood, Betty L. (Taylor) | East Lawn Memorial Park | Sacramento, CA |

(*maiden name*)

* Still in service as a WASP; however, killed in private plane crash.

** No longer in WASP service, but died in airplane crash while WASP program was still active.

# TYPE OF AIRCRAFT FLYING AT TIME OF DEATH

| WASP | AIRCRAFT | LOCATION |
|---|---|---|
| Champlin, Jane Dolores | Vultee BT-15 | Westbrook, TX |
| Clarke, Susan Parker | Vultee BT-13 | Columbia, SC |
| Davis, Marjorie Laverne | North American AT-6 | Walnut, MS |
| Dussaq, Katherine (Applegate) | North American AT-6 | New Carlisle, OH |
| Edwards, Marjorie Doris | North American AT-6 | Childress, TX |
| Erickson, Jayne Elizabeth | North American AT-6 | Sweetwater, TX |
| Fort, Cornelia | Vultee BT-13 | Abilene, TX |
| Grimes, Frances Fortune | Douglas A-24 | Otis Field, MA |
| Hartson, Mary P. | Vultee BT-13 | Sherman, TX |
| Howson, Mary Holmes | North American AT-6 | Sweetwater, TX |
| Keene, Edith Clayton | North American AT-6 | Mission, TX |
| Lawrence, Kathryn Barbara | Fairchild PT-19 | Sweetwater, TX |
| Loop, Paula R. | Vultee BT-13 | Medford, OR |
| Louie, Hazel Ying (Lee) | Bell P-63 | Great Falls, MT |
| Lovejoy, Alice E. | North American AT-6 | Brownsville, TX |
| Martin, Peggy (Wilson) | Vultee BT-13 | Marana, AZ |
| McDonald, Lea Ola | Douglas A-24 | El Paso, TX |
| Moffatt, Virginia C. | Vultee BT-15 | Ontario, CA |
| Moses, Beverly Jean | Beechcraft AT-11 | Las Vegas, NV |
| Nichols, Dorothy Mae | Bell P-39 | Bismarck, ND |
| Norbeck, Jeanne (Lewellen) | Vultee BT-13 | Shaw Field, SC |
| Oldenburg, Margaret (Sanford) | Fairchild PT-19 | Houston, TX |
| Rawlinson, Mabel Virginia | Douglas A-24 | Camp Davis, NC |
| Roberts, Gleanna | Boeing PT-17 | Lorraine, TX |
| Robinson, Marie N. (Michell) | North American B-25 | Victorville, CA |
| Scott, Dorothy F. | North American BC-1 (AT-6)* | Palm Springs, CA |
| Scott, Elizabeth Mae | Vultee BT-13 | Waco, TX |
| Seip, Margaret June | Cessna UC-78 | Big Spring, TX |
| Severson, Helen Jo (Anderson) | Cessna UC-78 | Big Spring, TX |
| Sharon, Marie Ethel (Cihler) | North American B-25 | Tecumseh, NE |
| Sharp, Evelyn | Lockheed P-38 | New Cumberland, PA |
| Silver, Gertrude Vreeland | North American P-51 | Southern California ? |
| Stine, Betty Pauline | North American AT-6 | Tucson, AZ |
| Toevs, Marian J. | Vultee BT-13 | San Jose, CA |
| Trebing, Mary Elizabeth | Fairchild PT-19 | Blanchard, OK |
| Webster, Mary Louise | Cessna UC-78 | Claremore, OK |
| Welz, Bonnie Jean (Alloway) | Vultee BT-13 | Randado, TX |
| Wood, Betty L. (Taylor) | Douglas A-24 | Camp Davis, NC |

* Trainer version of the AT-6.
(*maiden name*)

# THE DEADLIEST PLANES FLOWN BY THE WASP

**Eleven women lost their lives in the Vultee BT-13 and its variant the BT-15. –** ***Air Force photo 020903-0-9999j-001.***

**Nine women died flying the North American AT-6. –** ***Air Force photo 090821-F-1234S-001***

# NUMBER OF TRAINEES AND GRADUATES FROM EACH CLASS

- *The WAFS trained and graduated at New Castle Army Air Base, near Wilmington, Delaware.*
- *Classes 43-W-1, 43-W-2, 43-W-3, and one-half of Class 44-W-4 trained at Houston Municipal Airport in Houston, Texas.*

| Class | Trainees | Begin Training | Graduated | Graduation Date |
|---|---|---|---|---|
| WAFS | 31 | September 1942 | 28 | * *various* |
| 43-W-1 | 29 | November 15, 1942 | 23 | ** April 24, 1943 |
| 43-W-2 | 51 | December 13, 1942 | 43 | *** May 28, 1943 |
| 43-W-3 | 55 | January 16, 1943 | 43 | *** July 3, 1943 |
| 43-W-4 | 152 | February 16, 1943 | 112 | **** August 7, 1943 |
| 43-W-5 | 124 | March 26, 1943 | 85 | September 11, 1943 |
| 43-W-6 | 123 | April 25, 1943 | 84 | October 4, 1943 |
| 43-W-7 | 101 | May 23, 1943 | 59 | November 13, 1943 |
| 43-W-8 | 98 | July 5, 1943 | 48 | December 17, 1943 |
| 44-W-1 | 99 | August 9, 1943 | 49 | February 11, 1944 |
| 44-W-2 | 109 | September 6, 1943 | 49 | March 11, 1944 |
| 44-W-3 | 96 | October 4, 1943 | 57 | April 15, 1944 |
| 44-W-4 | 104 | November 1, 1943 | 52 | May 23, 1944 |
| 44-W-5 | 124 | December 7, 1943 | 71 | June 27, 1944 |
| 44-W-6 | 136 | January 8, 1944 | 72 | August 4, 1944 |
| 44-W-7 | 98 | February 12, 1944 | 59 | September 8, 1944 |
| 44-W-8 | 114 | March 14, 1944 | 49 | October 18, 1944 |
| 44-W-9 | 98 | April 13, 1944 | 55 | November 8, 1944 |
| 44-W-10 | 121 | May 26, 1944 | 68 | December 7, 1944 |

**All training and graduations were at Avenger Field, Sweetwater, Texas, with the following exceptions:**

* New Castle Army Air Base, Wilmington, Delaware.
** Ellington Field, Houston, Texas.
*** Trained in Houston but graduated at Avenger Field, Sweetwater, Texas
**** 76 trainees from class 43-W-4 trained in Houston

# THE LONG ROAD TO RECOGNITION

"The only reason they still aren't considered veterans is they are women. … The only thing wrong with those girls was that they were girls."

— Senator Barry Goldwater

December 20, 1944, Women Airforce Service Pilots program is deactivated. All records are sealed for over 30 years.

Nearly 33 years after WASP deactivation, the United States Congress passed, and on November 23, 1977 President Carter signed, Public Law 95-202 granting veteran status to all former WASPs. At the time, about 800 of the original women still survived, yet no WASPs were invited to the signing. Previous bills introduced in Congress in 1972, 1975, and 1976 had failed to pass.[1]

To further recognize WASP service, Congress amended Public Law 95-202 on September 24, 1983, by awarding the WWII Victory Medal and the American Campaign Medal to any WASP who had received an honorable discharge under the original 1977 law.[2]

"The Women Airforce Service Pilots courageously answered their country's call in a time of need while blazing a trail for the brave women who have given and continue to give so much in service to this nation."

— President Barack Obama.

On March 12, 2009, Public Law 111-40, authorizing a Congressional Gold Medal to honor the Women Airforce Service Pilots, quickly passes through the Congress. In a signing ceremony held in the Oval Office, July 1, 2009, President Obama signs the legislation into law. Present at the ceremony are WASPs Elaine Danforth Harmon (44-W-9), Lorraine H. Rodgers (44-W-2), and Bernice Falk Haydu (44-W-7).[3]

"We acknowledge that for too long the proud service of the WASPs was not recognized in word or in deed. Today, we honor you as the heroes that you are."

— Speaker of the House of Representatives Nancy Pelosi.

On March 10, 2010, more than 2,000 people, including over 200 surviving WASPs, gathered in Washington, D.C. to see all Women Airforce Service Pilots receive the Congressional Gold Medal. The original medal was donated to the Smithsonian Institution's collection, while each WASP received a smaller bronze version.

The previous day, at the Air Force Memorial in Arlington, Virginia, a wreath-laying and remembrance ceremony was held. The ceremony included a wreath and roses dedicated to the 38 women who died while flying as WASPs.[4]

President Obama signs the Congressional Gold Medal bill, July 1, 2009. The women in the photo are Rep. Ileana Ros-Lehtinen, WASP pilots Elaine Danforth Harmon, Lorraine H. Rodgers, and Bernice Falk Haydu; and active duty USAF pilots Col. Dawn Dunlop, Col. Bobbi Doorenbos, Lt. Col. Wendy Wasik, Maj. Kara Sandifur, and Maj. Nicole Malachowski. - *US Air Force Public Affairs photo.*

WASP Deanie Parrish (44-W-4) receives the Congressional Gold Medal, March 10, 2010, on behalf of all 1,102 Women Airforce Service Pilots at the Capitol Visitors Center, as members of Congress and several speakers look on. – *Department of Defense photo 100310-D-0653H-004.*

WASP Deanie Parrish (44-W-4) accepts the Congressional Gold Medal, March 10, 2010, on behalf of her fellow WASPs. Presenting the medal are Speaker of the House of Representatives Nancy Pelosi; Rep. John Boehner, House minority leader; Sen. Harry Reid, Senate majority leader; and Sen. Mitch McConnell, Senate minority leader. – *Department of Defense photo 100310-F-2418B-237a.*

At the WASP wreath-laying and remembrance ceremony held at the Air Force Memorial in Arlington, VA, March 9, 2010, WASP Dawn Seymour (43-W-5) receives a wreath honoring the 38 Women Airforce Service Pilots who lost their lives while flying for their country during WWII. – *Department of Defense photo _100309-D-0653H-019.*

During the wreath-laying and remembrance ceremony, Jan Nicolai holds a photo of Helen Jo Anderson Severson, one of the 38 deceased pilots who flew with the Women Airforce Service Pilots. – *Department of Defense photo 100309-D-0653H002.*

# CHAPTER NOTES

## *Chapter 1*

[1] Interview with Paula Williams, October 2012.

[2] (Medford, OR) *Mail Tribune*, 9 July 1944, 1.

[3] The Forest Service report followed procedures outlined in the National Environmental Policy Act of 1969 (NEPA) "requiring policies and procedures that will have a minimal environmental impact on National Forest lands."

[4] U.S. Department of Agriculture, Weather Bureau Chart, Medford Experiment Station, July 1944, www.ncdc.noaa.gov/IPS/coop/coop.html (9 October 2014). Ron Bartley, "BT-13 Wreckage Recovered from WWII Crash Site," *Oregon Aviation Historical Society Newsletter* 13.1 (August 2004): 4.

[5] "The Loop Family in America," www.theloopfamilyinamerica.org (3 January 2013). Government Land Records, www.glorecords.blm.gov (15 November 2014). Text of an Oklahoma College for Women's history exhibit provided in correspondence with Randy Talley, Media and Community Relations, University of Science and Arts, Chickasha, Oklahoma (September 2012).

[6] Talley correspondence. "Northwestern State Teachers College," www.pubco.net/normalschool (13 June 2014). "Encyclopedia of Oklahoma History & Culture," http://digital.library.okstate.edu (13 June 2014). "Induction to Oklahoma Hall of Fame," *Chickasha* (OK) *Express Star*, Chickashanews.com, 2 November 2007 (7 July 2014).

[7] (Washington, D. C.) *Evening Star*, 5 March 1939, 1; 20 June 1939, 5; 16 July 1939, sect. 2:1.

[8] (Washington, D.C.) *Evening Star*, 3 March 1940, C4. *Boston Herald*, 11 September 1939, 6. *Seattle Daily Times*, 27 June 1939, 1.

[9] *Dallas Morning News*, 8 December 1939, 2. *Lawrence* (KS) *Journal World*, 7 December 1939, 14. Patricia Strickland, *The Putt-Putt Air Force* (Washington, D.C.: Federal Aviation Administration, 1971), 109.

[10] Talley correspondence.

[11] *Ibid.* "*Induction to Oklahoma Hall of Fame*," *Chickasha* (OK) *Express Star*, Chickashanews.com, 2 November 2007 (7 July 2014). *Sweetwater* (TX) *Reporter*, 28 May 1943, 4.

[12] *Women Pilots With the AAF, 1941-1944, Army Air Forces Historical Studies No. 55*, (Washington, D.C.: Headquarters Army Air Forces, 1946), 23. *Boston Traveler*, 10 September 1942, 1, 2. (Sweetwater, TX) *The Avenger*, 28 June, 1943, 1.

[13] (Washington, D.C.) *Evening Star*, 4 July 1944, 1; 5 July 1944, 6.

[14] Texas Women's University, Women's Collection, Women Airforce Service Pilots, Mss 270.4, "Paula Loop Papers." *San Francisco Chronicle*, 8 July 1944, 8.

[15] *Medford* (OR) *Mail Tribune*, 9 July 1944, 1. Talley correspondence.

[16] Excerpts taken from death certificates posted on the FamilySearch.org website. Names of WASPs are not associated here with the cause of death, out of respect for surviving family members.

[17] Bert Andrews, "A Ladies Aid Society for the Air Corps?" *San Diego Union*, 14 May 1939, magazine section, 4.

[18] *Ibid.* The Ninety-Nines, Inc., "Betty Huyler Gillies," www.ninety-nines.org (13 April 2014).

[19] Andrews, "A Ladies Aid Society for the Air Corps?"

[20] *Ibid.*

## *Chapter 2*

[1] Jacqueline Cochran, "I Reached Stars the Hard Way," *Life* 37.7 (16 August 1954): 93, 95.

[2] ALLSTAR Network, www.allstar.fiu.edu/aero/cochran1.htm (05 May 2014). Doris L. Rich, "Cochran," *Notable American Women: A Biographical Dictionary Completing the Twentieth Century, Volume 5*, ed. Susan Ware (Boston: Harvard University Press, 2004) 131.

[3] Cochran, "I Reached Stars the Hard Way," 93, 95.

[4] *Ibid.* 98-99.

[5] *Ibid.* 101-102.

[6] U.S. Census Records, 1920, Florida, Walton County, Paxton Township, District: 148 , p. 2B. Cochran, "I Reached Stars the Hard Way," 104.

[7] Florida Memory, "WWI Service Cards," www.floridamemory.com (3 April 2014). U.S. Census Records, 1920, Florida, Escambia County, Pensacola City, District: 30, p. 1A; Florida, Holmes County, Noma Township, District: 40, p. 6B. www.Findagrave.com (3 April 2014). Florida, Death Index. Rich, "Cochran," 131. ALLSTAR Network, www.allstar.fiu.edu/aero/cochran1.htm (05 May 2014).

[8] Cochran, "I Reached Stars the Hard Way," 107.

[9] *San Diego Union*, 28 September 1947, 1, 2. *Cleveland* (OH) *Plain Dealer*, 24 March 1940, 28A.

[10] Cochran, "I Reached Stars the Hard Way," 107. *Dallas Morning News*, 17 March 1955, 1, 13. *Springfield* (MA) *Republican*, 5 December 1937, 2D.

[11] *Philadelphia Inquirer*, 8 October 1935, 28.

[12] *Springfield* (MA) *Republican*, 11 June 1934, 6; 7 August 1934, 6; 1 November 1934, 9. *Seattle Daily Times*, 18 October 1934, 14. *Trenton* (NJ) *Evening Times*, 20 October 1934, 2.

[13] *Springfield* (MA) *Republican*, 10 August 1934, 5; 18 August 1934, 2. "The History of Air Racing and Record Breaking," www.airracinghistory.freeola.com. (Washington, D.C.) *Evening Star*, 21 September 1937, 1.

[14] *Boston Herald*, 25 July 1939, 1; 2 October 1939, 8. *Springfield* (MA) *Republican*, 28 November 1939, 14.

[15] Women Pilots with the AAF, 2.

[16] *Boston Herald*, 8 December 1940, B3. *Omaha World Herald*, 28 May 1941, 4. *Kansas City* (MO) *Star*, 29 May 1941, 8.

[17] *Seattle Daily Times*, 16 June 1941, 7. *Dallas Morning News*, 6 July 1941, 3.

[18] *Springfield* (MA) *Republican*, 22 June 1941, 2. *Greensboro* (NC) *Daily News*, 21 June 1941, 1.

[19] *Ibid. Omaha World Herald*, 23 June 1941, 6.

[20] (Rockford, Ill) *Morning Star*, 2 July 1941, 5. (Springfield) *Illinois State Journal* 2 July 1941, 1. *Springfield* (MA) *Republican*, 2 July 1941, 1.

[21] San Francisco Chronicle, 3 July 1941, 5; 6 September 1941, 13. Women Pilots with the AAF, 5.

[22] Jacqueline Cochran, "Final Report on Women Pilot Program," Army Air Forces Report 6-1262, Headquarters Army Air Forces, 1945, 1. *Women Pilots with the AAF*, 6-7. (Washington, D.C.) *Evening Star*, 12 August 1941, B2. Eisenhower archives, "Letter and Survey to all women holders of licenses," July 29, 1941, Dwight D. Eisenhower Presidential Library, www.eisenhower.archives.gov (23 June 2013).

[23] *Kansas City* (MO) *Star*, 5 August 1941, 18.

[24] Women Pilots with the AAF, 10.

[25] *Dallas Morning News*, 24 January 1942, 4. Eisenhower archives, "Jacqueline Cochran's employment with the British Air Transport Auxiliary," February 10, 1943; "Air Transport Auxiliary Agreement," January 24, 1942. *Women Pilots with the AAF*, 11-12.

[26] Women Pilots with the AAF, 12.

[27] (Washington, D.C.) *Evening Star*, 10 June 1942, B7. *San Francisco Chronicle*, 9 March 1942, 5. Eisenhower archives, Jacqueline Cochran, "Form letter regarding the British Air Transport Auxiliary," undated.

[28] Greensboro (NC) Record, 10 July 1941, 7. San Diego Union, 17 September 1942, 4. British Air Transport Auxiliary, www.airtransportaux.com (20 July 2013). The four ATA pilots who later became WASPS were: Mikki Allen, Emily Chapin, Hazel Raines, and Helen Richey. KayVan Dooze returned as a Wasp flight instructor.

[29] *Kansas City* (MO) *Star*, 1 September 1942, 22.

[30] (Washington, D.C.) *Evening Star*, 10 September 1942, 1. *Women Pilots with the AAF*, 14-16.

[31] *Women Pilots with the AAF*, 17-21. Eisenhower archives, "Press release regarding Jacqueline Cochran's appointment as Director of Women's Flying Training," September 14, 1942.

## *Chapter 3*

[1] Gloversville (NY) Leader Republican, 28 May 1940, 8. (Washington, D.C.) *Evening Star*, 31 July 1940, B1.

[2] Women Pilots with the AAF, 3-4.

[3] Ibid.

[4] Laura White, "She Flew Flying Fortresses," *Boston Herald*, 29 October 1972, sect. 5:9.

[5] *Escanaba* (MI) *Daily Press*, 20 March 1928, 19; 29 November 1928, 1, 7; 20 May 1930, 2.

[6] "1903-1963 - Six Decades of Service," *Milwaukee School of Engineering Bulletin* 16.1 (1 January 1964): 27, 31. William Manly, "Milwaukee Pilot Taught Headline Winners to Fly," *Milwaukee Journal*, 13 October 1942, Green Sheet, 1. Federal Census Records. Ellis Island Foundation, http://libertyellisfoundation.org/passenger (12 December 2014).

[7] Deborah G. Douglas, "Nancy Harkness Love: Female Pilot and First to Fly for the U.S. Military," www.historynet.com/nancy-harkness-love-female-pilot-and-first-to-fly-for-the-us-military.htm (03

July 2014). Manly, 1.

[8] Manly, 1. *San Francisco Chronicle*, 28 May 1930, 23. *Kansas City* (MO) *Star*, 27 September 1942, C4.

[9] *Kansas City* (MO) *Star*, 27 September 1942, C4.

[10] Laura White, 9. *Escanaba* (MI) *Daily Press*, 8 January 1943, 2.

[11] "Freshman Does Stunt Flying Over Po'keepsie," (Poughkeepsie, NY) *Vassar Miscellany* News, 20 February 1932, 4. *Boston Herald*, 11 September 1942, 4. Vassar Encyclopedia, "Nancy Harkness Love" http://vcencyclopedia.vassar.edu (20 October 2014)

[12] "Freshman Does Stunt Flying Over Po'keepsie,"

[13] *Poughkeepsie* (NY) *Eagle-News*, 16 April 1932, 7. (Yonkers, NY) *Herald Statesman*, 3 June 1932, 7. *Chicago Tribune*, 29 January 1934, 8.

[14] (Poughkeepsie, NY) *Vassar Miscellany News*, 20 February 1932, 4. *Boston Herald*, 10 June 1934, society section, 6.

[15] (Poughkeepsie, NY) *Vassar Miscellany News*, 20 February 1932, 4. *Boston Herald*, 2 August 1935, 11; 12 January 1936, 21; 30 January 1936, 13. *Poughkeepsie* (NY) *Eagle-News*, 3 August 1935, 4. (Albany, NY) *Knickerbocker News*, 22 September 1942, 4B.

[16] "Woman Flyer Interests Uncle Sam in Plan to Mark Airway Trail," (Baton Rouge, LA) *Morning Advocate*, 21 November 1935, 7. *Brooklyn* (NY) *Eagle*, 16 September 1937, 6. Deborah G. Douglas, "Nancy Harkness Love:"

[17] J. H. Meyer, "The 1936 National Air Races," *Popular Aviation* 14.5 (Nov 1936): 20. *Kansas City* (MO) *Star*, 27 September 1942, C4.

[18] *Brooklyn Daily Eagle*, 16 September 1937, 6.

[19] (Biloxi, MS) *Daily Herald*, 31 August 1937, 3. *Cleveland Plain Dealer*, 12 September 1937, 31. "Two *Aircar*s for Every Garage," *San Francisco Chronicle*, 20 February 1938, Magazine Section, 15.

[20] *Niagara Falls Gazette*, 29 September 1937, 13. "Aircraft Owners and Pilots Association," *Popular Aviation* 26.3 (March 1940): 5.

[21] Hamilton Thornquist, "Love Birds," *Popular Aviation* 24.2 (February 1939): 44, 46.

[22] *Gloversville* (NY) *Leader Republican*, 28 May 1940, 8. (Washington, D.C.) *Evening Star*, 31 July 1940, B1.

[23] Boston Traveler, 5 February 1942, 9. Boston Herald, 12 September 1945, 18. Women Pilots with the AAF, 13.

[24] William H. Tunner, *Over the Hump* (Washington, D.C.: U.S. Air Force, 1998), 26-27.

[25] Tunner, 34-35.

[26] (Baton Rouge, LA) *Advocate*, 18 July 1942, 14. *Boston Herald*, 11 September 1942, 4.

### *Chapter 4*

[1] Oscar Schisgall, "The Girls Deliver the Goods," *Boston Herald*, 28 February 1943, magazine section, 8.

[2] (Albany, NY) *Knickerbocker News*, 22 September 1942, 4B. *Kansas City* (MO) *Star*, 27 September 1942, 3C.

[3] Schisgall, 8, 10. *Kansas City* (MO) *Star*, 27 September 1942, 3C.

[4] Schisgall, 10. *Women Pilots with the AAF*, 18, 22. (Albany , NY) *Knickerbocker News*, 22 September 1942, 4B. *San Diego Union*, 17 September 1942, 2.

[5] Women Pilots with the AAF, 15, 17.

[6] (Albany , NY) *Knickerbocker News*, 22 September 1942, 4B. (New Orleans, LA) *Times-Picayune*, 17 September 1942, 24. *Greensboro* (NC) *Daily News*, 25 October 1942, 9. Schisgall, 10.

[7] *Women Pilots with the AAF*, 30-31. (Boise) *Idaho Statesman*, 12 October 1942, Society Section, 10.

[8] *Women Pilots with the AAF*, 35. *San Diego Union*, 17 September 1942, 2. Schisgall, 10.

[9] Schisgall, 10.

[10] *Ibid.*

[11] "WAFS Uniforms," www.blitzkriegbaby.de/wasp/wasp3a.htm (3 August 2014).

[12] "Pioneer in Flight: Cornelia Fort and the WAFS," Nashville Public Library, http://nashvillepubliclibrary.org (3 January 2015).

[13] Women Pilots with the AAF," 72-71.

[14] Women Pilots with the AAF," 77.

[15] Schisgall, 10.

[16] Women Pilots with the AAF, 38-39.

[17] Women Pilots with the AAF, 67, 69.

[18] Women Pilots with the AAF," 61.

### *Chapter 5*

[1] Marjorie Kumler, "They've Done It Again!" *Ladies Home Journal* 61.3 (March 1944): 29.

[2] *Ibid.* Cochran, "Final Report on Women Pilot Program," 19.

[3] Cochran, "Final Report on Women Pilot Program," 4-5, 9.

[4] Kumler, "They've Done It Again!" 29.

[5] Ibid.

[6] Cochran, "Final Report on Women Pilot Program," 16-17.

[7] Kumler, "They've Done It Again!" 29.

[8] *Ibid. Seattle Daily Times*, 31 July 1938, sect. 4:12. *Dallas Morning News*, 1 December 1938, 9.

[9] "The 1940 Air Terminal Museum," www.1940airterminal.org (7 July 2014). Kumler, "They've Done It Again!" 29.

[10] Kumler, "They've Done It Again!" 29.

[11] *Ibid.*

[12] (Sweetwater, TX) *The Avenger*, 22 October 1943, 6.

[13] *Ibid.*

[14] *Ibid.*

[15] (Houston, TX) *The Fifinella Gazette*, 1 April 1943, 2.

[16] Marianne Verges, *On Silver Wings* (New York: Ballantine Books, 1991), 82. WASP Deanie Bishop Parrish, "History of The Uniforms of the Wasp of WWII," www.wingsacrossamerica.us/wasp/gallery (4 April 2014).

[17] (Sweetwater, TX) *The Avenger*, 22 October 1943, 6.

[18] *Wichita Falls* (TX) *Times*, 9 April 1972, 17. *Springfield* (MA) *Republican* (Springfield, MA), 14 March 1942, 4.

[19] (Houston, TX) *The Fifinella Gazette*, 1 April 1943, 6; 24 May 1943.

[20] *Canton* (OH) *Repository*, 31 October 1942, 6. *Dallas Morning News*, 22 November 1942, sect. 2:7. Kumler, "They've Done It Again!" 168. *Women Pilots with the AAF*, 25.

[21] Cochran, "Final Report on Women Pilot Program," 16.

[22] Kumler, "They've Done It Again!" 167-168.

[23] *Ibid.*

[24] *Ibid.* (Houston, TX) *The Fifinella Gazette*, 10 February 1943, 3. Cochran, "Final Report on Women Pilot Program," 14-15. (Sweetwater, TX) *The Avenger*, 22 October 1943, 6.

[25] Kumler, "They've Done It Again!" 167-168. (Sweetwater, TX) *The Avenger*, 7 January 1944, 1.

[26] Walt Disney, "Pukka Gen on Gremlins," *Richmond* (VA) *Times Dispatch*, 25 December 1942, 15. Peter Edson, "Gremlins Ride With Pilots of the R.A.F.," *Canton* (OH) *Repository*, June 1942, 4. *Greensboro* (NC) *Record*, 7 November 1942, 5.

[27] (Houston, TX) *The Fifinella Gazette*, 10 February 1943, 3, 4.

[28] Kumler, "They've Done It Again!" 169.

[29] "Class Rosters and Graduation Data," Women Airforce Service Pilots Digital Archive, Texas Woman's University, http://twudigital.contentdm.oclc.org (15 November 2014).

[30] *Ibid.* (Houston, TX) *The Fifinella Gazette*, 1 March 1943, 2.

## *Chapter 6*

[1] "In Memoriam," (Houston, TX) *The Fifinella Gazette*, 1 April 1943, 1. New York State Census, 1915, 1925.U.S. Census Records. United States World War I Draft Registration Cards, 1917-1918. "The Centennial of The University of California, 1868-1968," http://www.oac.cdlib.org (24 August 2014).

[2] National Archives, Hawaii, Honolulu Passenger Lists, 1900-1953, Roll 235 vol. 355, 1941-1942.U.S. Census Records. *Architect and Engineer* 151.1 (October 1942): 42.

[3] *Galva* (IL) *News*, 26 May 1938, 2; 24 July 1941, 1, 9; 22 July 1954, sect. 5:5.

[4] *Galva* (IL) *News*, 11 February 1943, 5; 12 February 1943, 5.

[5] Dallas Morning News, 8 March 1943, 1. San Luis Obispo (CA) Daily Telegram, 8 March 1943, 3.

[6] Ibid.

[7] *Galva* (IL) *News*, 18 March 1943, 2.

[8] *History of the WASP Program. Army Air Forces Central Flying Training Command* (Randolph Field, TX: Army Air Forces Central Flying Command, 20 January 1945), 9.

[9] Nashville Public Library, http://nashvillepubliclibrary.org (3 January 2015).

[10] John Trotwood Moore, Austin P Foster, *Tennessee- The Volunteer State, Vol. 2* (Chicaco: S.J. Clarke, 1923), 778-779. *Nashville Banner*, 22 March 1940, 1.

[11] PBS (Public Broadcasting Service), "American Experience: Fly Girls," www.pbs.org/wgbh/amex/flygirls (10 May 2014).

[12] *Philadelphia Inquirer*, 10 June 1945, "Everybody's Weekly," 4. *Nashville Banner*, 22 March 1940, 1. "Cornelia Fort," Tennessee Encyclopedia of History and Culture, http://tennesseeencyclopedia.net (9 September 2014). *Women Pilots with the AAF*, 81.

[13] *Women Pilots with the AAF*, 82. "Cornelia Fort," SF-260, http://sf260w.com/corneliatxt.html (6 June 2014).

[14] "Cornelia Fort '39 in 1942," Sarah Lawrence College, www.slc.edu/magazine/meaningful-life/alumni/cornelia-fort-39.html. "Cornelia Fort," SF-260.

[15] *San Diego Union*, 1 October 1941, 4.

[16] "Cornelia Fort," SF-260.

[17] *San Francisco* (CA) *Chronicle*, 4 March 1942, 9. Cornelia Fort, "At the twilight's last gleaming," *Woman's Home Companion* (July 1943): 19.

[18] *Ibid. San Diego Union*, 13 December 1941, 3.

[19] *San Francisco* (CA) *Chronicle*, 4 March 1942, 9. "Cornelia Fort," SF-260

[20] *Ibid. San Diego Union*, 17 September 1942, 4.

[21] "Cornelia Fort," SF-260.

[22] *Ibid.*

[23] Marianne Verges, *On Silver Wings*, 88-89. Rob Simbeck, *Daughter of the Air: The Brief Soaring Life of Cornelia Fort* (New York: Grove Press, 1999) 226.

[24] National Archives, "Access to Archival Databases" http://aad.archives.gov (06 May 2013). California Death Index.

[25] Kumler, "They've Done It Again!" 169. (Houston, TX) *Fifinella Gazette*, 23 April 1943, 2.

[26] Kumler, "They've Done It Again!" 169.

[27] *Ibid. Dallas Morning News*, 23 April 1943, 14.

[28] "Graduation Program Notes," http://wingsacrossamerica.us/records_all/documents.htm (4 April 2014). Kumler, "They've Done It Again!" 169.

[29] Verges, *On Silver Wings*, 82. "Silver Wasp Wings," http://wingsacrossamerica.us/elements/index.htm (4 April 2014).

[30] "Graduation Program Notes."

[31] *Ibid.* Kumler, "They've Done It Again!" 169.

[32] *Ibid. Washington* (D.C.) *Daily Star*, 25 April 1943, A13.

[33] Kumler, "They've Done It Again!" 169. *Dallas Morning News*, 25 April 1943, 9.

[34] *Ibid.*

## *Chapter 7*

[1] (Sweetwater, TX) *The Avenger*, 17 December, 1943, 5.

[2] *Sweetwater* (TX) *Reporter*, 29 December 1944, 1, 6. *Laredo* (TX) *Times*, 23 March 1930, 1. *Sweetwater* (TX) *Reporter*, 11 August 1937, 1; 15 August 1937, 1.

[3] *Sweetwater* (TX) *Reporter*, 9 July 1939, 8; 7 April 1940, 3; 9 July 1940, 1.

[4] *Dallas Morning News*, 17 March 1941, 4; 28 March, 3. *Sweetwater*

(TX) *Reporter*, 28 December 1941, 1; 29 December 1944, 1.

[5] *Sweetwater* (TX) *Reporter*, 1 April 1943, 1; 29 December 1944, 1, 6. (Sweetwater, TX), *Nolan County News*, 16 April 1942, 1; 23 April 1942, 1; 30 April 1942, 1.

[6] (Sweetwater, TX), *Nolan County News*, 7 May 1942, 3.

[7] *Ibid.* (Sweetwater, TX), *Nolan County News*, 16 April 1942, 1; 14 May 1942, 5.

[8] (Sweetwater, TX) *Nolan County News*, 2 July 1942, 7. *Sweetwater* (TX) *Reporter*, 6 July 1942, 1, 2; 29 December 1944, 1.

[9] (Sweetwater, TX) *Nolan County News*, 9 July 1942, 1; 10 July 1942, 1; 6 August 1942, 1. *Sweetwater* (TX) *Reporter*, 14 August 1942, 1.

[10] (Sweetwater, TX) *The Avenger*, 22 October 1943, 1; 3 March 1944, 7.

[11] (New Orleans, LA) *Times-Picayune*, 21 January 1943, 12. *Sweetwater* (TX) *Reporter*, 16 April 1943, 1; 28 April 1943, 1. *History of the WASP Program*, 25-34.

[12] *History of the WASP* Program, 25-26. (Sweetwater, Tex.) *Sweetwater Reporter*, 1 April 1943, 1.

[13] (Houston, TX) *The Fifinella Gazette*, 23 April 1943, 1, 4. (Sweetwater, TX) *The Avenger*, 11 May 1943, 1; 22 October 1943, 6.

[14] (Sweetwater, Tex.) *Sweetwater Reporter*, 28 May 1943, 1, 4. *Dallas Morning News* (Dallas, TX), 30 May 1943, 8.

[15] (Sweetwater, TX) *The Avenger*, 26 July, 1943, 3. *Sweetwater* (TX) *Reporter*, 17 June 1943, 1.

[16] (Sweetwater, TX) *The Avenger*, 26 July, 1943, 1. *Dallas Morning News*, 4 July 1943, 4.

[17] "Eleven Fatalities During Training," http://wwii-women-pilots.org (8 August 2014). (Sweetwater, Tex.) *Sweetwater Reporter*, 8 June 1943, 1. Sally Van Wagenen Keil, *Those Wonderful Women in Their Flying Machines* (New York: Rawson, Wade Publishers, 1979), 160.

[18] Saint Louis University Libraries Digital Collections, "The Archive of Saint Louis University, 1937" (yearbook), 112, http://cdm.slu.edu (5 October 2014).

[19] *Sweetwater* (TX) *Reporter*, 9 June 1943, 1. (Sweetwater, TX) *The Avenger*, 28 June 1943, 2.

[20] Saint Louis University, http://www.slu.edu (5 October 2014).

[21] *Waco* (TX) *News-Tribune*, 9 June 1943, 1. *Dallas Morning News*, 9 June 1943, sec. 2:8. (Sweetwater, TX) *The Avenger*, 28 June 1943, 2.

[22] (Houston, TX) *The Fifinella Gazette*, 23 April 1943, 1. "Deanie Parrish, Women Airforce Service Pilot," *Texas Heritage* v. 4 (2008):25.

[23] *Ibid. Boston Traveler* , 27 April 1943, 10.

[24] Deanie Parrish, 24. (Sweetwater, Tex.) *Sweetwater Reporter*, 6 December 1943, 1.

[25] Deanie Parrish, 24-25.

[26] (Sweetwater, Tex.) *Sweetwater Reporter*, 6 December 1943, 6.

[27] (Sweetwater, TX) *The Avenger*, 19 November 1943, 6. Cochran, "Final Report on Women Pilot Program," 21.

[28] Cochran, "Final Report on Women Pilot Program," 9. *Boston Traveler*, 12 March 1943, 30.

[29]U.S. Census Records. *The 1939 Dacotah*, University of North Dakota Yearbook, 197. *The 1942 Dacotah*, University of North Dakota Yearbook, 42. (Rolla, ND) *Turtle Mountain Star*, 18 January 1940, 8.

[30] (Rolla, ND) *Turtle Mountain Star*, 18 January 1940, 8. *The 1942 Dacotah*, University of North Dakota Yearbook, 96. *Bismarck* (ND) *Tribune*, 22 April 1940, 4.

[31] *Omaha World Herald*, 6 August 1943, 30. *Sweetwater* (TX) *Reporter*, 5 August 1943, 1. (Sweetwater, TX) *The Avenger*, 2 September 1943, 3.

## Chapter 8

[1] *Sweetwater* (TX) *Reporter*, 14 May 1943, 1.

[2] *Sweetwater* (TX) *Reporter*, 13 April 1943, 2; 2 May 1943, 1, 8.

[3] *Sweetwater* (TX) *Reporter*, 6 July 1943, 2. Cochran, "Final Report on Women Pilot Program," 22. *Boston* (MA) *Traveler*, 20 August 1943, 2.

[4] "Women Pilots of the AAF," 48.

[5] "Women Pilots of the AAF," 47.

[6] (Washington, D.C.) *Evening Star*, 25 October 1943, 2. *Omaha World Herald*, 26 October 1943, 12. John Stuart, "The WASP," *Flying* 34.1 (January 1944): 74.

[7] PBS (Public Broadcasting Service), "American Experience: Fly Girls," www.pbs.org/wgbh/amex/flygirls (10 May 2014).

[8] *Rockford* (IL) *Morning Star*, 21 November 1943, 6.

[9] John Stuart, "The WASP," 74.

[10] (Sweetwater, TX) *The Avenger*, 21 January 1944, 5.

[11] John Stuart, "The WASP," 163. *Kansas City* (MO) *Star*, 7 November 1943, C2.

[12] (Washington, D.C.) *Evening Star*, 25 October 1943, 2. *Canton* (OH) *Repository*, 27 October 1943, 5.

[13] *Kansas City* (MO) *Star*, 7 November 1943, C2.

[14] "Mabel Virginia Rawlinson," http://wingsacrossamerica.us/web/obits/rawlinsom_mabel.htm

[15] *Ibid.* (Adrian, Michigan) *Daily Telegram*, 31 August 1943, 10.

[16] (Troy, NY) *Times Record*, 28 November 1942, 3; 25 August 1943, 16. National Archives, "Access to Archival Databases" http://aad.archives.gov (07 July 2014).

[17] U.S. Naval Observatory, Astronomical Applications Department, http://aa.usno.navy.mil (14 January 2015). "Mabel V. Rawlinson - AAF Accident Report," http://wwii-women-pilots.org/WASP_KIA/MRawlinsonAAR (1 July 2014).

[18] NPR (National Public Radio), "Female WWII Pilots: The Original Fly Girls," www.npr.org/2010/03/09/123773525/female-wwii-pilots-the-original-fly-girls (17 July 2014).

[19] Deborah G. Douglas, *United States Women in Aviation: 1940-1985*, (Washington, D.C.: Smithsonian Institution Press, 1990), 51.

[20] PBS, "American Experience: Fly Girls."

[21] "Mabel V. Rawlinson - AAF Accident Report." *Richmond* (VA) *Times Dispatch*, 2 September 1943, 15.

[22] National Museum of the Air Force, www.nationalmuseum.af.mil/factsheets (05 June 2014).

[23] "Women Airforce Service Pilots," http://wwii-women-pilots.org (8 August 2014),

[24] *Ibid. Big Spring* (TX) *Daily Herald*, 31 August 1943, 5. Texas Death Certificates, www.FamilySearch.org.

[25] South Dakota Department of the Military, "Fallen Sons and Daughters of South Dakota in WWII." http://mva.sd.gov/sdwwiimemorial/subpages/profiles (3 August 2014).

[26] *Ibid.* South Dakota Department of the Military, "In Memory of U.S. Army Trainee, Women's Auxiliary Air Corps Helen Anderson Severson," http://mva.sd.gov/sdwwiimemorial/subpages/profiles (3 August 2014). *New York Sun*, 16 January 1939, 29. Katherine J. Mehrer, "Dakota Images," *South Dakota History* 33.3 (Fall 2003): 286.

[27] *Ibid.*

[28] *Milwaukee Journal*, 7 March 1939, 7; 1 September 1943, 1. *Appleton* (WI) *Post-Crescent*, 13 June 1938, 11.U.S. Census Records. Ralph M. Immell, "Wisconsin's Future in Aviation," *Wisconsin Blue Book, 1940* (Madison, WI: Legislative Reference Bureau, 1940), 179.

[29] *Milwaukee Journal*, 1 September 1943, 1; 11 July 1945, Green Sheet, 1. Liam Callanan, "Field of Dreamers," *Milwaukee Magazine*, www.milwaukeemag.com/article/10212012-FieldofDreamers (7 August 2013).

[30] North Texas State Teacher's College, *The Yucca, Yearbook of North*

*Texas State Teacher's College, 1941. Denton, Texas.* http://digital.library.unt.edu/ark:/67531/metapth61012 (5 February 8, 2015.

[31] (Sweetwater, TX) *The Avenger*, 28 June 1943, 3; 26 July 1943, 1.

[32] Meg Jones, "WWII pilot to finally get her honors," (Milwaukee, WI) *Journal Sentinel*, 14 July 2010. *Sweetwater (TX) Reporter*, 1 September 1943, 3.

[33] South Dakota Department of the Military, "In Memory of U.S. Army Air Corps Captain Robert A. Severson," http://mva.sd.gov/sdwwiimemorial/subpages/profiles (3 August 2014).

[34] Ozzie Roberts, "Winged Victory. WWII female pilots getting long-overdue recognition," *San Diego Union Tribune*, 29 August 2009.

[35] *Sweetwater* (TX) *Reporter*, 10 August 1943, 3.

[36] *Ibid.*

[37]U.S. Census Records. *Auburn* (CA) *Journal-Republican*, 19 August 1943, 1; 30 September 1943, 1. "Placer and Sierra College Timeline, www.sierracollege.edu/about-us/history (10 December 2014).

[38] *Sweetwater* (TX) *Reporter*, 26 September 1943, 1.

[39] *Ibid. Dallas Morning News*, 26 September 1943, 2. *Greensboro* (NC) *Daily News*, 27 September 1943, 9.

[40] *Sweetwater* (TX) *Reporter*, 26 September 1943, 1.

[41] *Auburn* (CA) *Journal-Republican*, 30 September 1943, 1.

## *Chapter 9*

[1] Library of Congress Veterans History Project, "Interview Transcript: Marion Foster Stegeman Hodgson," http://lcweb2.loc.gov/diglib (2 February 2014).

[2] (Sweetwater, TX) *The Avenger*, 8 October 1943, 5.

[3] *Ibid.* Alisha Semchuck, "Fly Girls recount their trials, triumphs in World War II flight," *Antelope Valley* (Palmdale, CA) *Press*, 30 March 2007.

[4] WASP Virtual Collection, Texas Woman's University Library, "319th AAFFTD Alphabetical List of Delinquencies and Demerits," www.twu.edu/library/wasp_virtual_collection.asp (15 February 2014).

[5] (Sweetwater, TX) *The Avenger*, 3 December 1943, 5-6.

[6] *Sweetwater* (TX) *Reporter*, 15 June 1943, 5. (Sweetwater, TX) *The Avenger*, 28 June, 1943, 8; 8 October 1943, 3.

[7] (Sweetwater, TX) *The Avenger*, 26 July, 1943, 1, 6.

[8] *Ibid.* (Sweetwater, TX) *The Avenger*, 14 July 1944, 7.

[9] *Sweetwater* (TX) *Reporter*, 9 June 1943, 6; 14 June 1943, 2, 6.

[10] *Sweetwater* (TX) *Reporter*, 6 June 1943, 2; 24 June 1943, 2; 28 June 1943, 2.

[11] *Sweetwater* (TX) *Reporter*, 15 June 1943, 1, 5.

[12] Helen Kelly Drake, "Memories of Other Times and Other Places," www.wingsacrossamerica.us/records_all/wasp_articles/memories.htm (09 September 2014.)

[13] *Sweetwater* (TX) *Reporter*, 1 July 1943, 1; 7 July 1943, 2.

[14] *Sweetwater* (TX) *Reporter*, 19 July 1943, 1.

[15] *Sweetwater* (TX) *Reporter*, 15 July 1943, 1; 20 July 1943, 1.

[16] *Sweetwater* (TX) *Reporter*, 7 September 1943, 2; 15 September 1943, 2. (Sweetwater, TX) *The Avenger*, 8 October 1943, 1; 22 October 1943, 5.

[17] (Sweetwater, TX) *The Avenger*, 28 June 1943, 8. (Cheyenne) *Wyoming State Tribune*, 16 March 1917, 3; 20 March 1917, 5. *House Journal of the Thirteenth State Legislature of Wyoming*, (Laramie, WY: Laramie Republican Company, 1915), 47.

[18] (Cheyenne) *Wyoming State Tribune*, 19 September 1917, 5. *Los Angeles City Directory, 1929* (Los Angeles: Los Angeles Directory Company, 1929), 1555.

[19] *San Bernardino* (CA) *County Sun*, 6 October 1943, 10. *Seattle Daily Times*, 6 October 1943, 17.

[20] (Sweetwater, TX) *The Avenger*, 8 October 1943, 1.

[21] (Sweetwater, TX) *The Avenger*, 2 September 1943, 1.

[22] *Ibid.*

[23] *Sweetwater* (TX) *Reporter*, 21 September 1943, 6. (Sweetwater, TX) *The Avenger*, 22 October 1943, 1; 19 November 1943, 8.

[24] *Sweetwater* (TX) *Reporter*, 2 November 1943, 4.

[25] Illinois Dept. of Mines and Minerals, *Coal Report, Volume 38* (Springfield, IL: Illinois State Journal Company, 1919), 229. "William Edward Trebing, Myrtle Mae DeWitt, and Bill Otis Trebing," http://trees.ancestry.com (15 January 2015).

[26] U.S. Census Records. *Sweetwater* (TX) *Reporter*, 8 November 1943, 1.

[27] "Mary Elizabeth Trebing," http://wingsacrossamerica.us/wasp/38/mary_elizabeth_trebing.htm (23 October 2014). Aviation Safety Network, http://aviation-safety.net/wikibase/wiki.php?id=106417 (23 October 2014).

[28] *Sweetwater* (TX) *Reporter*, 4 November 1943, 1; 11 November 1943,

1; 12 November 1943, 1; 14 November 1943, 1, 6.

[29] (Sweetwater, TX) *The Avenger*, 3 December 1943, 1. *Sweetwater* (TX) *Reporter*, 23 November 1943, 1; 28 November, 1943, 1.

## *Chapter 10*

[1] *Seattle Daily Times*, 23 February 1941, 5; 18 March 1941, 18.

[2] *Seattle Daily Times*, 30 March 1941, 12.

[3] *Ibid. Seattle Daily Times*, 21 February 1943, 20.

[4] U.S. Census Records. (Oroville, WA) *Okanogan Valley Gazette-Tribune*, 12 April 2012, A4; 10 May 2012, A4. *Seattle Daily Times*, 18 April 1948, 9; 11 March 1949, 16.

[5] *Riverside* (CA) *Daily Press*, 6 December 1943, 8.

[6] Women Pilots With the AAF, 59.

[7] *Riverside* (CA) *Independent Enterprise*, 4 December 1943, 3; 6 December 1943, 8. *Seattle Daily Times*, 5 December 1943, 1, 8. *The Rhinelander* (WI) *Daily News*, 6 December 1943, 2.

[8] (Sweetwater, TX) *The Avenger*, 11 May 1943, 6. *The Rhinelander* (WI) *Daily News*, 6 December 1943, 2.

[9] *Riverside* (CA) *Independent Enterprise*, 6 December 1943, 8. *Seattle Daily Times*, 5 December 1943, 1, 8.

[10] *Seattle Daily Times*, 18 April 1948, 9; 1 July 1953, 11.

[11] (Sweetwater, TX) *The Avenger*, 8 October 1943, 2.

[12] *Ibid.* (Sweetwater, TX) *The Avenger*, 7 January 1944, 6.

[13] (Sweetwater, TX) *The Avenger*, 22 October 1943, 2, 7; 3 December, 1943, 5.

[14] *Boston Herald*, 17 November, 1943, 11. Cochran, "Final Report on Women Pilot Program," 19. Sweetwater, TX) *The Avenger*, 3 December 1943, 1; 7 January 1944, 1, 7; 4 February 1944, 1; 3 March 1944, 2, 3.

[15] (Sweetwater, TX) *The Avenger*, 22 October 1943, 7.

[16] (Sweetwater, TX) *The Avenger*, 22 October 1943, 2; 3 December 1943, 2.

[17] (Sweetwater, TX) *The Avenger*, 3 December 1943, 5; 17 December 1943, 1; 7 January 1944, 1, 6, 3.

[18] *Dallas Morning News*, 13 January 1944, sect. 2:1; 14 January 1944, sect. 2:1. (Sweetwater, TX) *The Avenger*, 21 January 1944, 1, 4.

[19] *Sweetwater* (TX) *Reporter*, 19 December 1943, 1.

[20] *Miami* (OK) *Daily News-Record*, 4 February 1944, 7.

[21] Federal Census Records.

[22] "Oklahoma County Marriages," FamilySearch,

https://familysearch.org (2 January 2016).

[23] *Williamsport* (PA) *Sun Gazette*, 4 February 1944, 1. (Hagerstown, MD) *Daily Mail*, 5 February 1944, 2.

[24] (Bingen, WA) *Mt. Adams Sun*, 3 March 1944, 8. (Watervliet, MI) *Tri-City Record*, 14 February 2008, 4

[25] (Bingen, WA) *Mt. Adams Sun*, 3 March 1944, 8. *San Jose* (CA) *Evening News*, 18 February 1944, 1.

[26] (Bingen, WA) *Mt. Adams Sun*, 19 March 1942, 6; 3 March 1942, 8. *San Jose* (CA) *Evening News*, 18 February 1944, 1. (Newton, KS) *Christlicher Bundesbote*, 14 March 1944, 14.

[27] (Newton, KS) *Christlicher Bundesbote*, 14 March 1944, 14.

[28] (Sweetwater, TX) *The Avenger*, 18 February 1943, 1.

[29] Santa Barbara Unified School District, "Regular Meeting Board of Education, June 8, 1939," p. 10, www.sbunified.org (06 February 2015). (Santa Barbara, CA) *Daily Sound*, 6 November 2007. Will Rogers, Steven K. Gragert, M. Jane Johansson, *The Papers of Will Rogers, v. 3*, ed. Arthur Frank Wertheim and Barbara Bair (Oklahoma City: University of Oklahoma Press, 2001), 133-134, 336.

[30] U.S. Census Records. *Cleveland Plain Dealer*, 30 June 1929, 12. "Texas, Birth Index, 1903-1997," https://familysearch.org (06 February 2015). "Women Airforce Service Pilots Killed in Service," http://wwii-women-pilots.org/WASP_KIA/38KIA.html (6 July 2014).

[31] *Riverside* (CA) *Daily Press*, 26 February 1944, 1. Aviation Archeology, www.aviationarchaeology.com (7 July 2014).

[32] (Sweetwater, TX) *The Avenger*, 19 May 1944, 5.

[33] (Sweetwater, TX) *The Avenger*, 19 May 1944, 5; 17 March 1944, 7. U.S. Department of Agriculture, Weather Bureau Chart, Blythe, California Station, February 1944, www.ncdc.noaa.gov/IPS/coop/coop.html (14 February 2015).

[34] (Sweetwater, TX) *The Avenger*, 4 February 1944, 3, 7; 7 April 1944, 5; 19 May 1944, 1.

## *Chapter 11*

[1] *Omaha World Herald*, 10 October 1941, 12. *Dallas Morning News*, 22 July 1943, 5. M. J. Joslow, "The Week in Aviation," *Springfield* (MA) *Republican*, 13 January 1944, 9.

[2] (Baton Rouge, LA) *Advocate*, 31 January 1944, 6. *San Francisco Chronicle*, 21 January 1944, 1. John Stuart, "The Wasp," 73. *New York*

*Times*, 4 January 1944, Sports section, 14.

[3] Costello, Rep. John. HR 3358, A bill to provide for the appointment of female pilots in the Air Forces of the Army, 30 September 1943, 78th Congress, 1st Session; HR 4219, A bill to provide for the appointment of female pilots and aviation cadets in the Air Forces of the Army, 17 February 1944, 78th Congress, 2nd Session.

[4] *Omaha World Herald*, 22 March 1944, 2. *Kansas City* (MO) *Star*, 22 March 1944, 8. *Springfield* (MA) *Republican*, 23 March 1944, 11.

[5] (Sweetwater, TX) *The Avenger*, 5 May 1944, 1.

[6] (Sweetwater, TX) *The Avenger*, 3 March 1944, 1.

[7] Sweetwater, TX) *The Avenger*, 18 February 1944, 1, 3. Maj. Gen. Barton K. Yount, "Airmen By the Thousands," *Flying* 31:1 (July 1942): 81.

[8] "West Virginia Letter," (Cleveland) *Ohio Farmer*, 11 April 1914, 9. (Washington, D.C.) *Evening Star*, 5 November 1933, 1, 2. *Cumberland* (MD) *News*, 5 September 1957, 7.

[9] (Washington, D. C.) *Evening Star*, 28 December 1942, B1. *Richmond* (VA) *Times Dispatch*, 28 March 1944, 7; 9 March 1975, G4.

[10] *Richmond* (VA) *Times Dispatch*, 27 October 1943, 12. "Betty Deuser Budde Letters, 1943-1944," The Woman's Collection, Texas Woman's University.

[11] *Ibid. Columbus* (GA) *Daily Enquirer*, 16 December 1943, 2. *Richmond* (VA) *Times Dispatch*, 18 December 1943, 7; 9 March 1975, G4.

[12] *Richmond* (VA) *Times Dispatch* , 28 March 1944, 7; 29 March 1944, 10; 9 March 1975, G4.

[13] *The Canton* (OH) *Repository*, 3 April 1944, 2. *Riverside* (CA) *Daily Press*, 17 January 1944, 13.

[14] *Omaha* (NE) *World Herald*, 5 April 1944, 2; 7 July 1979, 20.

[15] *The Ord* (NE) *Quiz*, 13 April 1944, 1.

[16] *The Ord* (NE) *Quiz*, 13 April 1944, 3.

[17] *Omaha* (NE) *World Herald*, 7 July 1979, 20.

[18] National Park Service, "Evelyn Sharp," www.nps.gov/home/learn/historyculture (6 August 2014). *The Ord* (NE) *Quiz*, 2 June 1932, 1; 2 April 1936, 1; 6 April 1944, 1; 9 August 1934, 10. Heloise Bresley, "Recalling Evelyn Sharp, as a child," *Grand Island* (NE) *Independent*, 15 August 2002.

[19] *The Ord* (NE) *Quiz*, 3 November 1932, 5.

[20] *The Ord* (NE) *Quiz*, 11 December 1930, 8; 9 September 1948, 1, 4.

[21] *The Ord* (NE) *Quiz*, 30 April 1936, 1.

[22] *Trenton* (NJ) *Times Advertiser*, 17 May 1936, "Parade of Youth," 3. *The Ord* (NE) *Quiz*, 31 January 1935, 1.

[23] *The Ord* (NE) *Quiz*, 16 May 1935, 1; 6 June 1935, 4; 30 April 1936, 1.

[24] *The Ord* (NE) *Quiz*, 30 April 1936, 1. *Trenton* (NJ) *Times Advertiser*, 17 May 1936, "Parade of Youth," 3. *Omaha* (NE) *World Herald*, 15 November 1936, 11.

[25] *The Ord* (NE) *Quiz*, 28 January 1937, 1; 7 April 1937, 8; 16 June 1937, 6; 23 June 1937, 1; 21 July 1937, 1; 13 April 1944, 1.

[26] *The Ord* (NE) *Quiz*, 28 July 1937, 1; 25 August 1937, 1. *Omaha World Herald*, 19 August 1937, 13.

[27] *The Ord* (NE) *Quiz*, 22 September 1937, 1; 29 September 1937, 1; 27 October 1937, 1.

[28] *The Ord* (NE) *Quiz*, 3 November 1937, 1.

[29] *The Ord* (NE) *Quiz*, 8 December 1937, 1; 22 December 1937, 3.

[30] *The Ord* (NE) *Quiz*, 12 January 1938, 1, 6; 26 January 1938, 1; 18 May 1938, 1, 25 May 1938, 1, 12.

[31] *The Ord* (NE) *Quiz*, 25 May 1938, 1; 27 July 1938, 10; 8 February 1939, 10; April 1944, 1; 13; April 1944, 1.

[32] *The Ord* (NE) *Quiz*, 12 June 1940, 1; 19 June 1940, 5; 17 July 1940, 1; 31 July 1940, 1.

[33] *Bakersfield* (CA) *Californian*, 24 February 1941, 8. (Rockford, IL) *Register-Republic*, 16 June 1941, 6. *Lincoln* (NE) *Star*, 27 June 1942, 6.

[34] *The Ord* (NE) *Quiz*, 6 April 1944, 1; 13 April 1944, 1; 9 September 1948, 4. *Lincoln* (NE) *Star*, 6 November 1942, 10. Historical Branch, Intelligence and Security Division, Air Transport Command, *History of the Air Transport Command: Women Pilots in the Air Transport Command*, 1946, 30, 34.

[35] *San Francisco Chronicle*, 16 March 1944, 12.

[36] *Omaha World Herald*, 10 April 1944, 1; 11 April 1944, 7. U.S. Department of Agriculture, Weather Bureau Chart, Nebraska City, NE, April 1944, www.ncdc.noaa.gov/IPS/coop/coop.html (12 April 2015). Aviation Archaeological Investigation & Research, www.aviationarchaeology.com (15 April 2015).

[37] *Women Pilots in the Air Transport Command*, 44. Status Report from Jacqueline Cochran to Commanding General, Army Air Forces, 1 August 1944, http://wingsacrossamerica.us/records (14 May 2014).

[38] Findagrave.com (6 April 2014). R. L. Polk, Bozeman, Montana *1912 City Directory*.

[39] R. L. Polk, Helena, Montana *1922 City Directory*. 1930 Census Records. *San Francisco Chronicle*, 7 September 1930, 5.

[40] *Bend* (OR) *Bulletin*, 14 November 1940, 5; 12 April 1944, 1.

[41] The Rainbow: A Combined Yearbook of The Junior College Of

Augusta And The Academy Of Richmond County, for the Year 1933, 44, 60. Augusta (GA) Chronicle, 13 November 1935, 9; 8 July 1936, 5; 13 January 1943, 3; 15 May 1943, 3.

[42] (Portland, OR) *Oregonian*, 13 April 1944, 13. *Augusta* (GA) *Chronicle*, 1 July 1982, B3.

[43] (Washington, D.C.) *Evening Star*, 16 April 1944, 1, 5.

[44] (Washington, D.C.) *Evening Star*, 14 April 1944, 6.

[45] *Issaquah* (WA) *Press*, 9 November 1983, 1. FOSTER v. PRESTON MILL CO., No. 32630, Supreme Court of Washington, Department 1, 19 March 1954, p. 442.

[46] *Issaquah* (WA) *Press*, 9 November 1983, 1.

[47] *Ibid. Seattle Daily Times*, 9 February 1941, 19, 8 January 1943, 5.

[48] *Seattle Daily Times*, 7 November 1943, 10. *Issaquah* (WA) *Press*, 9 November 1983, 1.

[49] *North American Newspaper, Philadelphia and Popular Philadelphians*, (Philadelphia: American Printing House, 1891), 61-62. Charles R. Deacon, *A Biographical Album of Prominent Pennsylvanians*, (Philadelphia: American Biographical Publishing Co., 1888), 445-446. (Philadelphia) *Evening Public Ledger*, 26 December 1917, 9. Richard Howson, WWI Draft Registration Card.

[50] Joseph S. Kennedy, "Teacher Took To The Sky To Serve in WWII," *Philadelphia Inquirer*, http://articles.philly.com/1999-03-14/news/25513086_1 (6 June 2014). "In Memoriam" *Smith Alumni Quarterly* 33.2 (February 1942): 145; 35:1 (November 1942): 61; 35.4 (August 1944): 208.

[51] (Sweetwater, TX) *The Avenger*, 21 April 1944, 7. *Issaquah* (WA) *Press*, 9 November 1983, 1. Joseph S. Kennedy, Philadelphia Inquirer, http://articles.philly.com/1999-03-14/news/25513086_1 (6 June 2014).

[52] Elin Stebbins Waldal, "My Mother the WASP," http://beyondthebackyardblues.com/veterans-day-mother-wasp (23 July 2014).

[53] "Remembering Mary," www.wingsacrossamerica.us/wasp/memorial/mary.htm (14 May 2014). Joseph S. Kennedy, Philadelphia Inquirer, http://articles.philly.com/1999-03-14/news/25513086_1 (6 June 2014).

[54] (Washington, D.C.) *Evening Star*, 18 April 1944, 1.

[55] (Sweetwater, TX) *The Avenger*, 5 May 1944, 1. The Woman's Collection, Texas Woman's University, *Marjorie Osborne Nicol, WASP Letters, April-December 1944* (Denton, TX: Texas Woman's University,

1995), 11.

## *Chapter 12*

[1] "Battle of the Sexes," *Time* 43.19 (8 May 1944): 68.

[2] "Women Pilots with the AAF,"93. *Marjorie Osborne Nicol, WASP Letters*, 11.

[3] Joe Blackstock, "WASP pilots gave lives during WWII," www.whittierdailynews.com/general-news/20110912/wasp-pilots-gave-lives-during-wwii (5 June 2014). Paul McClure, Los Angeles Department of Public Works, "Brackett Field," http://dpw.lacounty.gov/avi/airports (5 June 2014). *Register -University of California, Volume 2*, (Berkeley, CA: University of California Press, 1943), 25.

[4] National Archives, "Access to Archival Databases" http://aad.archives.gov (23 July 2014). U.S. Department of Agriculture, Weather Bureau Chart, McAllen, Texas Station, April 1944, www.ncdc.noaa.gov/IPS/coop/coop.html (13 August 2014). *Brownsville* (TX) *Herald*, 26 April 1944, 11. (Ontario, CA) *Inland Valley Daily Bulletin*, www.dailybulletin.com/20110926/readers-offer-their-own-historical-tidbits (5 June 2014).

[5] *Sacramento* (CA) *Bee*, 5 May 1944, 2. *Boston Herald*, 10 May 1944, 20. (Boise) *Idaho Statesman*, 12 May 1944, 4.

[6] (Washington, D.C.) *Evening Star*, 15 May 1944, 2.

[7] (Washington, D.C.) *Evening Star*, 18 May 1944, 6.

[8] *Sweetwater* (TX) Reporter, 21 May 1944, 1. *WASP Newsletter*, v. 4 (June 1968):5.

[9] U. S. Congress, House, Concerning Inquiries Made of Certain Proposals for the Expansion and Change in Civil Service Status of the WASP, 78th Cong., 2d sess., 1944, H. R. 1600.

[10] (Sweetwater, TX) *The Avenger*, 9 June 1944, 1. Franklin D. Roosevelt Presidential Library, "A Mighty Endeavor," www.fdrlibrary.marist.edu/aboutfdr/d-day.html (17 July 2015).

[11] (Sweetwater, TX) *The Avenger*, 19 May 1944, 1; 9 June 1944, 1, 4.

[12] (Houston, TX) *The Fifinella Gazette*, 10 February 1943, 6.

[13] UCLA Yearbook, *Southern Campus, v. XIX*, (Los Angeles: UCLA Associated Students, 1938), 85. *University of California at Los Angeles. The Twenty-First Commencement, 15 June 1940* (Berkeley, CA: University of California Press, 1940), 40. (Baton Rouge, LA) *State Times Advocate*, 8 February 1941, 3.

[14] *Bakersfield* (CA) *Californian*, 22 September 1941, 7.

[15] Jary Johnson Mckay, "Women of Courage," *The 461st Liberaider* 17.2 (December 2000): 11.

[16] Jary Johnson Mckay, 31.

[17] *Ibid.* www.aviationarcheology.org/src/db.asp (6 January 2015).

[18] (Washington, D.C.) *Evening Star*, 10 June 1944, 2.

[19] *Ibid.*

[20] (Washington, D.C.) *Evening Star*, 11 June 1944, 12. *Sweetwater* (TX) *Reporter*, 18 June 1944, 1.

[21] 1920 Census Records, Anaheim, Orange County, CA. Frederick C. Edwards, The Fortnightly Club of Redlands, California, " The Mickey Before the Mouse," www.redlandsfortnightly.org/papers/EdwardsFredrick10.html. "Association Laboratory Now in Full Operation in Anaheim," *The California Citrograph* 7.11 (September 1922): 360.

[22] *Santa Ana* (CA) *Register*, 9 September 1942, 11. (Santa Ana, CA) *Orange County Register*, 17 September 2013. *La Cumbre 40*, "Graduates," v. 20 (Santa Barbara, CA: Students of Santa Barbara State College, 1940), 52.

[23] *Sweetwater* (TX) *Reporter*, 14 June 1944, 1.

[24] "WASP Crash Victim Honored With a Plaque," *Wasp News* 37.2 (Summer/Fall 1999): 12. Texas Death Certificate No. 26760, 15 June 1944.

[25] Elin Stebbins Waldal, http://beyondthebackyardblues.com/veterans-day-mother-wasp (23 July 2014). "All in a Life's Work," *Sweet Briar Alumnae Magazine*, 81.1 (Summer 2010): 15.

[26] Darna L. Dufour, "Alice Mossie Brues: 1913-2007," *American Journal of Human Biology* 19.4 (July/August 2007): 597. *Binghamton* (NY) *Press*, 19 June 1944, 17.

[27] *Daily* (Iowa City, IA) *Iowan*, 21 June 1944, 3. *Kalona* (IA) *News*, 16 July 2009, 1.

[28] *Daily* (Iowa City, IA) *Iowan*, 21 June 1944, 3. *Kalona* (IA) *News*, 11 May 1936. (Oxford, IA ) *Johnson County Democrat*, 13 February 1936, 1. Johnson County Planning and Zoning Department, Johnson County, Iowa, "Sharon Center Village Plan, 2014," Resolution #02-13-14-07, Adopted by the Johnson County Board of Supervisors: 13 February 2014, 2. *Omaha World Herald*, 17 December 1940, 8. *Iowa City* (IA) *Press-Citizen*, 2 June 1941, 5.

[29] *Cedar Rapids* (IA) *Tribune*, 5 February 1942, 5; 29 June 1944, 8. Jack Alicoate, ed., *The 1944 Radio Annual* (New York: The Radio Daily,

1944), 225. Daily (Iowa City, IA) Iowan, 21 June 1944, 3.

[30] *Kalona* (IA) *News*, 16 July 2009, 1.

[31] *Daily* (Iowa City, IA) *Iowan*, 5 July 1944, 3.

[32] *Sweetwater* (TX) *Reporter*, 22 June 1944, 1.

[33] *Sweetwater* (TX) *Reporter*, 22 June 1944, 1; 10. (Portland, OR) *Oregonian*, 19 June 1944, 5. (Washington, D.C.) *Evening Star*, 22 June 1944, 5. *San Diego Union*, 22 June 1944, 5.

[34] Lenore Olsen and Robin Weidner, "Women on the Wings of War," *Spectrum* 11.1 (Spring 1997): 12-13. Texas Death Certificate No. 27411, 22 June 1944.

[35] *Lubbock* (TX) *Avalanche*, 23 April 1944, 10; 22 June 1944, 7. *Canyon* (TX) *News*, 29 June 1944, 6. Lenore Olsen and Robin Weidner, 13.

[36] (Washington, D.C.) *Evening Star*, 27 June 1944, 2. Cochran, "Final Report on Women Pilot Program," 47.

[37] 1920, 1930, 1940 Census Records, *Dodge* City (KS) *Globe*, 15 October 1943. *Sweetwater* (TX) *Reporter*, 6 October 1943, 4. *Red Bluff* (CA) *Daily News*, 8 May 1970, 5.

[38] B. J. Welz, "Out in the Blue," (Sweetwater, TX) *The Avenger*, 2 September 1943, 1.

[39] "Roster Women Airforce Service Pilots," Women Airforce Service Pilots Digital Archive, Texas Woman's University, http://twudigital.contentdm.oclc.org/cdm/landingpage/collection/p214coll2 (15 June 2014). Frederick A. Johnson, *Martin B-26 Marauder*, "Warbird Tech Series, v. 29 (North Branch, MN: Specialty Press Publishers, 2000), 57, 76.

[40] (Harlingen, TX) *Valley Morning Star*, 21 January 1944, 1; 23 January 1944, 3.

[41] Harlingen, TX) *Valley Morning Star*, 30 June 1944, 1; 30 July 1944, 13.

[42] C. Andy Hailey, "Bonnie Jean Welz—Killed in Service," http://wwii-women-pilots.org/WASP_KIA/bjwelz.html (06 July 2014). Texas Death Certificate No. 28986, 1 July 1944. (Harlingen,TX) *Valley Morning Star*, 30 June 1944, 1.

## *Chapter 13*

[1] U.S. Congress, Senate Committee on Claims, *M. Elizabeth Quay (to accompany H.R. 1320)*, 79th Congress, 1st sess., 1945, S. Rep. 389, 1-3.

[2] Ibid.

[3] (Washington, D.C.) *Evening Star*, 2 July 1944, 9.

[4] *Abilene* (TX) *Reporter-News*, 1 July 1944, 1. (Washington, D.C.) *Evening Star*, 2 July 1944, 9.

[5] *Lexington* (KY) *Leader*, 6 August 1944, 24.

[6] *Fayette* (IA) *County Leader*, 17 August 1944, 2.

[7] (Sweetwater, TX) *The Avenger*, 14 July 1944, 3. U.S. Congress, Senate Committee on Claims, *Margaret M. Meersman (to accompany H.R. 1241)*, 79th Congress, 1st sess., 1945, S. Rep. 211, 1-3. U.S. Congress, Senate Committee on Claims, *Dorothy M. Moon (to accompany H.R. 1601)*, 79th Congress, 1st sess., 1945, S. Rep. 436, 1-3.

[8] (Pulaski VA) *Southwest Times*, 9 July 1944, 8.

[9] South Carolina Death Index. "Emily Ryerson Clarke Sues for Divorce," *New York Times*, 3 June 1932. *Buffalo* (NY) *Courier-Express*, 13 December 1933, 4.

[10] *Otsego* (Cooperstown, NY) *Farmer and Republican*, 11 June 1937, 5; 25 June 1937, 1; 1 October 1937, 7; 7 July 1944, 3. (Sweetwater, TX) *The Avenger*, 2 September 1943. 4.

[11] Bradford (PA) Evening Star and Daily Record, 27 June 1940, 17. Dallas (TX) Morning News, 15 April 1942, 2.

[12] *Otsego* (NY) *Farmer and Republican*, 18 June 1943, 1; 25 June 1943, 4.

[13] (Sweetwater, TX) *The Avenger*, 2 September 1943, 4; 8 October 1943, 4; 7 January 1944, 5. *Otsego* (Cooperstown, NY) *Farmer and Republican*, 10 September 1943, 5.

[14] *Binghamton* (NY) *Press*, 6 July 1944, 5. *Otsego* (Cooperstown, NY) *Farmer and Republican*, 7 July 1944, 3.

[15] U.S. Department of Agriculture, Weather Bureau Chart, Columbia, SC, July 1944, www.ncdc.noaa.gov/IPS/coop/coop.html (10 January 2015). WWII Women Pilots, http://wwii-women-pilots.org/WASP_KIA/38KIA2.html (07 October 2014). Aviation Safety Network, http://aviation-safety.net/wikibase/wiki.php?id=120458 (07 October 2014).

[16] *Otsego* (Cooperstown, NY) *Farmer and Republican*, 7 July 1944, 3.

[17] *Otsego* (Cooperstown, NY) *Farmer and Republican*, 14 July 1944, 4.

[18] *Medford* (OR) *Mail Tribune*, 3 June 1947, 1.

[19] *Monrovia* (CA) *Daily News-Post*, 8 July 1944, 1. *Los Angeles Times*, 9 July 1944, 11. "Monrovia Police Department's Historical Brief," www.cityofmonrovia.org (23 October 2014).

[20] *Monrovia* (CA) *Daily News-Post*, 8 July 1944, 1.

[21] "Betty Mae Scott," http://wwii-women-pilots.org (20 October 2014). Texas Death Certificate No. 34755, 15 July 1944.

[22] "Rites conducted for Betty Scott," *Los Angeles Times*, 13 July 1944,

A2.

[23] History of the WASP Program. Army Air Forces Central Flying Training Command, 130-131.

[24] "Beverly Jean Moses," http://wwii-women-pilots.org (15 November 2014). *Reno Evening Gazette*, 21 July 1944, 18. (Mattoon, IL) *Daily Journal-Gazette*, 21 July 1944, 1. *Boston Herald*, 22 July 1944, 5. *Bakersfield* (CA) *Californian*, 27 April 1946, 5. *Springfield* (MA) *Republican*, 27 July 1944, 12.

[25] (Reno) *Nevada State Journal*, 23 July 1944, 20.

[26] *Omaha* (NE) *World Herald*, 2 May 1942, 2. "Beverly Jean Moses," http://wwii-women-pilots.org (15 November 2014).

[27] *Los Angeles Times*, 17 January 1942, 1.

[28] (Sweetwater, TX) *The Avenger*, 4 August 1944, 1, 3.

[29] (Sweetwater, TX) *The Avenger*, 14 July 1944, 6; 4 August 1944, 7. *Abilene* (TX) *Reporter-News*, 5 August 1944, 5.

[30] (Uniontown, PA) *Morning Herald*, 3 August 1944, 6. *Flying*, "Model Airmen," 35.2 (August 1944): 158.

[31] *Troy* (NY) *Record*, 8 August 1944, 1.

[32] "Director of Women Pilots Asks Military Status for Wasps," War Department News Release, 8 August 1944. "Women Airforce Service Pilots," Report to General Arnold, Commanding General, Army Air Forces from Jacqueline Cochran, Director of Women Pilots, Army Air Forces, 1 August 1944.

[33] Federal Census Records. (Portland, OR) *Oregonian*, 6 November 1952, 26. Family Search, "Idaho Marriages, https://familysearch.org (23 August 2014).

[34] (Portland, OR), *Oregonian*, 1 June 1941, 18; 21 September 1943, 8; 6 January 1944, 7.

[35] U.S. Department of Agriculture, Weather Bureau Chart, Sherman, Texas Station, August 1944, www.ncdc.noaa.gov/IPS/coop/coop.html (13 March 2015). Aviation Archeology, www.aviationarchaeology.com (13 March 2015).

[36] History of the WASP Program. Army Air Forces Central Flying Training Command, 145-146.

[37] (Portland, OR) *Oregonian*, 18 August 1944, 15. *Council Bluffs* (IA) *Nonpareil*, 18 August 1944, 19.

[38] (Massillon, OH) *Evening Independent*, 28 August 1944, 4. *Sweetwater* (TX) *Reporter*, 21 August 1944, 1, 6; 22 August 1944, 1.

[39] Sweetwater (TX) *Reporter*, 20 August 1944, 1.

[40] (Sweetwater, TX) *The Avenger*, 24 August 1944, 1, 4.

[41] Sweetwater (TX) *Reporter*, 24 August 1944, 2.

[42] (Sweetwater, TX) *The Avenger*, 24 August 1944, 7.

[43] (Yonkers, NY) *Herald Statesman*, 16 September 1944, 1.

[44] *Ibid. Scarsdale* (NY) *Inquirer*, 17 January 1930, 5; 7 December 1934, 3.

[45] *Scarsdale* (NY) *Inquirer*, 10 March 1923, 3; 1 June 1928, 9; 6 December 1929, 10; 23 January 1931, 8.

[46] *Scarsdale* (NY) *Inquirer*, 16 June 1933, 1; 23 June 1933, 4; 23 October 1936, 6. (Yonkers, NY) *Herald Statesman*, 16 September 1944, 1. *Broadcasting: The Weekly News Magazine of Radio*, (25 September 1944): 67.

[47] (Harlingen, TX) *Valley Morning Star*, 14 September 1944, 1; 15 September 1944, 5. (Yonkers, NY) *Herald Statesman*, 16 September 1944, 1. *Brownsville* (TX) *Herald*, 14 September 1944, 7.

[48] Kendal at Hanover Residents Association, ed., "The Flight of the WASP- Louise Bowden Brown," *World War II Remembered* (Lebanon, NH: University Press of New England, 2012).

[49] *Abilene* (TX) *Reporter-News*, 15 September 1944, 14.

[50] (Massillon, OH) *Evening Independent*, 16 September 1944, 8.

[51] *Brooklyn* (NY) *Eagle*, 21 September 1944, 10.

## *Chapter 14*

[1] Oral History "Maurice E. Zetterholm" (1971), http://digitalcommons.iwu.edu/oral_hist/43 (07 July 2015). Federal Census Records.

[2] Oral History "Maurice E. Zetterholm."

[3] H.G. Reza, "Her Memory Still Soars," *Los Angeles Times*, 30 May 2005. *Sweetwater*(TX) *Reporter*, 3 October 1944, 1. Federal Census Records.

"Alumni of Extinct School Gather for Luncheon Monday," *Cleveland* (OH) *Plain Dealer*, 21 December 1943, 14.

[4] "WW2 'Fly Girl' to Finally Get Military Honors," *Detroit* (MI) *Free Press*, 27 May 2013. (Helena, MT) *Independent Record*, 25 June 1944, 12.

[5] (Reno) *Nevada State Journal*, "Reno Army Airbase News" section, 19 August 1944, 8.

[6] *San Bernardino* (CA) *County Sun*, 3 October 1944, 9; 10 October 1940, 15. *San Diego* (CA) *Union*, 2 June 1942, B1.

[7] G. Pat Macha, *Aircraft Wrecks of San Bernardino County* (Charleston, SC: History Press, 2013), 48. *San Bernardino* (CA) *County Sun*, 3 October 1944, 9.

[8] Arlington National Cemetery, "Elizabeth MacKethan Magid," www.arlingtoncemetery.net (04 November 2014).

[9] *Victoria* (TX) *Advocate*, 10 February 1988, 12A.

[10] *WASP News* 31.1 (April 1993): 5. Federal Census Records. WWI Draft Registration Card, Carl Elmo Wilson.

[11] Aviation archeological research, www.aviationarchaeology.com (05 November 2014). *Tucson* (AZ) *Daily Citizen*, 4 October 1944, 18.

[12] *Tucson* (AZ) *Daily Citizen*, 4 October 1944, 18.

[13] Abilene (TX) Reporter-News, 4 October 1944, 1. Sweetwater (TX) Reporter, 8 October 1944, 1. History of the WASP Program, 149.

[14] History of the WASP Program, 150.

[15] Eisenhower archives, "Letter, Cochran to WASPs regarding disbandment," October 12, 1944.

[16] History of the WASP Program, 132-135.

[17] *Sweetwater* (TX) *Reporter*, 17 October 1944, 1. *Salt Lake* (City, UT) *Tribune*, 18 October 1944, 5.

[18] "Class of 1941," *Poinsettia, Hollywood High School Annual 1940*, 47. *Van Nuys* (CA) *News*, 30 May 1968, 31A. "Veteran Memorial Plaque Dedicated," *Newsletter of the UCLA Department of Military Science* 2:3 (Fall 2007): 6. "Prepare Yourself as a Pilot," *San Francisco Chronicle* 24 May 1942, Want Ads, 2.

[19] Federal Census Record. Clinton Carr Davis, WWI and WWII Draft Registrations.

[20] "Sun and Moon Data for One Day," U.S. Naval Observatory Astronomical Applications Department, http://aa.usno.navy.mil/data/docs/RS_OneDay.php (04 September 2015). U.S. Department of Agriculture, Weather Bureau Chart, Corinth, MS, October 1944, www.ncdc.noaa.gov/IPS/coop/coop.html (04 September 2015). *Sweetwater* (TX) *Reporter*, 17 October 1944, 1.

[21] WWII Women Pilots, http://wwii-women-pilots.org (06 April 2015).

[22] Rod Lewellen and Margaret Marnitz, "About Jeanne L. Norbeck," Atterbury-Bakalar Air Museum, www.atterburybakalarairmuseum.org (09 January 2015). Department of Agriculture, Weather Bureau Chart, Sumter, SC, October 1944, www.ncdc.noaa.gov/IPS/coop/coop.html (06 September 2015). (Columbus, IN) *The Republic*, 17 October 1944, 1.

[23] *Cincinnati* (OH) *Enquirer*, 31 October 1921, 4. *Indianapolis* (IN) *News*, 31 March 1924, 10.

[24] (Columbus, IN) *The Republic*, 17 October 1944, 1; 26 September 1993, A4.

[25] "About Jeanne L. Norbeck,"

www.atterburybakalarairmuseum.org. Christine M. Sakumoto Drake, "Edward Norbeck," *Rice University Studies* 66.1 (Winter 1980): iii.

[26] "Hawaii, Honolulu Passenger Lists," Vancouver and Victoria, B.C. Passenger Lists, FamilySearch, https://familysearch.org (09 January 2015). (Columbus, IN) *The Republic*, 29 March 1939, 3. "Edward Norbeck," *Rice University Studies*, iii.

[27] Social Security Death Index.

[28] National Archives, "Access to Archival Databases" http://aad.archives.gov (06 January 2015).

[29] *Honolulu* (HI) *Star-Bulletin*, 9 November 1944, 1. (Columbus, IN) *The Republic*, 17 October 1944, 1. "Jeanne L. Norbeck," *Washington State Alumni Pow Wow* v. 34, no. 1&2, (September-October, 1944): 16.

[30] *Brooklyn* (NY) *Daily Eagle*, 19 February 1950, 14. "Edward Norbeck," *Rice University Studies*, iii-iv. *Salt Lake* (City, UT) *Tribune*, 13 May 1952, 12. *Van Nuys* (CA) *News*, 13 August 1959, 23A. *Corpus Christi* (TX) *Caller-Times*, 26 October 1969, 6B.

[31] (New Jersey) *Star-Ledger*, 31 May 2004.

[32] *Ibid.* The *Engineers List*, 10.8 (August 1901): 52. Passenger Records, New York, Los Angeles, and New Zealand, FamilySearch, https://familysearch.org (09 January 2015).

[33] (New Jersey) *Star-Ledger*, 31 May 2004.

[34] Phillips Academy Pot Pourri, (Andover, MA: Andover Press, 1922), 35. Yale University-Banner and Pot Pourri Yearbook Class of 1926 (New Haven, CT, 1926), 293.

Phillips Bulletin, Phillips Academy, Andover, MA 39.2 (Winter 1945):22.

[35] *New York Times*, 1 December 1943, 18. *Brooklyn* (NY) *Daily Eagle*, 27 September 1944, 17.

[36] Department of Agriculture, Weather Bureau Chart, Santa Monica, CA, October 1944, www.ncdc.noaa.gov/IPS/coop/coop.html (11 January 2015). *Dallas Morning News*, 2 November 1944, 5.

[37] *East Hampton* (NY) *Star*, 10 September 1964, 2; 4 March 1965, 3.

## *Chapter 15*

[1] *Wilkes-Barre* (PA) *Record*, 3 November 1944, 30.

[2] Sweetwater (TX) Reporter, 6 November 1944, 1, 6.

[3] Ibid.

[4] (Greenville, MS) *Delta Democrat-Times*, 14 November 1944, 2. *Lubbock* (TX) *Avalanche-Journal*, 19 November 1944, 21.

[5] "Proposed Air Stop to be Club Topic," *Sweetwater* (TX) *Reporter*, 19 November 1944, 3.

[6] Ibid.

[7] (Lincoln) *Nebraska State Journal*, 1 August 1944, 3; 20 November 1944, 1-2.

[8] (Lincoln) *Nebraska State Journal*, 20 November 1944, 1-2. *Dallas Morning News*, 1 September 1974, 38A.

[9] (Sweetwater, TX) *The Avenger*, 28 June, 1943, 6.

[10] (Sweetwater, TX) *The Avenger*, 28 June 1943, 8.

[11] *Ibid.*

[12] Federal Census Record.

[13] (Portland, OR) *Oregonian*, 30 May 1921, 14; 5 June 1921, 16; 7 June 1925, sect. 3:1; 26 June 1927, sect. 3:3; 4 June 1930, 6.

[14] (Portland, OR) *Oregonian*, 12 February 1933, 13.

[15] *Ibid.* (Portland, OR) *Oregonian*, 12 May 1935, magazine section, 2.

[16] (Portland, OR) *Oregonian*, 12 May 1935, magazine section, 2.

[17] (Portland, OR) *Oregonian*, 12 February 1933, 13. *Brownsville* (TX) *Herald*, 1 October 1944, 2.

[18] *Brownsville* (TX) *Herald*, 1 October 1944, 2. (Rome, NY) *Daily Sentinel*, 16 February 1944, 5. *Abilene* (TX) *Reporter-News*, 25 April 1943, society section, 2. (Portland, OR) *Oregonian*, 12 May 1935, magazine section, 2; 22 December 1938, 3.

[19] Washington and Seattle Passenger Lists, (Portland, OR) *Oregonian*, 22 December 1938, 3.

[20] (Portland, OR) *Oregonian*, 22 December 1938, 3. (Salem, OR) *Daily Capital Journal*, 7 March 1939, 1.

[21] Federal Census Records. (Sweetwater, TX) *The Avenger*, 11 May 1943, 6. *Abilene* (TX) *Reporter-News*, 14 May 1943, 12. *Brownsville* (TX) *Herald*, 1 October 1944, 2.

[22] *Brownsville* (TX) *Herald*, 1 October 1944, 2. *Sweetwater* (TX) *Reporter*, 7 November 1943, 5. "Biplane Fighter Aces,: http://surfcity.kund.dalnet.se/china_louie.htm (6 November 2-14).

[23] (Sweetwater, TX) *The Avenger*, 11 May 1943, 6. *Abilene* (TX) *Reporter-News*, 25 April 1943, Society, 2. *Circleville* (OH) *Herald*, 24 August 1943, 3. *Richmond* (VA) *Times Dispatch*, 12 October 1943, 9. (Rome, NY) *Daily Sentinel*, 16 February 1944, 5.

[24] (Sweetwater, TX) *The Avenger*, 7 April 1944, 6.

[25] *Brownsville* (TX) *Herald*, 1 October 1944, 2.

[26] *Havre* (MT) *Daily News*, 24 November 1944, 1. (Helena, MT) *Independent Record*, 24 November 1944, 3; 25 November 1944, 5.

[27] 1st Lt. Harold H. Eby, ed., *Tank Busters. The History of the 607th*

*Tank Destroyer Battalion in Combat* (Munich, Germany: Knorr & Hirth, n.d.), sections 4 & 6.

[28] (Portland, OR) *Oregonian*, 30 November 1944, 15.

[29] (Portland, OR) *Oregonian*, 11 April 1946, 7.

[30] *San Antonio* (TX) *Express*, 28 November 1944, 5.

[31] Federal Census Records. *Walla Walla* (WA) *Union Bulletin*, 13 June 1947, 11. *Kappa Alpha Theta, "Leading Women, "http://www.kappaalphatheta.org* (02 February 2015). (Salem) *Oregon Statesman*, 3 August 1924, sect. 2:2.

[32] *Santa Ana* (CA) *Register*, 4 May 1927, 4.

[33] *Manitowoc* (WI) *Herald*, 25 January 1936, 8. (Canton, OH) *The Repository*, 7 April 1936, 6. *Oakland* (CA) *Tribune*, 19 June 1931, 3.

[34] *Ibid.*

[35] *Decatur* (IL) *Herald*, 14 June 1938, 1. *Decatur* (IL) *Herald and Review*, 24 July 1938, 12. *Omaha* (NE) *World Herald*, 20 May 1941, 1.

[36] (Valparaiso, IN) *Vidette-Messenger*, 2 December 1944, 2. *Bradford* (PA) *Evening Star and Daily Record*, 3 March 1941, 2. (Rockford, IL) *Morning Star*, 8 March 1942, 11.

[37] *Lock Haven* (PA) *Express*, 30 October 1943, 1. (Harlingen, TX) *Valley Morning Star*, 9 June 1944, 12. (Sweetwater, Tex.) *Sweetwater Reporter*, 24 August 1944, 8. *Wasp Newsletter*, 1.5 (10 December 1944): 4.

[38] *Decatur* (IL) *Review*, 21 September 1949, 2. *Los Angeles Times*, 15 June 1996.

[39] History of the WASP Program, 149-150.

## *Chapter 16*

[1] *Sweetwater* (TX) *Reporter*, 7 December 1944, 1.

[2] *WASP Newsletter* 1.6 (20 December 1944): 7.

[3] NPR Radio, "All Things Considered: The Wasps: Women Airforce Service Pilots of World War II," broadcast 18 December 2002.

[4] *WASP Newsletter* 1.6 (20 December 1944): 7.

[5] "Remembering – fifty years ago," *WASP News* 33.3 (December 1994): 29. *Council Bluffs* (IA) *Nonpareil*, 8 December 1944, 1. *Omaha* (NE) *World-Herald*, 8 December 1944, 1.

[6] (Canton, OH)*The Repository*, 12 December 1934, 2. *Cleveland Plain Dealer*, 23 June 1935, magazine section, 1. *Buffalo* (NY) *Courier-Express*, 21 October 1941, sect. 6:16.

[7] Minnesota History Center, www.MinnesotaHistoryCenter.org/Virginia-Mae-Hope-Resources (25

January 2015). *History of the AAF Weather Service: Special Study No. 2, Utilization of WASPS in AAF Weather Service* (Ashville, NC: Headquarters, AAF Weather Wing, February 1945), 2.

[8] History of the AAF Weather Service, Appendix 10.

[9] Ibid.

[10] Texas Birth Index. "Baylor Bears Football," http://old.lostlettermen.com/football/baylor (16 November 2014). "Degrees and Diplomas Conferred Commencement, 1911," *Baylor University Bulletin*, 15.3 (May 1912): 85. Texas Death Certificate #53949, 26 December 1932.

[11] *Lubbock* (TX) *Avalanche*, 30 May 1942, 1. *Sweetwater* (TX) *Reporter*, 10 November 1943, 7.

[12] History of the AAF Weather Service: Special Study No. 2, Appendix 12.

[13] *Council Bluffs* (IA) *Nonpareil*, 8 December 1944, 1. *Omaha* (NE) *World-Herald*, 8 December 1944, 1. *Paris* (TX) *News*, 20 December 1944, 4.

[14] *Ibid.*

[15] *WASP News* 38.3 (September 1989): 20. *WASP News* 39.1 (January 1990): 29.

[16] *Miami* (OK) *News Record*, 10 December 1944, 1. U.S. Department of Agriculture, Weather Bureau Chart, Muskogee, Oklahoma Station, December 1944, www.ncdc.noaa.gov/IPS/coop/coop.html (18 January 2015). *Seattle Daily Times*, 11 December 1944, sect. 2:11.

[17] Federal Census Records. *Ellensburg* (WA) *Daily Record*, 23 December 1957, 1.

[18] (Ellensburg WA) *Daily Record*, 18 August 1989, 14D. *Seattle Daily Times*, 11 December 1944, sect. 2:11.

[19] *Racine* (WI) *Journal Times*, 11 December 1944, 5. *Vernon* (TX) *Daily Record*, 11 December 1944, 1.

[20] (Ellensburg WA) *Daily Record*, 18 August 1989, 14D. *Seattle Daily Times*, 11 December 1944, sect. 2:11.

[21] (Ellensburg WA) *Daily Record*, 11 December 1944, p. 1.

[22] *Greensboro* (NC) *Daily News*, 11 December 1944, 10. (West Lebanon, NH) *Valley News*, 22 February 2013.

[23] *Augusta* (GA) *Chronicle*, 17 December 1944, 10.

[24] *Ibid. Fresno* (CA) *Bee*, 26 December 1944, sect. 6B.

[25] "Requiem for the Wasp," *Flying* 35.6 (December 1944): 55-56, 146, 148.

[26] "WASP Still Stings," *Flying*, 36.2 (February 1945): 81,144

[27] Women Pilots With the AAF, 101.

[28] *WASP Newsletter* 1.4 (1 December 1944): 4.

[29] History of the WASP Program, 150-151. WASP Newsletter 1.6 (20 December 1944): 7.

[30] *Sweetwater* (TX) *Reporter*, 15 December 1944, 1; 28 December 1944, 1; 28 January 1945, 1.

[31] *Lubbock (TX) Avalanche-Journal*, 24 June 1972, B1. *WASP Newsletter* 1:5 (10 December 1944): 4.

[32] *WASP Newsletter* 1.4 (1 December 1944): 6.

[33] *Wasp Newsletter* 1.6 (20 December 1944): 12.

[34] *Augusta* (GA) *Chronicle*, 17 December 1944, 10.

[35] *WASP Newsletter* 2.3 (20 May 1945): 1.

[36] *Daytona Beach* (FL) *Morning Journal*, 27 August 1946, 3. *Indiana* (PA) *Gazette*, 27 August 1946, 2. (Bradford, PA) *Evening Star*, 27 August 1946, 2.

[37] *Van Nuys* (CA) *News*, 13 September 1948, 13. *San Bernardino* (CA) *County Sun*, 17 September 1948, 11. *WASP Newsletter* 5.3 (December 1948): 6-7.

[38] Cochran, "Final Report on Women Pilot Program," 1.

[39] Cochran, "Final Report on Women Pilot Program," 3. (Portland, OR) *Oregonian*, 24 November 1977, 25.

[40] *Kingsport* (TN) *News*, 1 February 1973. 16.

## *Appendices*

[1] (Washington, D.C.) *Evening Star*, 23 October 1977, 5. *GI Bill Improvement Act of 1977*, November 23, 1977, Title IV, "Women's Air Forces Service Pilots," Public Law 95-202, Sec. 401.

[2] *Department of Defense Authorization Act, 1984*, September 24, 1983, "Award of Campaign and Service Medals to Certain Persons," Public Law 98-94, Sec. 1263.

[3] "President Obama Signs Bill Awarding Congressional Gold Medal to Women Airforce Service Pilots," www.whitehouse.gov (26 June 2015). *An Act to Award a Congressional Gold Medal to the Women Airforce Service Pilots (WASP)*, July 1, 2009, Public Law 111-40.

[4] "Women Airforce Service Pilots Gold Medal Ceremony," C-Span, www.c-span.org/video/?292460-1/women-airforce-service-pilots-gold-medal-ceremony (26 June 2015). "Women Airforce Service Pilots," Department of Defense, http://archive.defense.gov/home/features/2010/0310_wasp/index.html (26 June 2015).

# BIBLIOGRAPHY


**Newspapers**

*Abilene* (TX) *Reporter-News*
*Advocate* (Baton Rouge, LA)
*Antelope Valley* (Palmdale, CA) *Press*
*Appleton* (WI) *Post-Crescent*
*Auburn* (CA) *Journal-Republican*
*Augusta* (GA) *Chronicle*
*The Avenger* (Sweetwater, TX)
*Bakersfield* (CA) *Californian*
*Bend* (OR) *Bulletin*
*Big Spring* (TX) *Daily Herald*
*Binghamton* (NY) *Press*
*Bismarck* (ND) *Tribune*
*Boston* (MA) *Herald*
*Boston* (MA) *Traveler*
*Bradford* (PA) *Evening Star and Daily Record*
*Brooklyn* (NY) *Eagle*
*Brownsville* (TX) *Herald*
*Buffalo* (NY) *Courier-Express*
*Canton* (OH) *Repository*
*Canyon* (TX) *News*
*Cedar Rapids* (IA) *Tribune*
*Chicago* (IL) *Tribune*
*Christlicher Bundesbote* (Newton, KS)
*Cincinnati* (OH) *Enquirer*
*Circleville* (OH) *Herald*
*Cleveland* (OH) *Plain Dealer*
*Columbus* (GA) *Daily Enquirer*
*Corpus Christi* (TX) *Caller-Times*
*Council Bluffs* (IA) *Nonpareil*
*Cumberland* (MD) *News*
*Daily Capital Journal* (Salem, OR)
*Daily Herald* (Biloxi, MS)
*Daily Iowan* (Iowa City)
*Daily Journal Gazette* (Mattoon, IL)
*Daily Sentinel* (Rome, NY)
*Daily Sound* (Santa Barbara, CA)
*Daily Telegram* (Adrian, MI)
*Dallas* (TX) *Morning News*
*Daytona Beach* (FL) *Morning Journal*
*Decatur* (IL) *Review*
*Decatur* (IL) *Herald*
*Decatur* (IL) *Herald and Review*
*Delta Democrat-Times* (Greenville, MS)
*Detroit* (MI) *Free Press*
*Dodge City* (KS) *Globe*
*East Hampton* (NY) *Star*
*Ellensburg* (WA) *Daily Record*
*Escanaba* (MI) *Daily Press*
*Evening Independent* (Massillon, OH)
*Evening Public Ledger* (Philadelphia, PA)
*Evening Star* (Bradford, PA)
*Evening Star* (Washington, D.C.)
*Fayette* (IA) *Leader*
*The Fifinella Gazette* (Houston, TX)
*Fresno* (CA) *Bee*

*Galva* (IL) *News*
*Gloversville* (NY) *Leader Republican*
*Grand Island* (NE) *Independent*
*Greensboro* (NC) *Daily News*
*Greensboro* (NC) *Record*
(Hagerstown, MD) *Daily Mail, 5 February 1944, 2.*
*Havre* (MT) *Daily News*
*Herald Statesman* (Yonkers, NY)
*Honolulu* (HI) *Star-Bulletin*
*Idaho Standard* (Boise)
*Idaho Statesman* (Boise)
*Illinois State Journal* (Springfield)
*Independent Record* (Helena, MT)
*Indiana* (PA) *Gazette*
*Indianapolis* (IN) *News*
*Iowa City* (IA) *Press-Citizen*
*Issaquah* (WA) *Press*
*Johnson County Democrat* (Oxford, IA)
*Journal Sentinel* (Milwaukee, WI)
*Kalona* (IA) *News*
*Kansas City* (MO) *Star*
*Kingsport* (TN) *News*
*Knickerbocker News* (Albany, NY)
*Laredo* (TX) *Times*
*Lawrence* (KS) *Journal World*
*Lexington* (KY) *Leader*
*Lincoln* (NE) *Star*
*Lock Haven* (PA) *Express*
*Los Angeles* (CA) *Times*
*Lubbock* (TX) *Avalanche*
*Lubbock* (TX) *Avalance-Journal*
*Manitowoc* (MI) *Herald*
*Medford* (OR) *Mail Tribune*
*Miami* (OK) *News-Record*
*Milwaukie* (WI) *Journal*
*Monrovia* (CA) *Daily News-Post*
*Morning Herald* (Uniontown, PA)
*Morning Star* (Rockford, IL)
*Mt. Adams Sun* (Bingen, WA)
*Nashville* (TN) *Banner*
*Nebraska State Journal* (Lincoln)
*Nevada State Journal* (Reno)
*New York Sun*
*New York Times*
*Niagara Falls* (NY) *Gazette*
*Nolan County News* (Sweetwater, TX)
*Oakland* (CA) *Tribune*
*Ohio Farmer* (Cleveland)
*Okanogan Valley Gazette-Tribune* (Oroville, WA)
*Omaha* (NE) *World Herald*
*Orange County Register* (Santa Ana, CA)
*The Ord* (NE) *Quiz*
*Oregon Statesman* (Salem)
*Oregonian* (Portland)
*Ostego Farmer and Republican* (Cooperstown, NY)
*Philadelphia* (PA) *Inquirer*
*Poughkeepsie* (NY) *Eagle News*
*Racine* (WI) *Journal Times*
*Red Bluff* (CA) *Daily News*
*Register-Republic* (Rockford, IL)
*Reno* (NV) *Evening Gazette*
*The Repository* (Canton, OH)
*The Republic* (Columbus, IN)
*The Rhinelander* (WI) *Daily News*
*Richmond* (VA) *Times Dispatch*
*Riverside* (CA) *Daily Press*
*Riverside* (CA) *Independent Enterprise*
*Rockford* (IL) *Morning Star*
*Sacramento* (CA) *Bee*
*Salt Lake City* (UT) *Tribune*
*San Antonio* (TX) *Express*
*San Bernardino* (CA) *County Sun*
*San Diego* (CA) *Union*
*San Diego* (CA) *Union Tribune*
*San Francisco* (CA) *Chronicle*
*San Jose* (CA) *Evening News*
*San Luis Obispo* (CA) *Daily Telegram*
*Santa Ana* (CA) *Register*
*Scarsdale* (NY) *Inquirer*
*Seattle* (WA) *Daily Times*
*Southwest Times* (Pulaski, VA)
*Springfield* (MA) *Republican*
*Star-Ledger* (Newark, New Jersey)
*State Times Advocate* (Baton Rouge, LA)

*Sweetwater* (TX) *Reporter*
*Times-Picayune* (New Orleans, LA)
*Times Record* (Troy, NY)
*Trenton* (NJ) *Evening Times*
*Trenton* (NJ) *Times Advertiser*
*Tri-City Record* (Watervliet, MI)
*Troy* (NY) *Record*
*Turtle Mountain Star* (Rolla, ND)
*Tucson* (AZ) *Daily Citizen*
*Valley Morning Star* (Harlingen, TX)
*Valley News* (West Lebanon, NH)
*Van Nuys* (CA) *News*
*Vassar Miscellany News* (Poughkeepsie, NY)
*Vernon* (TX) *Daily Record*
*Vidette-Messenger* (Valparaiso, IN)
*Victoria* (TX) *Advocate*
*Waco* (TX) *News-Tribune*
*Walla Walla* (WA) *Union Bulletin*
*Washington Daily Star*
*Wichita Falls* (TX) *Times*
*Wilkes-Barre* (PA) *Record*
*Williamsport* (PA) *Sun Gazette*
*Wyoming State Tribune* (Cheyenne)

**Books**

Bowden Brown, Louise. "The Flight of the WASP," *World War II Remembered,* edited by Kendal at Hanover Residents Association. Lebanon, NH: University Press of New England, 2012.

"Class of 1941," *Poinsettia, Hollywood High School Annual 1940.*

Deacon, Charles R. *A Biographical Album of Prominent Pennsylvanians.* Philadelphia: American Biographical Publishing Co., 1888.

Douglas, Deborah G. *United States Women in Aviation: 1940-1985.* Washington, D.C.: Smithsonian Institution Press, 1990.

*History of the AAF Weather Service: Special Study No. 2, Utilization of WASPS in AAF Weather Service.* Ashville, NC: Headquarters, AAF Weather Wing, 1945.

*House Journal of the Thirteenth State Legislature of Wyoming.* Laramie, WY: Laramie Republican Company, 1915.

Illinois Dept. of Mines and Minerals. *Coal Report, Volume 38.* Springfield, IL: Illinois State Journal Company, 1919.

Immell, Ralph M. "Wisconsin's Future in Aviation," *Wisconsin Blue Book, 1940.* Madison, WI: Legislative Reference Bureau, 1940.

Johnson, Frederick. *Martin B-26 Marauder*, "Warbird Tech Series, v. 29. North Branch, MN: Specialty Press Publishers, 2000.

*La Cumbre 40*, "Graduates," v.20. Santa Barbara, CA: Students of Santa Barbara State College, 1940.

*Los Angeles City Directory, 1929.* Los Angeles: Los Angeles Directory Company, 1929.

Macha, G.Pat. *Aircraft Wrecks of San Bernardino County.* Charleston, SC: History Press, 2013.

Moore, John Trotwood and Austin P Foster. *Tennessee - The Volunteer State, Vol. 2.* Chicago: S.J. Clarke, 1923.

*The 1944 Radio Annual,* edited by Jack Alicoate. New York: The Radio Daily, 1944.

*North American Newspaper*, *Philadelphia and Popular Philadelphians.* Philadelphia: American Printing House, 1891.

*Phillips Academy Pot Pourri.* Andover, MA: Andover Press, 1922.

*Register - University of California, Volume 2.* Berkeley, CA: University of California Press, 1943.

Rich, Doris. *Notable American Women: A Biographical Dictionary Completing the Twentieth Century, Volume 5*, edited by Susan Ware. Boston: Harvard University Press, 2004.

Rogers, Will, Steven K. Gragert and M. Jane Johansson. *The Papers of Will Rogers, v.3,* edited by Arthur Frank Wertheim and Barbara Bair. Oklahoma City: University of Oklahoma Press, 2001.

Simbeck, Rob. *Daughter of the Air: The Brief Soaring Life of Cornelia Fort.* New York: Grove Press, 1999.

Strickland, Patricia. *The Putt-Putt Air Force.* Washington, D. C.: Federal Aviation Administration, 1971.

*Tank Busters. The History of the 607th Tank Destroyer Battalion in Combat,* edited by 1st Lt. Harold H. Eby. Munich, Germany: Knorr & Hirth, n.d.

Tunner, William H. *Over the Hump.* Washington, D.C.: U.S. Air Force, 1998.

UCLA Yearbook, *Southern Campus, v. XIX.* Los Angeles: UCLA Associated Students, 1938.

*University of California at Los Angeles. The Twenty-First Commencement, 15 June 1940.* Berkeley, CA: University of California Press, 1940.

University of North Dakota. Yearbook: *The 1939 and 1942 Dacotah.*

Van Wagenen Keil, Sally. *Those Wonderful Women in Their Flying Machines.* New York: Rawson, Wade Publishers, 1979.

Verges, Marianne. *On Silver Wings.* New York: Ballantine Books, 1991.

*Women Pilots With the AAF, 1941-1944, Army Air Forces Historical Studies No. 55.* Headquarters Army Air Forces, 1946.

*Yale University-Banner and Pot Pourri Yearbook Class of 1926.* New Haven, CT, 1926.

**Periodicals**

"Aircraft Owners and Pilots Association," *Popular Aviation* 26.3 (March 1940).

"All in a Life's Work," *Sweet Briar Alumnae Magazine*, 81.1 (Summer 2010).

*Architect and Engineer* 151.1 (October 1942).

"Association Laboratory Now in Full Operation in Anaheim," *The California Citrograph* 7.11 (September 1922).

Bartley, Ron. "BT-13 Wreckage Recovered from WWII Crash Site," *Oregon Aviation Historical Society Newsletter* 13.1 (August 2004).

"Degrees and Diplomas Conferred Commencement, 1911," *Baylor University Bulletin*, 15.3 (May 1912).

*"Broadcasting" The Weekly News Magazine of Radio, (September 1944).*

Cochran, Jacqueline. "I Reached Stars the Hard Way," *Life* 37.7 (August 1954).

"Deanie Parrish, Women Airforce Service Pilot," *Texas Heritage* v. 4 (2008).

Dufour, Darna L. "Alice Mossie Brues: 1913-2007," *American Journal of Human Biology* 19.4 (July/August 2007).

The *Engineers List*, 10.8 (August 1901).

Fort, Cornelia. "At the twilight's last gleaming," *Woman's Home Companion* (July 1943).

"In Memoriam," *Smith Alumni Quarterly* 33.2 (February 1942,

November 1942, August 1944).
"Jeanne L. Norbeck," *Washington State Alumni Pow Wow* v. 34, no. 1&2, (September-October, 1944).
Kumler, Marjorie. "They've Done It Again!" *Ladies Home Journal* 61.3 (March 1944).
McKay, Jary Johnson. "Women of Courage," *The 461st Liberaider* 17.2 (December 2000).
Mehrer, Katherine J. "Dakota Images," *South Dakota History* 33.3 (Fall 2003).
Meyer, J.H. "The 1936 National Air Races," *Popular Aviation* 14.5 (November 1936).
"Model Airmen," *Flying* 35.2 (August 1944).
"1903-1963 - Six Decades of Service," Milwaukee School of Engineering Bulletin 16.1 (January 1964).
Olsen, Lenore and Robin Weidner. "Women on the Wings of War," *Spectrum* 11.1 (Spring 1997).
*Phillips Bulletin, Phillips Academy, Andover, MA* 39.2 (Winter 1945).
"Requiem for the Wasp," *Flying* 35.6 (December 1944).
Sakumoto, Christine M. "Edward Norbeck," *Rice University Studies* 66.1 (Winter 1980).
Stuart, John. "The WASP," *Flying* 34.1 (January 1944).
Thornquest, Hamilton. "Love Birds," *Popular Aviation* 24.2 (February 1939).
"Veteran Memorial Plaque Dedicated," *Newsletter of the UCLA Department of Military Science* 2:3 (Fall 2007).
"Wasp Crash Victim Honored With a Plaque," *Wasp News* 37.2 (Summer/Fall 1999).
*Wasp News* 31.1 (April 1993); 33.3 (December 1994); 38.3 (September 1989); 39.1 (January 1990).
*WASP Newsletter*, 1.4, 1.5, 1.6 (December 1944); 2.3 (May 1945); 5.3 (December 1948); v.4 (June 1968).
"WASP Still Stings," *Flying*, 36.2 (February 1945).
Yount, Maj. Gen. Barton K. "Airmen By the Thousands," *Flying* 31:1 (July 1942).

**Correspondence/Interview**

Talley, Randy. Media and Community Relations, University of Science and Arts, Chickasha, Oklahoma.
Williams, Paula. U.S. Forest Service (Ret.), Tiller Ranger District Silviculturist and Environmental Documentation Coordinator.

**Internet**

ALLSTAR Network, www.allstar.fiu.edu/aero/cochran1.htm.
Arlington National Cemetery, www.arlingtoncemetery.net.
Lewellen, Rod and Margaret Marnitz, "About Jeanne L. Norbeck," Atterbury-Bakalar Air Museum, "www.atterburybakalarairmuseum.org.
Aviation Archeology Investigation & Research, www.aviationarchaeology.com.
Aviation Safety Network, http://aviation-safety.net.
"Baylor Bears Football," http://old.lostlettermen.com/football/baylor.
"Biplane Fighter Aces,: http://surfcity.kund.dalnet.se.

Blackstock, Joe. "WASP pilots gave lives during WWII," www.whittierdailynews.com.

British Air Transport Auxiliary, www.airtransportaux.com.

Callanan, Liam. "Field of Dreamers," *Milwaukee Magazine*, www.milwaukeemag.com/article/10212012-FieldofDreamers.

"The Centennial of The University of California, 1868-1968," http://www.oac.cdlib.org.

"Cornelia Fort," SF-260, http://sf260w.com/corneliatxt.html.

"Cornelia Fort," Tennessee Encyclopedia of History and Culture, http://tennesseeencyclopedia.net.

"Cornelia Fort '39 in 1942," Sarah Lawrence College, www.slc.edu/magazine/meaningful-life/alumni/cornelia-fort-39.html.

C-Span, "Women Airforce Service Pilots Gold Medal Ceremony," www.c-span.org.

Department of Defense, "Women Airforce Service Pilots," http://archive.defense.gov/home/features/2010/0310_wasp/index.html.

Douglas, Deborah G. Harkness Love: Female Pilot and First to Fly for the U.S. Military," www.historynet.com/nancy-harkness-love-female-pilot-and-first-to-fly-for-the-us-military.htm.

Edwards, Frederick C. The Fortnightly Club of Redlands, California, "The Mickey Before the Mouse," www.redlandsfortnightly.org.

Eisenhower archives, Dwight D. Eisenhower Presidential Library, www.eisenhower.archives.gov.

"Encyclopedia of Oklahoma History & Culture," http://digital.library.okstate.edu.

Family Search, https://familysearch.org.

Federal Census Records, Ellis Island Foundation, http://libertyellisfoundation.org/passenger.

Find A Grave, http://findagrave.com.

Florida Memory, "WWI Service Cards," www.floridamemory.com.

Franklin D.Roosevelt Presidential Library, "A Mighty Endeavor," www.fdrlibrary.marist.edu.

Government Land Records, www.glorecords.blm.gov.

"The History of Air Racing and Record Breaking," www.airracinghistory.freeola.com.

Illinois Wesleyan University, Oral History http://digitalcommons.iwu.edu/oral_hist.

"*Induction to Oklahoma Hall of Fame*," *Chickasha* (OK) *Express Star*, Chickashanews.com.

*Inland Valley Daily Bulletin* (Ontario, CA) www.dailybulletin.com.

*Kappa Alpha Theta, "Leading Women, "http://www.kappaalphatheta.org.*

Kennedy, Joseph S., "Teacher Took To The Sky To Serve in WWII," *Philadelphia Inquirer*, http://articles.philly.com.

Library of Congress Veterans History Project, "Interview Transcript: Marion Foster Stegeman Hodgson," http://lcweb2.loc.gov/diglib.

"The Loop Family in America," www.theloopfamilyinamerica.org.

McClure, Paul, Los Angeles Department of Public Works, "Brackett Field," http://dpw.lacounty.gov/avi/airports.

Minnesota History Center, www.MinnesotaHistoryCenter.org/Virginia-Mae-Hope-Resources.

"Monrovia Police Department's Historical Brief," www.cityofmonrovia.org.

Nashville Public Library, http://nashvillepubliclibrary.org.

National Archives, "Access to Archival Databases," http://aad.archives.gov.

National Museum of the Air Force, www.nationalmuseum.af.mil/factsheets.

National Park Service, "Evelyn Sharp," www.nps.gov/home/learn/historyculture.

"The 1940 Air Terminal Museum," www.1940airterminal.org.

The Ninety-Nines, Inc., "Betty Huyler Gillies," www.ninety-nines.org.

North Texas State Teacher's College, *The Yucca, Yearbook of North Texas State Teacher's College, 1941. Denton, Texas.* http://digital.library.unt.edu/ark.

NPR (National Public Radio), "Female WWII Pilots: The Original Fly Girls," www.npr.org.

PBS (Public Broadcasting Service), "American Experience: Fly Girls," www.pbs.org/wgbh.

"Placer and Sierra College Timeline," www.sierracollege.edu/about-us/history.

Saint Louis University Libraries Digital Collections, "The Archive of Saint Louis University, 1937" (yearbook), http://cdm.slu.edu.

Santa Barbara Unified School District, "Regular Meeting Board of Education, June 8, 1939," www.sbunified.org.

South Dakota Department of the Military, http://mva.sd.gov.

U.S. Department of Agriculture, Weather Bureau Chart: ww.ncdc.noaa.gov/IPS/coop/coop.html.

U.S. Naval Observatory, Astronomical Applications Department, http://aa.usno.navy.mil.

Vassar Encyclopedia, "Nancy Harkness Love" http://vcencyclopedia.vassar.edu.

"WAFS Uniforms," www.blitzkriegbaby.de/wasp/wasp3a.htm.

Waldal, Elin Stebbins, "My Mother the WASP," http://beyondthebackyardblues.com.

WASP Virtual Collection, Texas Woman's University Library, www.twu.edu/library/wasp.asp.

"President Obama Signs Bill Awarding Congressional Gold Medal to Women Airforce Service Pilots," www.whitehouse.gov.

"William Edward Trebing, Myrtle Mae DeWitt, and Bill Otis Trebing," http://trees.ancestry.com.

Wings Across America, www.wingsacrossamerica.us/wasp.

WWII Women Pilots, http://wwii-women-pilots.org.

**Other Reference Sources**

*An Act to Award a Congressional Gold Medal to the Women Airforce Service Pilots (WASP)*, July 1, 2009, Public Law 111-40.

California Death Index.

Cochran, Jacqueline "Women Airforce Service Pilots," Report to General Arnold, Commanding General, Army Air Forces, 1944; "Final Report on Women Pilot Program," Army Air Forces Report 6-1262, Headquarters Army Air Forces, 1945.

Costello, Rep. John. *HR 3358, A bill to provide for the appointment of female pilots in the Air Forces of the Army*, 30 September 1943, 78th Congress, 1st Session; *HR 4219, A bill to provide for the appointment of female pilots and aviation cadets in the Air Forces of the Army*, 17 February 1944, 78th Congress, 2nd Session.

*Department of Defense Authorization Act, 1984*, September 24, 1983, Public Law 98-94.

Florida Death Index.

FOSTER v. PRESTON MILL CO., No. 32630. Supreme Court of Washington, Department 1, 19 March 1954.

*GI Bill Improvement Act of 1977*, November 23, 1977, Public Law 95-202.

Historical Branch, Intelligence and Security Division, Air Transport Command, *History of the Air Transport Command: Women Pilots in the Air Transport Command*, 1946, 44.

*History of the WASP Program. Army Air Forces Central Flying Training Command* (Randolph Field, TX: Army Air Forces Central Flying Command, 20 January 1945).

Johnson County Planning and Zoning Department, Johnson County, Iowa, "Sharon Center Village Plan, 2014," Resolution #02-13-14-07.

National Archives, Hawaii, Honolulu Passenger Lists, 1900-1953, 1941-1942.

NPR Radio, "All Things Considered: The Wasps: Women Airforce Service Pilots of World War II," broadcast 18 December 2002.

R.L. Polk, Helena, Montana *1922 City Directory*.

*The Rainbow: A Combined Yearbook of The Junior College Of Augusta And The Academy Of Richmond County* for the Year 1933, 44, 60.

Social Security Death Index.

South Carolina Death Index.

Texas Birth and Death Indexes.

Texas Death Certificates.

U.S. Census Records.

U. S. Congress, House, 78th Cong., 2d sess., 1944, H. R. 1600.

U.S. Congress, Senate Committee on Claims, accompaniment to H.R. 1241, 1320, 1601, 79th Congress, 1st sess., 1945.

U.S. Forest Service Report. Procedures outlined in the National Environmental Policy Act of 1969.

U.S. War Department News Release, 8 August 1944.

U.S. World War I and II Draft Registration Cards.

# INDEX

## ABOUT THE AUTHOR

William M. Miller is a writer and lecturer who has lived in Southern Oregon for nearly 20 years. For nearly eight years, he was a newspaper reporter and history columnist for the Mail Tribune newspaper, in Medford, Oregon. Previously he was the Southern Oregon Historical Society Historian. He lives in Shady Cove, Oregon.
*WilliamMMiller.com*

Printed in Great Britain
by Amazon

40813478R00167